Nomads of the Borneo Rainforest

Nomads of the Borneo Rainforest

The Economics, Politics, and Ideology of Settling Down

BERNARD SELLATO *Translated by Stephanie Morgan*

 UNIVERSITY OF HAWAII PRESS / Honolulu

First published as *Nomades et sédentarisation à Bornéo: Histoire économique et sociale*, by Bernard Sellato, © 1989 École des Hautes Études en Sciences Sociales

© 1994 University of Hawaii Press
Printed in the United States of America

98 97 96 95 94   5 4 3 2 1

Library of Congress Cataloging-in-Publication Data
Sellato, Bernard.
   [Nomades et sédentarisation à Bornéo. English]
   Nomads of the Borneo rainforest : The Economics, Politics, and Ideology of Settling Down / Bernard Sellato ; translated by Stephanie Morgan.
      p.   cm.
   Includes bibliographical references and index.
   ISBN 0-8248-1566-1
   1. Punan (Bornean people)—Social conditions.   2. Punan (Bornean people)—Economic conditions.   3. Punan (Bornean people)—Agriculture.   4. Nomads—Borneo—Sedentarisation.   5. Shifting cultivation—Borneo.   6. Social change—Borneo.   I. Title.
DS646.32.P85S4513   1994
306.3'09598'3—dc20   94-4291
                              CIP

University of Hawaii Press books are printed on acid-free paper and meet the guidelines for permanence and durability of the Council on Library Resources

The publication of this translation was made possible in part by a grant from the French Ministry of Culture.

Designed by Kenneth Miyamoto

Aii' savilaa' Punaan ange, man ino' pelo' ne? . . .

"Hey friends, our Punan visitors, where are you from?"

"We're Punan from the headwaters, Punan who live in holes in the rocks. We've come to call on you people of Idaa' Beraan."

"Well, what a sight! Our Punan friends that we invite so often. What brings you here, friends, to our rice fields?"

"We've come from the headwaters to see the fine way of life you people have here at Idaa' Beraan. . . . Our names? We're just low-class, no-good Punan, Punan who smell like mud and snakes. . . . He's Apaa' *tere*-fruit, Punan from far upriver, guardian of the headwaters of the river Kalimaan. . . . And he's Baluluk, a Punan of the highlands, we met him on the way through your fields; he's a Punan who isn't used to eating rice, up there in the headwaters. . . . This Baluluk Punan, he's from far away, from far upriver; this is the first time he's met people. We just came along with him, we've got no idea how to talk with him. . . . You're the ones who can deal with him," says Lutaang Punan.

—From the Mendalam Kayan epic *Takna' Lawe' dahin Nyalo,* verses 497–498, 514, 517, 535, 539, 551–553.

Sung and transcribed by S. Lii' Long; translated into Indonesian by A. J. Ding Ngo; published in Kayan and Indonesian (Yogyakarta: Gadjah Mada University Press, 1984–1985)

Contents

Foreword by Georges Condominas   ix
Preface to the English Edition   xiii
Preface to the French Edition   xvii

Part One: Punan Histories
Data and Methodology   3
Chapter 1. Land and People   8
Chapter 2. The Bukat   18
Chapter 3. The Kereho of the Busang River   75

Part Two: Traditions and Changes
Origins of the Punan   115
Chapter 4. Traditional Nomad Culture   118
Chapter 5. Processes of Change   163
Chapter 6. Summary and Conclusion   215

Appendix: Maps and Charts   221
Abbreviations   253
Bibliography   257
Index   275

Photographs follow p. 100

FOREWORD

THE GREAT TROPICAL rainforest possesses its own special
magic. Most of the settled folk who venture into it find it terrifying
and take revenge for their fear by blindly felling the magnificent giants
that comprise it; but for a select few, on the contrary, it is fascinating.
Bernard Sellato is one of these. Having come to Borneo as a geologist,
duty-bound to range through the center of the island, he swiftly suc-
cumbed to the lure of the forest and the people who belong to it and
roam through it, people whom their swidden-farming neighbors call
Punan or Penan and think of as savages.

These swidden farmers, themselves only semisedentary, are in their
turn called savages by the fully settled farmers of the lowlands and the
coast. These latter groups live in contact with fishing peoples, some as
settled as they are, while others, the Bajau Laut, are as nomadic on the
sea as the Punan in the forest.

Although at first encounter one may fall under the spell of the splen-
dor of the vast primary forest, life in it takes on a deeper dimension
once the traveler meets the people who live there—people it is easy to
like and care about—and develops lasting and friendly relationships
with them. The kind of training that prepares a student for the natural
sciences, and in particular for the mineral world, has nothing in common with the training required for someone who seeks to fathom people of a different culture. Geologist Bernard Sellato, to gain a fuller
understanding of his new friends, buckled down to the human sciences
and managed to master the scientific tools of the historian and the
anthropologist. Returning to Borneo at his own expense, now
equipped with the necessary conceptual apparatus, Sellato devoted a
year and a half to the study of every aspect of the lives of nomadic and
formerly nomadic groups in one of the most isolated regions of the

island, the Müller mountains. After several other sojourns in Borneo, he produced his doctoral dissertation and the present work.

That the anthropologist's profession is a way of life *(un genre de vie)*, a life freely chosen, is something academics often prefer to overlook. The solitary ethnologist is clearly a free agent, and it should be realized that this is also true for the groups who live in the forest. In our Western society, straining toward an ideal—less unconscious than it seems—of material comfort, we imagine that every society shares the same ambition.

However, anyone, like Sellato and myself, who spends even a little time living among forest peoples quickly senses that what inspires them is an ideology of nomadism. Even when local circumstances, most often in fact produced by outside pressures, compel them to live with some minimal degree of permanence, these forest societies still find material or ritual reasons to move, as I discovered in my study of the Montagnards of Vietnam (Condominas 1977). To give the earth they farm the time to regain its fertility after one or two harvests, they go off to "eat another forest"; to give the land on which they live time to purify itself after a deadly epidemic or a great sacrifice of water buffalos (ritually equivalent to humans), they must leave the site of their settlement and reconstruct it elsewhere.

The exploitation of the forest's broad array of resources offers the social group that lives in it an equally broad range of choices, and thereby a highly flexible economic system. But increases in population, and the consequent incursions of neighboring groups into the forest, soon limit the land available to the forest people. Forced into closer contact with their neighbors, they develop trade relationships, in the course of which they gradually borrow elements of the neighbors' technology, sometimes along with associated ritual practices. Sellato, in his reconstruction of earlier forms of Punan society, shows that elements of technology such as the dog, metal, and the fishing net, borrowed in relatively recent times, have played a major role in the economic transformations of nomad societies.

But it is very clear that the Punan, in response to the temptation offered them or the demand made upon them to settle down and devote their energies to farming, often make a conscious decision to remain nomads. Whereas the settled farmer feels safe in his village, in his solidly anchored home, the nomad or seminomad feels fully alive only when he sets out with his weapons into the great forest so frightening to others, so welcoming to him.

This ideology of nomadism, which in the end enters deeply into the spirit even of the ethnologist who spends time with the forest peoples, can also be found among sea nomads like the Moken, whose lives center around their boats and the hunt for their sea-dwelling prey, as well as among desert nomads like the Australian Aborigines, who chose to elaborate their intellectual and spiritual life to an extraordinary degree, while reducing their material technology to the absolute minimum.

The reconstruction proposed by Sellato of the history of nomad groups has another merit. "I cannot attach to oral traditions any historical value whatsoever under any conditions whatsoever" was the categorical statement made by Robert Lowie in 1915; and not until much later, with Jan Vansina's *De la tradition orale* (published in 1961) and other studies from Africa, did the historical traditions of societies without writing begin to receive the respect they deserve. Sellato has been able to show here that oral tradition allows for the reconstruction not only of political history, but of economic and social history as well, even in the case of very small-scale acephalous or an-archic societies. Those who have been called "peoples without history," even those whose social space is most limited, nevertheless do have a history.

Finally, this book, the product of long familiarity with the forest nomads, will, I hope, dispel some of those culturally derogatory clichés that keep our consciences quiet. The nomads are not remnant groups left behind by progress, but human beings who have made a choice about their way of life. Our self-indulgent civilization, which finds its well-being and self-glorification only in personal comfort and various forms of ownership, is too frequently prone to equate its own lost and marginal people with these true nomads, whose joy is their mobility.

GEORGES CONDOMINAS

PREFACE TO THE ENGLISH EDITION

THIS BOOK is a translation of the original French work, *Nomades et sédentarisation à Bornéo: Histoire économique et sociale,* based on my doctoral dissertation of 1986. *Nomades et sédentarisation* was completed in 1987 and published in 1989, and received the Prix Jeanne-Cuisinier, an award for books on Southeast Asia in the social sciences.

The English version is not a revised edition. No substantial changes have been made. Constraints of the translation process have called for minor alterations and some reshuffling, as a close reader of both editions might notice, but these are meant only to make the data and the argument more easily accessible.

Maps are profoundly important to a study such as this. This book follows the French edition in presenting a set of detailed maps, their relationships clarified where necessary in one map on a larger scale. Here a grid has been provided to help the reader locate places mentioned in the text, through coordinates given in the Index.

Bibliographical references have also been slightly edited. The original list has been updated only by the inclusion of a few recent works of my own that seem relevant to the theme of the book and four important recent studies: Michael Heppell's report on the Bukat of Sarawak, the only study made of them so far (1989); Jérôme Rousseau's landmark book on the stratified societies of Central Borneo (1990); J. Peter Brosius' pioneering thesis on the Penan of Sarawak (1992); and a symposium paper on Punan hunting by Rajindra Puri (1992).

Besides the two histories presented here, the original dissertation also included monograph-length reconstructions of the history of the Aoheng (or Penihing) and the Punan of the rivers Murung and Ratah. These are being prepared for separate publication in English, along with other such studies drawn upon but not included in full in my dissertation and a study of the languages of the nomadic groups of Borneo. A more general work on the cultural history of the island will be published in 1994.

I would like to express my gratitude to Georges Condominas, who kindly offered to write a special foreword to this English edition; to Madame Marie-Louise Dufour, of the *Éditions de l'École des Hautes Études en Sciences Sociales* (EHESS) in Paris, for arranging the transfer of copyrights and other legal matters; to the Direction du Livre of the French Ministry of Culture, which offered a translation grant; and to Pamela Kelley, of the University of Hawaii Press, for her unstinting organizational and editorial effort and concern.

No translator could have been more appropriate than Stephanie Morgan, herself an ethnologist whose own experience of Borneo has considerable historical depth. I am much indebted to her for her outstanding translation, the fruit of many months of intense discussion, friendly argument, and close collaboration.

I would also like to take this opportunity to thank Jean Subra for his photographs and his friendship, and Allen Maxwell for his helpful suggestions.

Space prohibits here, as it did in the first edition, acknowledging my debt to each one of the hundreds of people, in dozens of locations in Borneo, who kindly and patiently gave me their time and shared their knowledge with me. I would like to make particular mention of the following persons: Temanggung Gemala and Temanggung Janen (Nanga Tepai); Nyopalo (Metelunai); Sawing Gemala (Nanga Balang); Berikum Ubai, Diam Da'o, Ngaun Bange' (Noha Tivap); Lipa Pisa and Ake' Doming, Subu, Dani Kujat (Tamalue); Umang, Singka, Lijuk, Temanggung Tapa and Temanggung Dalung, Guru Toto, Kaja', Ha'ang (Tanjung Lokang); Bujang (Nanga Lapung); Lige, Ake' Bungai (Bo'ung); Juba' (Belatung); Koeng Bato' and Jangin (Nanga Enap); Bacung (Nanga Ira'); Kamih, Sidik (Nanga Sopan); Pastor A. J. Ding Ngo (Padua); Abang Achmad (Lunsa Ra); Guru Sengek (Ukai); Di'ong, Nyiring, Tingang Bavong, Lisung (Long Apari); Ake' Majae and Anye' Majae, Ibo Ding (Ujoh Bilang); Inon Hului and Amun Ding, Tebon, Janin (Lirung Aham); Guru Kaya and Ake' Bulan, Ake' Sava, Josep Uvat (Long Kerio'); Anyang, Langa, Savang Bano (Tiong Bu'u); Inon Okan Buring, Ake' Tubung, Tingang Dia, Sula Aran, Bang Donggo, Ake' Anye', Guru Lavon, Ake' Borang, Ake' Jalung

Bulan, Irang Napap, Uvo Miang, Ake' Nyangun (Tiong Ohang, Long Doho', and Long Bagun Baru); Ajang Nalau, Jivan, Petrus Lijio, Berare', Sirang (Long Mutai); Timang, Awing, Ding (Long Lunuk); Bo' Belare' Liah, Bit, Anye' Pai (Long Tuyo'); Bo' Bayut (Long Kuling); Satu', Gawob, Inot, Luban (Muara Belinau); Ibeu (Sungai Lunuk); Pingai, Jenapui, Ibo Ajang (Muara Tubo'); Banying and Paran (Long Merah); Hamut and Telajan (Topus); Sidi' Bindih (Tujang); Jihat, Wardi Awan (Sungai Ratah). The languages they speak may have no specific word for "thank you," since in traditional Punan society mutual aid is taken for granted, but they know the feeling. Many of these people or their descendants may someday see their names here and understand that I thank them from my heart. Special thanks go also to my adopted Aoheng family, particularly to Amun Batang Dirung Dahing and Inon Batang Tuko', Amun Okan Oang, Ake' Paron, and Hangin Bang.

The Borneo of 1993, which I continue to revisit several times a year, is no longer the Borneo I knew in 1973. Many of my informants, already old in 1980, have died; and with them, fragments of their peoples' oral historical traditions have passed away. I hope that this book, to which the knowledge of so many persons was contributed, will help future generations to know and understand their own historical background, to find answers to questions about themselves and their ancient traditions that the elders of their people will no longer be able to give them, and to feel pride in themselves and their cultural heritage through the confrontations forced on them by this rapidly changing world. My informants, the grandfathers and grandmothers of these young people, enriched by their own existence the cultural diversity of the great lands they lived in, and made and proudly held to decisions that preserved their ideal of how their lives should be lived. For the young people of Borneo today, and for all of us, they set a good example.

Note on Transcription and Translation

In the original French edition, and to an even greater extent in this English edition, readability rather than phonological accuracy has been the prime concern. Names and terms in Punan languages are therefore presented in a highly simplified system of transcription, which does not take fully into account the phonologies of these languages, their rich system of vowel sounds in particular. More accurate descriptions can be found in my forthcoming study of these languages.

Several points may be noted here. In this transcription, "v" stands for the voiced bilabial fricative /β/, while in some cases (Punan Tubu, for instance), "f" stands for the voiceless equivalent /φ/. The phoneme noted "ɼ" in my study, a single flap from back to front, is phonologically distinct from either "r" (an alveolar flap) or "l" (/l/); here, "ɼ" and "r" are both represented by "r." The vowel close to /Y/ (noted in my study as "ü") and the centralized /U/ (noted there as "u") are both represented here by "u"; while the vowel corresponding to /i/ (noted there as "ï") and the centralized /I/ (noted there as "i") are both represented here by "i." The transcription does distinguish the vowel noted here as "ö," which in Bukat, as in some related languages (Lisum, Beketan), stands for a nasalized /o/.

French permits and indeed requires the use of "é" to represent /e/ (which may be locally realized as /E/ and /ε/); "e" then represents the schwa (which may sometimes be realized in morphological prefixes as /o/). This distinction is of great value in transcribing not only Punan languages but many others in the region. The constraints of English, however, have shaped the conventions of transcription in English writing, and the present translation follows these conventions in representing both sounds by "e."

Other points that may be noted with regard to the translation include the use of standard spellings from local languages for words brought into English in the past (damar, rotan, padi), the use of "farmers" in place of "agriculturalists" or "rice-cultivators," and a much more general use than in the French text of the past tense.

BERNARD SELLATO

Jakarta,
1993

Preface to the
French Edition

THIS STUDY, historical in perspective, is concerned with the processes of transformation undergone over the past two centuries by the societies of the nomadic hunter-gatherers of Borneo, collectively called Punan. The many factors—ecological, economic, commercial, political, social, cultural, and ideological—that have played a part in generating and mediating these processes will be treated diachronically, as elements in a global, constantly changing system. Emphasis will be placed in particular on the economic processes of conversion to commercial activity (the collecting of forest products for trade or sale) and to certain forms of agriculture, and on associated processes of social transformation. In the pages that follow I intend to show, with a respectful nod to the work of Fernand Braudel, that the historical traditions of peoples without writing may be sources for the development of fertile reconstructions of the past; that this is possible not only in the field of political history, but also in the more subtle fields of economic and social history; and that this can be done even for very small-scale acephalous societies.

Little is known of the origins of the hunter-gatherers of Borneo. Some specialists have taken the view that the Punan are groups left over from an evolutionary process, who stayed in the forests while their neighbors took to rice cultivation; others believe that there exists an autonomous hunter-gatherer culture, independent of the farming cultures; still others hold that the Punan groups are the products of a devolution, that they in fact consist of former cultivators turned nomad in order to specialize in the exploitation of the forest.

I have had the opportunity of spending time with more than a dozen of the nomadic or formerly nomadic ethnic groups that live in various

regions of Borneo. These include the Aoheng, the Seputan, the Hovongan, the Kereho of the regions along the Kapuas and Busang rivers, the Bukat of the river Mahakam and the Bukat of the Kapuas, the
Semukung of the Kapuas, the Punan of the river Murung and of the
Ratah, the Punah Merah of the Mahakam, and the Lisum and the
Beketan of the river Belayan; and I have collected information among
still other groups. As I worked to reconstruct their history, one fact
became obvious: all these groups, as far back in time as it is possible to
go, have been nomadic; and all have more or less recently, more or less
completely, taken to a sedentary way of life. A generalized process of
devolution is therefore out of the question, at least over the course of
the past two or three centuries. On the contrary, what can be observed
over this period is a general tendency among these groups toward the
more or less complete abandonment of a nomadic existence. This
indeed is a tendency that seems to hold true for all of Southeast Asia.

My intention was to make a particular study of the processes that
lead a nomadic group to change its traditional mode of life and take
up certain commercial strategies, some degree of sedentarization, and
certain forms of agriculture (varying by group). At the start it was my
desire to propose, within the framework of this study, a reconstruction of the history of all of the groups mentioned above. I meant to try
to find, throughout those histories, basic "themes" forming the constituent elements of these processes which, by the frequency of their
occurrence, would acquire a statistical value and therefore present a
high degree of reliability. Indeed, my work did bring out the particu-
lars of these processes, and causal relations among their episodes,
demonstrating a fair consistency among the different groups.

It was, however, hardly possible within the format of this volume to
include a dozen or so different historical monographs. I might have
chosen to present these reconstructions in highly simplified form,
including only data essential to a description of processes of change;
but this would have been to lose much of the interest that a global
reconstruction can offer. Since the processes under scrutiny are
involved with every aspect of the life of a human group, it has been
necessary to present their context as fully as possible. A study of all of
a group's interactions—with the environment, with neighboring ethnic groups, with commercial networks of trade—cannot be made
without a description of the partners in these interactions. Ultimately,
therefore, I chose to focus upon only two groups that seemed to me to
illustrate, each in its own way, the different aspects of processes of

change. Chapters 2 and 3 present their history, detailing the dynamics of their interactions, to provide a thorough description of the context for these transformations.

These two groups are the Bukat (Chapter 2) and the Kereho of the river Busang (Chapter 3). Some Bukat bands began to settle as early as the first half of the nineteenth century, adopting the way of life of the rice-farming Kayan. The rest of the Bukat settled gradually between 1900 and 1930; at the present time, though they probably depend upon rice for more than half their subsistence, they still rely heavily upon wild sago, and commercial collecting remains an important economic activity. The second group, the Kereho of the Busang, maintained their nomadic way of life until the beginning of the twentieth century. Their society has remained egalitarian, and their subsistence is based upon a combination of rice, cassava, and wild sago. Commercial collecting plays a prominent part in their economic system.

In the chapters that concern these groups, I will attempt to reconstruct their history as far back in time as their oral traditions allow, with particular emphasis upon the description of the changes that these societies have undergone in relation to the dynamics of political and economic change at the regional level. For the rest, I will let these reconstructions speak for themselves.

Following these examples of historical reconstruction, Chapters 4 and 5 will present an integration of the results of the study of these two groups, and of the other groups I have visited, with data from the literature on yet other groups in Sarawak and elsewhere.

Chapter 4 provides a description of the numerous cultural traits common to most Punan groups, which I believe justify the use of the term "Punan" as a collective designation for the nomadic hunter-gatherers of Borneo. By the same token, these similarities justify the use of the expression "traditional Punan culture" or "traditional nomad culture" to refer to a single cultural substratum common to all these groups. This first half of the chapter attempts a reconstruction of traditional culture in all its aspects, technological, economic, and social, with particular reference to its relationship to the forest environment, which is viewed as a special "economic niche" that offers to the nomads who live in it total dietary self-sufficiency. The subsistence economy of the nomads is described in detail, with particular attention to strategies that relate to the exploitation of sago and specific techniques of hunting and fishing. The patterns of Punan mobility, their concepts of territory, and their strategies of territorial defense are also examined, in the context of their interactions with their farming neighbors. The social, political, and ritual organization of the band, as it relates to economic organization, is also explored in detail. Finally, some information is provided on aspects of Punan religious and ritual practices.

Chapter 5 attempts an analysis of the economic, political, and social mechanisms of the changes that have taken place in this traditional nomad culture in the course of more or less intensive contacts with the cultures of the sedentary farmers.

The first phase of the discussion shows how the Punan, after the introduction of certain new items of technology such as metal, turn to the commercial collecting of forest products under the pressure of demand from downriver markets, and thereby find themselves integrated into regional networks of trade. The second phase focuses upon the process of conversion to agriculture, beginning with the cultivation of tuber crops and fruit trees in a mixed subsistence economy based upon cassava and sago, and moving on eventually to the cultivation of rice, in a subsistence system based upon three elements: rice, cassava, and sago.

Following this is a discussion of the social changes experienced by Punan groups in the course of their interactions with the farmers. The development of a sedentary mode of residence, in connection with economic changes linked to the practice of agriculture, leads to profound transformations in the organization of family and community, as well as in the sphere of religious and ritual practices. This study of historical processes of change in nomad societies demonstrates the persistence of certain traits characteristic of these societies through the emergence of new and specific models of socioeconomic organization.

Before entering upon the substance of my study, I will try to explain a more personal journey, that of a geologist possessed by the human sciences. It may seem a strange intellectual itinerary, this drifting from the exact sciences into the natural sciences, and on again into the human sciences; nevertheless, as I look back on it, it seems inevitable. Constant through all the chance wanderings of my research route was the presence of humanity, of human reality. I could not help meeting it; and having met it, I could not close my mind to it. Humanity was on my path, it is now the goal of my journey (for beyond humanity there is nothing to seek but the self—or God, or the void, philosophers would say).

Why travel so far to make this discovery? It was chance, undeniably, that sent me to Borneo rather than elsewhere. Chance must take the blame. I found myself set down, a young geologist with a brand-new diploma, in a market town of the Melawi river one day in September 1973, knowing nothing of Indonesia (after a transit time of four hours in Jakarta and an hour in Pontianak), speaking not a word of the language, empty-handed (my baggage, misrouted toward Tokyo, was never found). Twenty-two years old, a newborn babe. The circumstances were ripe for shock. But how did it happen that the setting for this cultural shock, so powerful and so welcome, so quickly became, first the object of fervent curiosity, then the partner in a quiet passion? I still wonder. Whatever the case may be, here is not the place to bare the shifting states of my soul.

There followed a period of more than two years of geological exploration in the interior of Borneo, particularly in the Müller mountains, one of the most inaccessible regions of the island. It was there, among the Aoheng, that I first broke through the barrier of the lingua franca, Indonesian, to begin to stammer a local language, and through it to collect oral literature, the elements of a lexicon, and information on the history and religious traditions of this group. I went so far as to spend my leave time on the spot, in order to join an Aoheng expedition across the mountains into Sarawak, as far as Kapit (from which I returned on foot to the Mahakam).

This was a bit too much for my bosses of the moment, who felt it wise, in order to "de-Indonesianize" me, to send me to the depths of the Sahara. After two years' roaming across the verdant landscapes of the borderlands of Niger with Libya and Chad, the Algerian and Mauritanian frontiers of Mali, and other far corners of western Africa (where I managed nevertheless to learn a bit of Tamachek, Hausa, Bambara, and . . . Japanese), I took back my liberty.

I set out again for Southeast Asia in 1978, after a brief passage through Denys Lombard's seminar on Indonesian studies and a brief article for *Archipel;* and at the end of a year of various peregrinations, including several months in Sarawak, Sabah, and East Kalimantan, I obtained a research permit from the Indonesian authorities (to whom, and to LIPI and Mr. Napitupulu in particular, I take this opportunity to express my gratitude). In this I had the help of letters of recommendation from Georges Condominas and Denys Lombard of the École des Hautes Études en Sciences Sociales (Sorbonne, Paris) and Jérôme Rousseau of McGill University in Montreal (to all three of whom I give heartfelt thanks for having been bold enough to support and encourage me) and the sponsorship of the Center of Linguistic Studies

(PPPB) in Jakarta and of Amran Halim (to whom I also express my liveliest gratitude).

I then spent eighteen months among the people of the interior, principally with my adoptive family among the Aoheng of the district of Long Apari, and traversing the Müller mountains for long stays with other groups that were still partially nomadic. I would gladly have stayed another year, especially as the authorities made no objection to extending my permit, but my savings were exhausted. With a thousand dollars obtained from the Ford Foundation, through the welcome intervention of George Appell (to whom, as to the foundation, I also offer my thanks), I was able to ship myself and my baggage back to France in June of 1981.

In the course of a difficult year of job-hunting (prospects were very bleak in the mining and petroleum sectors), and after enrolling in the École des Hautes Études en Sciences Sociales under the supervision of Professor Lombard, I managed to get my predoctoral degree (DEA) in 1982.

At the end of 1982, I finally signed a contract as consultant to a petroleum company (Elf Aquitaine Indonésie, to which I also pledge my gratitude), with the duty of conceiving, organizing, and carrying out exploratory expeditions in the vast uninhabited regions of Borneo's mountainous heartlands. This period lasted till the end of 1985, allowing me to rediscover the upper Mahakam and to meet again with my Aoheng friends, and also to revisit the Melawi, site of my first steps in Borneo. It was in 1983 that I formally became an Aoheng through the appropriate rituals of adoption, under the name of Suling, son of Dirung, an Aoheng notable of Long Bagun, and grandson of Dahing, dedicated headhunter, who took part, under the Dutch system of forced labor, in the first ascent of the highest peak in New Guinea.

I chose to withdraw from these contracts at the end of 1985 to give myself time to write my doctoral dissertation. Though a precise accounting of my stays in Borneo is not easily made, I would estimate that I have spent, all told, about six years in the interior up to the time of writing. The studies on which this book is based derive from data collected in the field between 1973 and 1985.

Here I must offer my thanks to the jurors of my committee, Georges Condominas, Pierre Labrousse, Denys Lombard, and Emmanuel Terray, who suggested that I publish my dissertation, as well as to the

Association Archipel, which made this possible; to my colleagues and friends, Jean-François Guermonprez, Gilbert Harmonic, Charles Macdonald, and Jérôme Rousseau, who, by their comments on my text, their advice, and our discussions, have brought me to this point in my meditations; and finally to Véronique Dorner, Elisabeth Sellato, Olivier Sieffer, and Philippe Sourin. May all find here the expression of my gratitude.

PART ONE

PUNAN HISTORIES

Data and Methodology

My field data, gathered over the course of a dozen years, represent more than two thousand transcribed interviews and about one hundred and fifty hours of tape recordings. The collection of these data was never a matter of formal sessions of fixed length, with selected paid informants. Nor did I ever require the services of a research assistant, and I never, except for rare instances, had recourse to an interpreter. In almost every case, my personal relationship with my informants extended over a far broader range than that of the classic relationship of investigator and informant.

Because of these factors, the circumstances in which the data were collected were unstandardized and extremely diverse, and the interviews were unequal in length and interest. I often joined old people who were resting or working at handicrafts during the quiet hours when most people in the community were at work in their fields, and we then held long, desultory conversations during which the investigator talked as much as the informant, conversations often interrupted by the little children that the old folk were supposed to be minding (and, for that matter, I did plenty of babysitting myself). Or the scene might be an informal group of people sitting around together in the evening, when I would lead the conversation toward particular points of interest. Sometimes, in such evening gatherings, it was I who would play tapes of an epic or a tale from a neighboring village; or I might tell folktales from my own European culture, Tom Thumb or Snow White, slightly modified, which were received with great enthusiasm. Often, too, when I visited people to provide medical care, I took advantage of the opportunity to hold a brief historical interview. My

3

regular participation in farm work gave me access to this specific context of ritual and literature, and, similarly, my active participation in certain rituals gave me an insider's perspective on their organization. Trips to other villages, where I stayed with my adoptive kinfolk, also offered chances for long nighttime discussions.

On geological expeditions into the forest, I frequently had the opportunity, late in the evening or during a day of heavy rain (at least when the tarpaulin roofing the shelter we had constructed turned out not to be too permeable), to question the members of my team, recruits from many different groups, porters, boatmen, and guides. This launched general discussions in which we compared the traditions, rituals, and history of the various ethnic groups whose members were present, all of whom were curious to learn about their neighbors. At times I was obliged to guide the conversation somewhat, but I soon realized that information of the greatest interest could appear spontaneously in such a setting, and often I let the discussion follow its natural course. One other benefit of such a discussion was that it gave me the chance to spot right away, among a score or more of newly hired strangers, those who would be most worth a private conversation.

This enormous body of data, heterogeneous in form and quality, has naturally not been easy to handle. Given its volume, there could be no question of presenting the raw material in the text. I made no a priori decision to deprive the reader of access to these raw data, but after considerable hesitation I chose to give none of them even in an appendix. Similarly, in order not to weigh down a text that was already fairly dense and hard to follow, I decided not to include references to specific interviews (place, date, number, or informant, though some informants' names are given in a general context). For this same reason, paradoxically, in order to make it easier to read the text straight through without interruption, I chose to avoid footnotes or endnotes altogether: every significant element of information that might have formed the subject of a note has been integrated into the text. Although I have paid the price of this system with a few digressions, these do not, I believe, break the continuity of the text, each having its link to the logic of the argument.

Field data, with related bibliographic sources, are presented in Chapters 2 and 3. Each chapter is a type of monograph corresponding to a single ethnic group. They are of unequal length, due to differences in the size of the ethnic groups considered, the number of subgroups given individual treatment and the amount of information available, and finally to my personal choice of specific aspects to be developed more fully. Nowhere near the whole of the data, whether from the field or from the literature, has been integrated into these monographs: I have included only that information which seemed to me pertinent within the framework of the study.

The study reported in these two chapters is based on a long-term knowledge of the region, its geography, and the pattern of its rivers (hydrography). This knowledge has proved indispensable to the understanding of the nomads' relationships with their environment and of the process of their sedentarization. The same is true of my firsthand knowledge of the ethnic, social, and cultural environment of the groups under consideration. By virtue of this experience, I have been able to consider these groups in the context of their integration into the political, economic, commercial, and social systems that surround and, in the end, encompass them.

Particular care has been taken with the maps that accompany the text, and with the representation upon these maps of the position and movements of these groups, along with dates of these movements, to facilitate a general view of patterns in time and space. Extremely detailed maps have been prepared to this end, the best to date for the interior of Borneo. Studies of historical processes sometimes have a tendency to detach themselves from their geographical setting; I felt it important, on the contrary, to anchor history in its landscape, to put time back into space. Summary tables provide the basis for a review of the chronological order of events.

To represent terms and expressions in local languages, I have adopted a highly simplified system of transcription (see the Note on Transcription and Translation following the Preface to the English Edition). A more complete study of Punan languages is still in progress.

In the two chapters of reconstructed history that follow, three-quarters of the data are drawn from the oral traditions of the people concerned and those of their neighbors, the rest being taken from the literature (which itself in many cases draws its material from oral tradition). Information whose source is the literature is routinely followed by a bibliographic citation. Any information not followed by a reference is therefore data from oral tradition, collected in the field.

Elements of historical information may be met with in oral literature, particularly in formal literary genres; but abundant historical material may also be collected in the course of informal conversations with old people of the group. In the case of long-settled groups, the oral literature is rich and varied. Certain epics contain references to events of long ago, unfortunately obscured by a linguistic encoding (archaisms, metaphors) to which the key has been lost. Other genres of literature transport the listener to a wide variety of settings—the world of the dead, of spirits, of folktale heroes and magicians; most of these contain no historical information. Among nomadic groups or those recently settled, informal conversation turns out to be the most fertile source for the studies undertaken here. These groups indeed have little oral literature, and all their historical knowledge is informally stored in the memories of the elderly.

Oral sources apparently only rarely conflict with written sources. It may indeed be emphasized that certain written sources, tales recounted by travelers or other visitors, should at times be regarded with more suspicion than certain oral sources. With regard to the historical value of the testimony, archival materials have no a priori superiority over oral materials. Among written as among oral accounts, there are good and bad sources.

It must be emphasized that in the study which follows, oral tradition may be the one and only source of historical information, in the absence of written documentation. The region of the Müller mountains was "discovered" only in the last years of the nineteenth century, and since numerous written sources provide no more than rumors about the area, oral tradition is a vital resource. Therefore it must necessarily be examined in great detail. In the case of the Aoheng (Sellato 1986b), oral tradition alone, or almost alone, provides the data for a convincing reconstruction of the history of the upper Mahakam (East Kalimantan) during the century and a half prior to colonial penetration.

Besides the explicit information contained in transcribed or tape-recorded documents, the investigator has available to him certain intertextual pieces of chronological information, which, though internal to the text, refer to things other than the text. These connotative markers may be explicit (toponyms, references to tools, animals, plants, or foodstuffs) or implicit (elements of language, social relationships). It is also possible to pick out historical markers that may be glottochronological (archaisms, borrowings), ecological, technoeconomic (technology, diet), or sociological (such as changes in the kinship system). One may also meet with markers that provide an absolute date, like the explosion of the volcano Krakatau, just west of Java, in August 1883 (heard in Borneo and far beyond), or the first visit of an explorer.

In the absence of trustworthy chronological landmarks, which exist only for the colonial period, an attempt at dating may be made through the use of genealogies and of village relocations. Dates are inevitably uncertain. In the text, and in maps and tables, they are given with a margin of error of ten years more or less for the beginning of the nineteenth century, and of five years more or less for the turn of the twentieth century.

CHAPTER 1
LAND AND PEOPLE

THIS CHAPTER includes an extremely summary description of the geographical and ethnological setting of this study, the island of Borneo.

Borneo: Landmarks

The island of Borneo, lying across the Equator, has an area of about 750,000 square kilometers and a population of less than ten million. Politically, as shown in Map 1, it is divided into three regions. The Indonesian portion, comprising two-thirds of its area, is made up of four provinces: West Kalimantan (145,000 square km, population 2.5 million, capital Pontianak), East Kalimantan (200,000 square km, population 1.3 million, capital Samarinda), Central Kalimantan (150,000 square km, population 1 million, capital Palangkaraya), and South Kalimantan (40,000 square km, population 2.3 million, capital Banjarmasin). Next in size are the two states that form part of the Federation of Malaysia, Sarawak (125,000 square km, population 1.2 million, capital Kuching) and Sabah (75,000 square km, population 800,000, capital Kota Kinabalu). Smallest is the independent sultanate of Brunei Darussalam (5,700 square km, population 200,000, capital Bandar Sri Begawan). Whereas Indonesians use the name Kalimantan to refer to the whole island of Borneo, including the northern states, the Malaysians group Sarawak and Sabah together under the name of East Malaysia.

Mountain ranges shape the interior of the island, particularly in the north, giving way in the south, the west, and to a lesser degree in the east to extensive flatlands. The highest point of the island (and indeed of all Southeast Asia) is Mount Kinabalu, at 4,170 meters (13,455

8

feet), located in Sabah. Certain peaks of the Müller and Schwaner mountains in Kalimantan rise above 2,000 meters. Powerful rivers furrow the island, radiating like the spokes of a cartwheel (Map 2). To the west the greatest of these is the Kapuas (about 1,300 km long); to the east, the Mahakam (about 1,000 km) and the Kayan; to the south, the Barito and the Kahayan; and to the northwest, the Rejang and the Baram.

The climate is equatorial, with average temperatures of between 25 and 35° C (about 70–95° F), and rainfall that varies by region from 2.5 to 4.5 meters per year. It rains all year round, though not quite so heavily during the "dry season," from June to September. A considerable portion of the territory is still covered by dense primary forests rich in animal life, despite the intensive exploitation to which they are subject (by loggers in particular).

There are still relatively few roads in Borneo, most of them restricted to the coastal regions. In the interior, rivers generally serve as the only means of communication, and private and commercial traffic of passenger and cargo vessels is considerably hampered by relatively sudden and unpredictable changes in water level, often of tens of meters between low water and flood, and by the effects of these changes on the difficulty for boats to pass upriver rapids.

Homo sapiens was apparently already present in Borneo some 35,000 years ago, and traces of a stone-tool industry have been found in the Niah Caves in Sarawak; but, in general, the prehistory of Borneo is very poorly known. Techniques of rice cultivation penetrated the island during the Neolithic period, possibly following a period of horticultural activity. Iron may have been introduced between the fifth and tenth centuries of the present era.

Relations with China had already been established via the northern part of Borneo by the time of the Sung dynasty (tenth to thirteenth centuries), and with Java, via the southern part, possibly by the ninth century. Traces of Hindu influence dating from the fourth century have been found on the eastern coast, and petty Hinduized kingdoms developed in the coastal regions of the island. The influence of the Javanese upon these kingdoms made itself felt from the ninth century, and even more strongly from the fourteenth century, particularly in the south. Islam apparently reached Borneo via the Malay peninsula during the thirteenth century, and the Hinduized kingdoms were replaced by Muslim sultanates, first appearing in the fifteenth or sixteenth centuries: Brunei in the north, Sambas, Landak, and Sukadana in the west, Kutai and others in the east, and Banjarmasin in the south.

Europeans made contact with the coasts of Borneo at the beginning of the sixteenth century, but neither the Spanish nor the Portuguese took enough interest in the island to establish control. Only in the nineteenth century did the English and the Dutch take effective possession of Borneo territories, respectively in the north (Sarawak and Sabah) and in the south (Kalimantan), conquering or establishing dominance over a large proportion of the coastal sultanates. For the purposes of this study, the details of colonial history are of no particular interest. The central regions of the island, which alone concern us directly, were penetrated by colonial powers only at the turn of the twentieth century, and definitively "controlled" only around 1930. The Japanese occupation of Borneo, from 1942 to 1945, had a lesser impact in the interior than in the coastal regions; the same holds true for the Indonesian struggle for independence lasting till 1949, which culminated in the establishment of the Republic of Indonesia. In 1963, Sarawak and Sabah were incorporated into the Federation of Malaysia. In what was called "Confrontation," Indonesia opposed the establishment of these new states all along their borders with Kalimantan. The Sultanate of Brunei, formerly under British control, achieved its independence in 1984 under the name of Brunei Darussalam.

The Dayak, who occupy the interior of the island, are considered to be the original inhabitants of Borneo. The term *Dayak* covers dozens —indeed hundreds—of ethnic groups, each of them distinctive in culture, social organization, and language. All of these groups cultivate rice, most often on temporary hill fields cleared for the purpose and fertilized with ash (slash-and-burn or swidden agriculture). It is necessary to distinguish between the Dayak and the Punan, with whom the present study is concerned. The term *Punan* encompasses a number of little local groups who have (or have had) in common a nomadic way of life and a subsistence economy based on forest hunting and gathering. Up to the present day, these groups live in the most inaccessible mountainous regions of the island's interior.

The Malays, Malay-speaking Muslims, occupy extensive territories in the coastal regions and in the low-lying plains along the great rivers. The great majority of them descend from Dayak groups converted to Islam, while others derive from Muslim populations coming from Sumatra or Java. They are fishermen, farmers, or traders. The Indonesian government's recent policy of transmigration (subsidized shifts of population from high-density regions of the country to those less peopled) has led to a massive and continuing influx of Javanese into Indonesian Borneo. Buginese from southern Celebes very early settled on the east coast, and in some places on the west coast. Madurese are also present in the Indonesian provinces of Borneo. Chinese settled in West Kalimantan and in Sarawak beginning in the eighteenth century. At present they can be found in every urban center of the island, and sometimes even far upriver, particularly in West Kalimantan, Sarawak, and Sabah. They make their living in a variety of ways, most particularly by commerce.

Finally, on the coasts of Sabah and East Kalimantan, one finds the so-called sea nomads, generally known by the name of Bajau Laut, who traditionally live by fishing, without permanent settlements on land, between northern Celebes, Borneo, and the southern Philippines.

Ethnic Groups of the Interior

THE DAYAK

What follows is a panoramic view, so to speak, of the principal Dayak groups, inspired by Avé and King (1986) and modified by myself. Map 3 gives a general picture of the location of these ethnic groups. For a description that focuses more closely upon the social organization of these groups, see Sellato (1987).

Iban: The Iban are a major ethnic group, widespread in Sarawak and to a lesser degree in West Kalimantan, where they originated and where several related groups still live, the "Ibanic" groups Kantu', Seberuang, Mualang, and Desa. The Iban have often been pioneer farmers in primary forest; their societies are rather egalitarian, and they have been renowned headhunters.

Barito Group: This other important group of peoples inhabits a large part of the southern half of Kalimantan. It includes the Ngaju, a large group living in the central and western regions of Central Kalimantan; the Ot Danum and related peoples, who live farther upriver and along the Melawi; the Siang and Murung of the upper Barito; the Luangan and Ma'anyan of the middle Barito; and the Benua', Bentian, and Tunjung of the middle Mahakam. A particular characteristic of these groups is the practice of elaborate funerary rituals, including secondary treatment of the bodies of the dead, suggesting a relationship to an ancient center of Hinduized culture in the south of Borneo. Cer-

tain groups of the Melawi (Limbai, Melahui, Payak, Tebidah, Kebahan, and others; see Sellato 1986a), though they speak dialects more
or less closely related to Malay, show distinct cultural affinities to the
Barito group.

Kayan-Kenyah-Modang: This group of related peoples occupies
vast territories in the center of Borneo. From the Apo Kayan plateau in
East Kalimantan, they spread out along the Rejang and the Baram in
Sarawak, the Mahakam in East Kalimantan, and even the upper
Kapuas in West Kalimantan. The societies of these swidden farmers
are rigidly stratified into aristocrats, commoners, and slaves, and they
have traditionally been a warlike and conquering people.

"Nulang Arc" Group: A certain number of relatively small groups
inside Sarawak and in the regions along its eastern border with Kalimantan, the Kajang, Melanau, Berawan, Lun Dayeh, Lun Bawang,
and Kelabit, show cultural similarities and historical links among
themselves, despite differences in their social organization and subsistence economy that relate to their differing natural and ethnic environ-
ments. The Melanau, for instance, are Muslims who cultivate sago
palms and fish along the coasts, while the Kelabit traditionally grow
wet rice in irrigated fields on the high plains of the interior. Some
among these groups have stratified social structures. On the whole,
these groups practice secondary treatment of the dead, or did so in the
past, in ways similar to the Barito groups; it has therefore been possible to group them together under the term *"nulang* arc," from the
name of these rituals.

Maloh: Another socially stratified group is the Maloh, including
three subgroups, Taman, Embaloh, and Kalis, living in the upper
Kapuas.

Bidayuh: The Bidayuh, formerly known as Land Dayak, are a heterogeneous group living along the lower Kapuas and in southwest
Sarawak. One characteristic of these ethnic groups is that they construct a "head house" which serves as a center for male activities and
rituals.

Along the western coast of the island there are Dayak groups like
the Selako and the Kendayan who, though they speak languages
closely related to Malay, are not Muslim and do not identify themselves with Malays. Finally, there are groups in Sabah, known collectively as Dusun and Kedazan, who grow rice either in swidden clearings or in irrigated rice fields, and whose languages show affinities
with those of the Philippines.

The way of life of all the above-mentioned Dayak groups is based with few exceptions upon the cultivation of hill or dry rice in forest clearings. Trees and other vegetation are felled, left to dry, and then burned, and the rice is planted in the ash-fertilized soil. This swidden field is generally used for no more than a single yearly harvest of rice, sometimes for two; cassava (manioc) may be planted after the rice, and then the field is normally left to lie fallow for ten to twenty years, during which time it becomes covered with secondary forest and so regains its fertility. Sowing generally takes place during August and September, the harvest around January or February, but this may vary by region, altitude, or the variety of rice that is grown.

Dayak villages, whether or not they take the form of a communal dwelling-place or longhouse, must shift their location from time to time as the lands farmed around the village cease to be productive. These ethnic groups, commonly (as here) referred to as settled or sedentary in contrast to the nomadic hunter-gatherers, are, strictly speaking, more appropriately called semisedentary.

As well as rice, these farming groups cultivate cassava, taro, yams or sweet potatos, corn or maize, sugarcane, a number of different vegetables including beans, cucumbers and leaf greens, and a wide variety of semi-wild fruit trees. Fishing and hunting also make regular contributions to their diet. Animal husbandry is generally limited to dogs (and cats), chickens, and pigs. Some groups have begun to keep ducks or market breeds of chicken, and some, who generally have commercial ties to the coastal regions, raise cattle or water buffalo. The cultivation of cash crops has been under way among certain ethnic groups for some time, and continues to spread at an increasing rate. These crops include pepper, cloves, coffee and cocoa, coconut and oil palms, and rubber.

THE PUNAN

Known by ethnonyms varying according to region, the Punan traditionally differ from the Dayak in their way of life, being nomadic hunter-gatherers. As nomads, they ranged in small bands through the vast primary forests of the interior of Borneo, farther up the rivers than the farming peoples. Their subsistence economy was based principally upon sago, a starch extracted from the pith of several genera of palm, and also upon hunting, gathering, and a little fishing. The band, an egalitarian society and an economic unit, was autonomous as far as diet was concerned. Band members gathered forest products

for barter, maintaining trade relationships with their sedentary neighbors. In the course of the past few centuries, and to an increasing
extent over recent decades (under the pressure of the authorities), the
Punan have formed more permanent settlements, converting to a more
sedentary way of life oriented toward certain forms of agriculture.

Map 3 outlines, in the center of the island, the vast mountainous
region that is the domain of a considerable number of Punan groups,
nomads or former nomads. Other pockets of Punan population exist
in mountain ranges in the center and near the coast of East Kalimantan. Map 4 locates the principal Punan groups mentioned throughout
this study. The last section of this chapter provides a brief look at the
ways in which these different groups have been named and may be
classified.

The Nomads of Borneo

The groups collectively known as Punan, traditionally nomadic hunter-gatherers but now in general fully or partially settled,
are spread out over the three northern provinces of Indonesian Kalimantan, Sarawak, and Brunei. They are for the most part very inade-
quately known. Dozens of groups exist for whom no ethnographic
data whatsoever have been gathered; even a complete inventory of
present-day Punan groups is still to be made. The absence of permanent autonyms, names that groups use to refer to themselves, and the
frequent migrations of the Punan, can make it hard to identify groups
mentioned in the literature at the beginning of the century with those
that exist today. Thus the literature includes an impressive number of
ethnonyms old and new (exonyms, names imposed by nonmembers),
corresponding to a more limited number of actual ethnic groups.

Apart from this characteristically meager array of ethnographic
source materials, and because of it, we have little understanding of
exactly who the Punan are, ethnically, culturally, and linguistically. A
further complication is that contacts between Punan and various
major groups of sedentary Dayak farmers have led to indisputable
similarities between the cultures and languages of the different Punan
groups and those of their more settled neighbors.

Sources and Studies

The colonial literature, in Kalimantan as in Sarawak, provides an enormous body of documentation, which entails a consider-

able effort of sifting and winnowing for the sake of very meager results. Indeed, though certain relatively old sources mention the existence of nomads in the interior of the island, almost nothing in the literature prior to 1900 provides more than occasional very brief notes about them, and almost always these notes are based on secondhand information or unfounded rumors. Only in the last few years of the nineteenth century, which saw the first major expeditions into the interior, does a more reliable body of data appear, based on firsthand information. Even this rarely consists of more than a few paragraphs, at best a few pages: no real studies are undertaken. Moreover, these data from the literature may be difficult to utilize, given their use of multiple and sometimes idiosyncratic ethnonyms. The difficulties will be clear from a glance at the first paragraphs of Chapters 2 and 3. Nevertheless, even such sparse scraps of information can be of some help in the development of historical reconstructions.

After 1950 the first serious articles about the nomads of Borneo began to appear, starting with Harrisson, Needham, and Urquhart, and continuing a little later with Tuton Kaboy, Benedict Sandin, and Johannes Nicolaisen. However, all of these studies focus exclusively upon groups living in Sarawak. Only after 1980 did the nomads become a specific topic of study, with dissertations and other entire works devoted to them, not only in Sarawak (Peter Kedit) but also in Kalimantan (Hildebrand's compilation of earlier sources, Hoffman's dissertation, and my own dissertation, upon which this present work is based). Other work in progress, notably that of Brosius, indicates that this area of study is at last developing, for which one can only be thankful. But the opportunity for fieldwork among true nomads may already be past, for the last of them are vanishing under the pressures of the modern world.

Classifications

In the different regions of Borneo, a variety of terms have been and still are used by the farming groups to refer to the nomads. Three main ideas emerge in the concept that the farmers have of the nomads: nomads live farther upstream, in the mountainous highlands; they live in the forest; they have no village, but are constantly moving. Hence the most common terms of reference: "upriver people" *(olo ot)*, in Central Kalimantan; "mountain people" *(ukit, tau 'ukit, bukit)* in Sarawak and West Kalimantan; "forest people" *(tau toan)* in West Kalimantan; and the terms *penan, pennan, punan* (of controversial etymology, but which some authors say may mean "to wander in the forest"), used in Kalimantan, Sarawak, and Brunei. The term Basap is also used, referring to the nomads who live close to the coasts of East Kalimantan.

It is important to emphasize from the start that all of these are exonyms. These first-order exonyms are generally followed by a second-order exonym, distinguishing the group more precisely, which is a toponym, a name referring to the place where the group lives: for example, the Olo Ot Nyawong (the nomads of Mount Nyawong), or the Punan Serata (nomads of the river Serata). Obviously, when the band of nomads living on the Serata leaves this river to make its home elsewhere, its new neighbors will know it by a different name. Thus, for example, the Punan Serata were successively called Punan Langasa, Punan Nya'an, and at last Punan Merah. The name of Olo Ot Nyawong, similarly, is that given in Central Kalimantan to the Kereho, who are known as Punan Keriau in West Kalimantan. One can imagine the difficulties that arise when it becomes necessary to identify the groups referred to by these different ethnonyms.

Generally speaking, moreover, the nomads themselves will confirm the exonym (or successive exonyms) by which others call them. In certain cases a toponym becomes their autonym, and the first-order exonym is dropped: thus the Lisum (or Punan Lisum). It would be no exaggeration to say that the nomads are not in the least concerned with the names used to refer to them, which hardly simplifies matters.

There are, or used to be, dozens of little nomadic groups in Borneo, and the linguistic and cultural relationships among them are yet to be definitively established, most particularly because of the notable scarcity of field data. In Sarawak, there have been attempts at classification (by Needham, for example). From my own data and on the basis of linguistic affinities, a significant subgrouping appears, which spread in the course of its migrations from western Sarawak and West Kalimantan (Bukat-Ukit, Beketan, Sru, Lugat) over to the middle Mahakam (Lisum, Beketan). Another subgroup that may be closely related to the first includes the Punan Aput-Busang of the Apo Kayan and the Punan Merah (or Kohi) of the Mahakam. A third major subgroup may unite the nomads of the northeast of Sarawak and those of the northern part of East Kalimantan, while the Basap and the Punan Kelai-Segah may form a fourth subgroup in the eastern part of East Kalimantan. The Kereho, Hovongan, Seputan, and Aoheng of the Müller and Schwaner mountain ranges form yet another subgroup. A group of related bands of nomads may also have existed along the border between East and Central Kalimantan, of which there only remain, in the north, the Punan of the Murung River (henceforth called Punan Murung), and perhaps the Bukit of the Meratus mountains in the south.

Whatever the validity of such a classification, it must remain merely hypothetical so long as a serious linguistic survey of all nomadic or formerly nomadic groups is still to be made. What can be said with certainty is that all these nomad languages appear to be more or less closely related. Moreover, the cultural similarities among all these groups have frequently been remarked upon. This aspect of the problem will be discussed in Chapter 4.

At the present day, very few truly nomadic groups still exist. Most of them, if not completely converted to a sedentary life and the cultivation of rice, have at least begun to live in relatively permanent villages for part of the year.

CHAPTER 2
THE BUKAT

THE BUKAT are a small group of hunter-gatherers whose original home is the upper Kapuas (West Kalimantan). The total number of individuals who answer to this ethnonym is estimated at 600. About 300 of them live in West Kalimantan, 150 in East Kalimantan, and perhaps 150 in Sarawak (see Map 5). I visited the first group in 1981 and the second in 1974, 1975, 1980, and 1981, but I have no firsthand information on the Sarawak group. Most of the Bukat began to adopt a sedentary life at the beginning of this century, but up to the present they still depend upon wild sago. After reconstructing the history of the various Bukat subgroups, I will describe the changes that have taken place in their culture and society in the course of the past century and a half. Places mentioned in the text can be located through the Index, which refers via grid coordinates to Maps 7.1 through 7.8, whose relationships are shown on the larger-scale Map 7.

Historical Reconstruction
Written Sources, Ethnonyms, and Ethnic Groups

All the Bukat locate the origins of their ethnic group along the river Mendalam, which they call the Buköt (see Map 6). The name of this river is the source of the ethnonym Buköt, which is the present autonym of the group, both in West and East Kalimantan. This ethnonym has, in its turn, given rise to the exonyms Bukot (in Aoheng), Hovukot (in Hovongan or Punan Bungan), Bohukot (in Kereho or Punan Keriau and in Seputan), and Bukat (in Kayan, and subsequently in the Dutch literature; in common use since Lumholtz 1920).

Another ethnonym that has been used to designate the Bukat is Ukit. The Maloh call all nomads or ex-nomads *tau 'ukit* (mountain people, hillmen) or *tau toan* (forest people; King 1985:52). The Iban call the Bukat Uket or Ukit, and in Sarawak the Bukat were regularly referred to as Ukit even in written sources (referring also to the Bukat of Kalimantan). This term would appear to be derived from the Malay *bukit,* mountain (see Anonymous 1882). The expression *orang bukit,* mountain people, is used in Malay dialects to refer to the Bukat of the Mahakam (Stolk 1907). One may also note the phonetic variant Buket in certain languages of Sarawak (see Guerreiro 1987). It is interesting to note the phonetic convergence between the autonym Buköt and the term *bukit/ukit,* and the semantic association between nomads and mountains that lies behind it.

The identification of Ukit with Bukat has been frequently pointed out, as long ago as the end of the nineteenth century (Büttikofer 1894: 438; Haddon 1905:314; up to King 1979b:94, and Seitz 1981:282). Harrisson (1965:324) reports the mention by his Maloh informants of Ukit on the Mendalam and the Sibau. The Ukit are sometimes called Punan Ukit on the upper Balui in Sarawak (J. Nicolaisen 1976b:43).

The old Dutch literature made the correct distinction between the "Mankettan," a general term for the nomads of the right bank of the Kapuas (the "true" right bank, facing downstream), and the Punan, nomads of the left bank (von Kessel 1849:167; Veth 1854:I, 57). However, it did not in general distinguish between the Bukitan (or Beketan) and the Bukat, the two nomadic groups of the right bank. This distinction is nevertheless essential to the history of these groups, since the Bukat-Ukit and the Bukitan-Beketan were notorious enemies.

The term *Bukat* seems to appear in the literature only with the period of the Nieuwenhuis expedition and the installation of a Dutch resident in the upper Kapuas (1893–1894), with Büttikofer (1894–1895), and subsequently Molengraaff (1900, 1902) and Nieuwenhuis himself (1900a and elsewhere). This does not prevent Nieuwenhuis (1900a:267), and after him Enthoven (1903:86), from noting the presence of "Punan" along the right bank of the Kapuas, in the Sibau and the Mendalam. Freeman, in Sarawak, clearly distinguishes the Ukit from the Beketan (1970:134).

With regard to the Mahakam region of East Kalimantan, the first mention of the Bukat in the literature seems to be that made by Tromp (1889:291), who calls them Penhing-Bahungan, and considers them to be Penihing (or Aoheng) originally from the river Bungan. Subsequently, Nieuwenhuis (1900a and elsewhere) and Molengraaff (1900) call them Bukat, confirming their identity with the Bukat of the Kapuas. Stolk (1907), meeting Bukat on the Kacu, proposes the ethnonym Punan Habungku.

Mention should be made here of a reference in the Sarawak literature to the Sru who lived on the river Baleh, perhaps in the eighteenth century, in the region of the river Gaat. These Sru were scattered by incoming Kayan at the start of the nineteenth century, and some of them left for the Kapuas, while others went down the river Rejang. Around 1850 this second group was once again attacked and dispersed, this time by the Iban (see Sandin 1956:68–69), and some of them fled toward "Lusum" (F. de R. 1963:259). Those who retreated downriver before the Kayan ultimately disappeared as a separate ethnic group after 1900 (Bailey 1963:251).

It appears that a group of these Sru did in fact come back to the Baleh after the Kayan had left it, settling more specifically along the Gaat (or Lugat), where they were known by the name Lugat; as late as 1882, reference is made to two of these Lugat villages (Low 1882). Some of the Sru who fled before the Kayan toward the Kapuas lived under this same name, Logat, first with the Maloh of the river Embaloh, then between 1840 and 1860 with the Aoheng of the upper Kapuas, and at last settled themselves on the upper Mahakam as an Aoheng subgroup (see Sellato 1986b:337–339). For more on the Sru, one may turn to Harrisson's manuscript (undated).

As for those who were said to have fled to Lusum, they are in fact the Lisum (also known as Uma Lisum or Uma Lissoom), who lived for some time on the upper Balui, above Belaga (Deshon 1901a:8, 1901b: 117; Anonymous 1907:135). Between 1910 and 1920, again under the pressure of Iban raids, they left Sarawak for the Apo Kayan region of East Kalimantan, where they placed themselves under the protection of the Lepo' Tau Kenyah. Despite this, they were yet again the victims of Iban raiding parties (Elshout 1926:243). The descendants of the few who escaped these massacres live today in the region of the Boh and the upper Belayan, still under the name of Lisum.

The Sru apparently represent a nomadic group distinct from the Bukat and the Beketan. Indeed, they have preserved their own identity throughout their history, even in their contacts with the Beketan (on the Embaloh and the Belayan) and the Bukat (on the Kapuas and the upper Mahakam). Sru, Ukit, and Beketan were three distinct groups despite the similarities in their language and way of life, just as the Lisum, the Bukat, and the Beketan are today.

If one sets aside a few descriptive remarks by explorers and colonial administrators, the Bukat are barely mentioned in the literature. Among the fullest, relatively speaking, of the descriptions that exist one may mention those of Veth (1854), Molengraaff (1900, 1902), Nieuwenhuis (1904–1907), Enthoven (1903), Lumholtz (1920), and Bouman (1924); but these consist in general of no more than a few paragraphs, or at best a few pages. One may also mention the more recent articles by King on the nomads of the upper Kapuas (1974b, 1975a, 1975b, 1979b), and Hildebrand's compilation of earlier material (1982).

No researcher has focused on the Bukat of the Kapuas, aside from Bücher who published nothing besides a series of articles in a Jakarta daily paper. With regard to linguistic research, though there exist a few word lists from Sarawak of Beketan (also called Mangkettan, Bukitan, Bakatan or Pakatan; Cense and Ühlenbeck 1958:36–37), very little is available on the Bukat-Ukit: a 1910 manuscript by Page-Turner (see Ray 1913:47) and another by Urquhart (1955), both concerning the Ukit of Sarawak. A list of 310 words was collected for the Ukit of the Balui by Rousseau in 1971. Bücher undoubtedly compiled a vocabulary for the Bukat of Kalimantan, but these data are inaccessible (see Bücher 1970).

The Bukat of the Mahakam have apparently been little visited, and material on them in the literature is almost nonexistent. One may note Vorstman (1952) and Lumholtz (1920), who provide some information, and a manuscript word-list of four pages (Lumholtz). I myself have collected 800 words and 250 phrases from the Bukat of the Kapuas (1981), and a shorter vocabulary from the Bukat of the Mahakam (1980).

The Regional Situation around 1800

The central region of Borneo (the watersheds of the upper Kapuas, the upper Barito, the upper Mahakam, and the Baleh) was the scene of notable changes in the last decades of the eighteenth century and the first decades of the nineteenth. Major groups of farming peoples, the Ot Danum in the south, Taman in the west, and Kayan and Long Gelat in the East, had some degree of hostile interaction with each other from one river basin to the next, while small bands of nomads held the vast central area, sparsely populated but important as a zone of transit.

The Bukat (to be called by this name, since this variant prevails locally as well as in the literature) locate their own origins in the upper Mendalam, right tributary of the upper Kapuas (see Map 6). Apparently they were already in this area when, at some indeterminate time in the past, the Taman (or Maloh) arrived there (King 1985:52). This latter group settled along the Sibau, the Mendalam, the Mandai, and the Embaloh, more precisely on the alluvial plains along the lower courses of these rivers, and along the Kapuas below the rapids. These Taman groups, farmers with a stratified society, assimilated some of the nomads and pushed others farther toward the headwaters (King 1985:52). At the turn of the nineteenth century, a group of Ot Danum (locally called Ulu Air, Ulu Ai', or Ulu Ayer) came from the south or the east to settle the upper Mandai; but though they no doubt had contacts with the nomads of their region, they had none to speak of with the Bukat. At that time Putussibau may have been no more than a simple trading center established by Malays and perhaps by Chinese, but the sultanate of Bunut (at Nanga Bunut) farther downstream was a local political power and economic center.

According to my informants, the Bukat territory in this region included the Mendalam above its junction with the Selua' (see Map 7.1), the high country around Mounts Paku and Selua', and the left tributaries of the Sibau. The far bank of the Sibau was probably the territory of the Bukitan (or Beketan), another nomad group also in contact with the Taman. The Bukat range spread southeastward as far as the north bank of the Kapuas, above the mouth of the Penyeriang (the area of the first rapids in the Kapuas itself, a little upstream from present-day Nanga Balang). Their neighbors on the south bank of the Kapuas were the nomadic Kereho (called at present Punan Keriau and Punan Bungan), who lived in the basins of the Kereho (or Keriau) and the Hovongan (or Bungan).

Some Bukat informants believe that the entire basin of the river Baleh in Sarawak formed part of the traditional territory of their ancestors. It may reasonably be accepted that they controlled, though they may not have permanently occupied, the left bank of the river: the Belatei and the Metevulu (if not the entire basin of the Menyivung). They did occupy this region up to the beginning of the twentieth century, and it is not inconceivable that their range may have extended much farther to the west at the beginning of the nineteenth century. Indeed, among the other ethnic groups known to exist at that time, the Tanyung and Kanowit lived much farther down the river Rejang; the Beketan were no doubt still farther to the west; and the Iban had not yet begun their migration up the Baleh. On the other hand, Kayan groups were beginning to arrive from the east, leaving the area of the Apo Kayan to occupy the Balui, and some of these may have already been passing through the Baleh as early as 1780. Some of these Kayan, the Uma' Aging, would be found a little later in the Kapuas river basin.

To the east, Bukat bands probably occupied all the northern part of the Müller mountains, as far as the right tributaries of the Mahakam above present-day Long Apari. As early as 1760, Kayan from the Apo Kayan had begun to settle in the upper Mahakam, dominating the native groups or driving them away. These local groups, known as Pin, are related to the present-day Ot Danum of the basin of the river Barito (for details, see Sellato 1986b, and Chapter 5 below). Some of these Pin fled toward the Barito, others toward the lower Mahakam (becoming the Tunjung Linggang), while others took refuge upstream. Of this last group some went to live along the Kacu, where they mingled with local nomads (no doubt a subgroup of the Kereho) to become the group called Seputan; others went to the Huvung, where they were to become a subgroup of the Aoheng; still others, close to the headwaters of the Mahakam, blended with Acue nomads from the east to form the upriver Aoheng subgroup. These are the people with whom, a little before 1800, nomads called Halunge came into contact. The Halunge, bearing the name of the river where they lived in the headwaters of the Mahakam, are unambiguously identified with the Bukat by their present-day descendants. These nomadic Halunge were later to assimilate completely into the future Aoheng, but other Bukat bands would range the same area after them.

Such, to the best of our knowledge, were the regions occupied by the Bukat just before the turn of the nineteenth century. The next section proposes a view of Bukat history through that of a number of local bands for which oral tradition and the rare written sources allow for a reconstruction.

1800–1850 (Map 8.1, Chronology I)

The oral tradition of the Bukat of the Kapuas mentions three groups: two in the Mendalam, the upriver Bukat (Buköt Ut) and the

downriver Bukat (Buköt Alung), and one in the Sibau, the Buköt
Hovut. The upriver Bukat comprised a certain number of autonomous
nomadic bands ranging the upper tributaries of the Mendalam and the
mountainous highlands around them. These included the Tayung,
Tovaliu, Mekajo, Temoan, Höloi, Soa Kalöp, Koyan, and the Tain
Kiat (or Taing Kiat), group names that correspond to local toponyms.
It may be that not all these bands existed at the same time, and that
two or more of these ethnonyms in fact refer to the same band. The
downriver Bukat were similarly divided into Salua' (living along the
Selua') and Hovat (living along the Hovat). These groups, by their
geographical location, were in direct contact with their farmer neighbors of the lower Mendalam. The Bukat of the Sibau lived along the
Hovut (which may be the stream the Taman call the Jut), a left tributary of the Sibau. These may in fact be the same bands as those of the
river Selua', whose nomadic range also included the Sibau. The
downriver Bukat and the Bukat of the Sibau had entered into relations
with the Taman groups that occupied the lowlands of the Mendalam
and the Sibau. It is probable that these Taman were already engaged in
barter with the nomads.

Whatever the situation, it was altered by the arrival of the Kayan,
coming from the Apo Kayan by way of Sarawak. Apparently they settled first in the upper Sibau; then, under the pressure of Iban raids,
some subgroups among them went back to Sarawak. The Kayan Uma'
Aging stayed, and eventually went on down toward the middle Sibau.
This Kayan group arrived, Bouman tells us (1924:181), at the very
start of the nineteenth century, under a chief named Batang Lalang.
Finding the land occupied by the Taman (see Enthoven 1903:79), and
not numerous enough to carve out a territory for themselves by force,
they had to acknowledge the overlordship of the Taman in order to
obtain one (Bouman 1924:181–182; 1952:86). The Taman subjected
them to a variety of aggravations, to the point that the Kayan, as they
report (Bouman 1924:182), called their Kayan brothers, who had
moved into the Mahakam, to come and rescue them. This was the
start of the great war expedition of the Mahakam people against
the Taman.

The opinions of informants from the different ethnic groups involved, and those of different authors, are not in agreement on the
exact origin of this war. According to the Taman, it was a matter of a
dispute between Liju, ruler of the Long Gelat of the Mahakam, and
Ajang (if that was his name), chief of the Taman of the Embaloh

(Maloh). According to the Aoheng, it was the harassment of Taman at the border of their territory by the Kereho and Semukung that led the Taman to launch an attack up the Kapuas as far as the Bungan, which Liju found unacceptable (see the discussion in Sellato 1986b).

Nieuwenhuis gives no other explanation than the desire of the Long Gelat to establish their hegemony over the peoples of the upper Kapuas and levy tribute upon them (1904–1907:I, 57–58). He suggests that Liju may possibly have tried to attack not only the Taman and the Ot Danum but also the Kayan Uma' Aging, whom he spared only through the efforts of a heroic Uma' Aging warrior named Bang. In this he is probably mistaken, because Liju was accompanied by other Kayan related to the Uma' Aging, and Bouman notes that some Taman who had been hidden by their Kayan neighbors were able to escape the massacre. It is entirely likely, on the other hand, that Liju did subsequently establish an alliance with the Uma' Aging through a marriage with the daughter of a ruler, as Nieuwenhuis reports (1904–1907:I, 57–58). He also formed an alliance with the sultan of Bunut (Bouman 1924:182).

Whatever the cause, Liju Li', called Liju Aya' (the Great), whom Bouman calls the Dayak Napoleon (1952:50), chief of a powerful army of Long Gelat warriors, took command of a coalition of Mahakam peoples, among them the Kayan Mahakam and the Kayan Uma' Suling and Uma' Wak, who had recently arrived from Sarawak. All of them assembled on the Serata in the upper Mahakam and, around 1830, entered the Kapuas. Liju's armies burned village after village, driving the Taman, it is said, as far downriver as Sintang (or Selimbau, according to Enthoven), and drove the Ot Danum toward the Melawi (Enthoven 1903:418). Only the Maloh of the Embaloh, who probably took refuge farther up their river, were able to remain in the region (Enthoven 1903:418). Liju went back to the Mahakam with an enormous amount of loot and a great number of captive slaves. Only then could the Kayan Uma' Aging settle the Mendalam in peace (Enthoven 1903:79).

It was during that same period that the Semukung (or Uheng, from the Punan name of the Kapuas), a nomadic group coming from Sarawak, began to establish themselves in the upper Kapuas, on the left bank. They are known to have had clashes with the Aoheng, but nothing is known of their relations with the Bukat. Hovongan and Kereho traditions, as well as that of the Semukung, report that Liju's military logistics entailed a demand for the services of these nomadic groups.

The downriver Bukat, too, are said to have been put to work, their contribution being the making of swidden farms at the mouth of the Muti, in the headwaters of the Kapuas, to feed Liju's armies.

For the moment we will postpone consideration of the upriver Bukat, isolated in the headwaters of the Mendalam, in order briefly to explore the situation of these downriver Bukat. They were called Salua', from the name of this right tributary of the Mendalam (variously transcribed as Selua' or Seluwa), and also Hovat, from the name of a left tributary (or Obat; in Kayan, Huvaat). These Bukat made very early contact with the Kayan, probably shortly after the arrival of this group, on the Sibau and then on the Mendalam. These contacts were no doubt made through the Taman. Tjilik Riwut (1979:234) notes that the *suku Mendalam* (the Mendalam group, the Bukat), after having been "subject" to the Taman, passed under the control of the Kayan.

Opinions differ on the nature of the relations between Kayan and Bukat. Some informants say that the Bukat were enemies of the Kayan, who, on the other hand, had good relations with the Bukitan (though this group was geographically more distant). Others say that relations between Kayan and Bukat were very close, as evidenced in particular by the alliance of the two groups against the Iban (though this dates from a later period).

According to Molengraaff, the Kayan had good relations with the Bukat (1900:177; 1902:169) and with the Beketan (1902:188). Among earlier authors, von Kessel (1849:187) notes that "Punan" and Pari (Kayan) were in close communication, but it is unclear whether his term "Punan" includes the Bukat. Veth, more precise, reports that the Mankettan (assumed to include both Bukat and Beketan) were at peace with the Pari (1854:I, 57), and elsewhere that Kayan, Punan, and Mankettan were allied against the Dayak of the Maloh—that is, the Taman of the Embaloh (1854:II, 372). This latter point implies that the Bukat were indeed on the side of the Kayan in Liju's great war against the Taman.

Were the downriver Bukat, then, or at least a portion of them, already undergoing a process of sedentarization around 1830? It is not unlikely that they did make swidden farms at the mouth of the Muti, which is quite close to the Hovat by overland travel. Bouman also affirms that Liju made farms in the headwaters of the Kapuas before going on downriver to attack the Taman (1924:182). One may consider the possibility that at this period the Bukat of the Selua' and the

Hovat already had sufficiently close relationships with the Kayan, perhaps by intermarriage, for the Kayan to have gotten them to participate, if not in the allied army's campaigns, at least in its provisioning. In any case, there are other examples of identical interaction: Liju had already gotten the nomads of the Kacu to settle, by marrying his brother to the daughter of a headman of the Pin, who controlled them (see Sellato 1986b). Apparently it was not uncommon for a ruler among the farming peoples to move "his" nomads around as he liked, and for his own purposes.

This is all that is known of the downriver Bukat. After Liju's invasion, they assimilated into Kayan communities in the Mendalam and ceased to exist as a separate ethnic group. Nevertheless, it is possible that some of them moved to (or back to) the Sibau, forming the group known as the Bukat of the Sibau.

Not long after the end of the war of Liju Aya', an Aoheng group led by Nyagang came to settle on the banks of the Kapuas, joining the first Semukung. In their final dispersal (1840–1850) the Semukung left the headwaters of the Kapuas. Some went off toward the Mahakam, others toward the Bungan (where they mingled with the Kereho to constitute the group called Hovongan), and yet others went down the Kapuas, settling first at Nanga Hakat, then around 1850 below the rapids, with the Aoheng.

The Bukat once again began to range from the northern part of the Müller mountains over to the right tributaries of the Mahakam, while, on the Mendalam, upriver Bukat little by little replaced the downriver Bukat in the region of the Hovat and the Selua'. Both of these processes will be discussed below.

To return to the upriver Bukat, at the start of the nineteenth century, according to informants, they were divided into eight bands: the Tayung, Tovaliu, Mekajo, Temoan, Höloi, Soa Kalöp, Koyan, and Tain Kiat. As noted, it is possible that rather than designating eight distinct bands, these terms refer to places in which a smaller number of bands may have successively lived; nevertheless, the Bukat tell the story of these bands as if they were distinct and synchronous. The mountain massifs of the Bukat range, as described above, are in any case vast enough to provide a living for eight bands of fifty or so people, or indeed for many more.

The Tayung and the Tovaliu appear never to have left the river Mendalam throughout their history. The Tayung must have eventually become part of the Tovaliu, since this latter band is best remembered today. Even so, little enough is known of the history of the Tovaliu. They ranged for decades along the Mendalam, took over the lands along the Hovat left free by the assimilation of the downriver Bukat to the Kayan, and finally settled themselves at Nanga Hovat (or Nanga Obat), probably around 1850. They lived there for a long time, in a camp of small huts. The location of this site is highly strategic, since it is precisely on the border between lowlands and mountains, at the limit of Kayan farmlands and consequently at the interface between Kayan and Bukat, the zone of contact between two economic systems. Nanga Hovat was a trading center for Kayan barter with these upriver Bukat come down from the hills, as it had no doubt been earlier for the downriver Bukat.

There was another reason besides trade for this closer relationship, a political reason: the pressure of the Iban upon the upper basins of the Sibau and the Mendalam. A little after 1800, the Iban had begun to move into Sarawak (Pringle 1970:214), and as early as 1830 they had established themselves on the Embaloh (Veth 1854:55), from which they staged headhunting raids against the Bukitan of the Embaloh and the Bukat of the Mendalam and the upper Baleh (Pringle 1970:214). The situation was to worsen in the second half of the century, with the alliance between Beketan and Iban and the intensification of their attacks.

Nothing is known of the Bukat bands who ranged the basin of the river Baleh, in Sarawak, at the start of the nineteenth century, not even their names. We do know that among the bands of upriver Bukat already mentioned, several—the Mekajo, the Temoan, and the Höloi —lived on the right tributaries of the upper Mendalam, in the region of the Ulu Selua' mountains. These three bands were the first to be exposed to the attacks of the Bukitan, then of the Iban, as early as the 1830s. The Mekajo were further decimated by disease.

Between raids and sickness, the few that remained of these three bands scattered. Some families went toward the headwaters of the Mendalam, farther to the east, and formed the band known as the Belatung, which managed to maintain itself in the same area until 1910, when it regrouped with other bands by administrative order to settle at Nanga Hovat. Other families crossed the mountains toward the Baleh (by the pass to the west of Mount Loi), and, possibly joining with other Bukat of that region, established themselves on the Metevulu, the Belatei, and the Halangi, left tributaries of the upper Baleh, most probably around 1840. It is to these Bukat, and their precursors in the area, that Bouman refers (1924:175) by the name of Dayak Menyimbung (meaning the stream variously transcribed as Menyivung or Mengiong), mistakenly concluding that the origin of the Bukat is to be sought on the Baleh.

These Bukat of the Baleh were then known by the name of Ukit. Brooke noted a little later (1866:II, 250) that the Ukit of the Baleh were on excellent terms with their Kayan neighbors of the Balui. Such, unfortunately, was not the case with the Iban, who were beginning to conquer the Rejang.

The Bukat Metevulu, on the front lines against the Iban and their Beketan allies (see Sandin 1967–1968:228), quickly separated around 1850 into two groups, one of which stayed to confront the enemy or slowly retreated to the east, while the other left the region for right tributaries of the high headwaters of the Kapuas, the Oseai, and Helevusu'. There, oral tradition knows them by the name of Helevusu'. Some of them will reappear a little later, on the Mahakam (below). The Bukat Belatei held their ground in Sarawak for about twenty more years before emigrating toward the headwaters of the Kapuas, around 1860–1870. This group, too, will be discussed later.

About the Bukat Halangi very little is known. Closer to the main river, they may have been more exposed to Iban attack. The ethnonym Halangi corresponds either to the Langei, a tributary of the Belatei, or to the Jalangi of the maps. In any case, the Halangi came back toward the Kapuas around 1850 (perhaps by way of the Helangi, a small left tributary) and rejoined the Belatung band in the headwaters of the Mendalam.

A word on the Bukat of the Sibau, mentioned above. These Bukat Hovut, as they were called, lived on the upper Sibau in the region of the Hovut, which may be the river the Tamans call the Jut. There is a footpath from the Hovut to the Mendalam, via the Selua'. It has been suggested that these Bukat formed part of the downriver Bukat, living in the mountains between Sibau and Selua', and controlling the left tributaries of the Sibau. Bücher (1970) states that the origin of the Bukat is to be sought along the Mendalam (or Buköt) and the Sibau (which the Bukat call Tawiou). It is likely that the Bukat of this mountainous highland split into two groups when the Kayan left the Sibau to settle the Mendalam, at the start of the nineteenth century. Some of them followed the Kayan to establish themselves on the Hovat and the Selua', while others stayed on the Hovut, maintaining a relationship with the Taman of the Sibau. The Bukat Hovut were undoubtedly subjected to attacks by the Beketan and the Iban after 1830. Indeed, tradition has it that they fled the area, returning to the Sibau only much later, at the start of the twentieth century.

On the Mahakam, we have already noted the presence of the Halunge, identified as a Bukat band (or several bands). Since some time prior to 1800 these Halunge had held all the right tributaries of the Mahakam above the Apari. Aoheng tradition reports that these nomads lived along the river Halunge at a place in the mountains called Hokuyat, and that they constantly harassed the groups of the left bank, nomads (Acue) as well as farmers (Amue and Auva). The Halunge apparently came to form two groups. One, under a leader named Utot, moved to the Bovasang (later also called Levusu') and at last made an alliance by marriage with the Amue of the other bank, settling near the Amue at Tomong Mo'ong. The other group stayed for some time on the Halunge, under a female leader named Penganun, then allied itself with the Acue and settled in Acue territory, at Takung Nanyang.

Subsequently, around 1800, Amue and Acue joined together under Tingang Senean, first historical chief of this core group of Aoheng. Toward 1820, the Halunge joined the Aoheng village of Long Acue, and from then on the Halunge, on their way toward sedentary living and ethnic assimilation, shared the fortunes of this emerging Aoheng subgroup (see Sellato 1986b), just as the downriver Bukat did those of the Kayan. In the village of Long Apari several families still remain today who say that they descend from the Halunge.

It may be noted in passing that in this instance Aoheng oral tradition provides precious information on a Bukat group (place-names and the names of leaders), information which moreover can be dated with some precision by means of genealogies. Bukat tradition itself, on the other hand, first gives a leader's name only at the start of the twentieth century.

1850–1900 (Map 8.2, Chronologies I and II)

At the start of the second half of the nineteenth century, the event of greatest importance in the upper Kapuas region was the massive population movement of Iban groups toward the north and west, and the ever-increasing pressure that they exerted on the upper Kapuas and the Baleh. The Bukitan, subject at first to Iban attacks (in 1860–1861, for which see Kater 1867:253, and again, later, Enthoven 1903:65), finally became their allies (Freeman 1970:34) and made more violent attacks upon their Bukat enemies of the Sibau, the Mendalam, and the upper tributaries of the Baleh. In 1855, the peoples of the upper Kapuas became Dutch subjects (Enthoven 1903:55), but the Bukat remained for the moment beyond the reach of colonial authority.

As noted above, some among the Bukat of the Metevulu left that area as early as 1850 for the headwaters of the Kapuas, around the Helevusu'. Since the Semukung had finally left this region, migrating downstream to the Kapuas, the Mahakam, and the Bungan, it was open for settlement. These Bukat Helevusu' will be discussed again a little further on. The other Bukat, who chose to stay on the Metevulu, are mentioned as nomads by the name of Ukit in the *Sarawak Gazette* (Anonymous 1882). Between 1860 and 1900, they gradually abandoned their lands before the joint attacks of Beketan and Iban, who were moving into the Baleh, and retreated toward the east. Some of them, perhaps the major portion, chose to return to the Mendalam. At last, at the turn of the century, led by a valiant fighter against the Iban named Sekudan (on whom more below), the last Bukat band left the Baleh river basin (probably via Mount Cemuki) to take refuge in the headwaters of the Mahakam. Freeman's sources confirm that the Bukat (Ukit) were driven toward the Mahakam (1970:150). After 1900 or 1905 there were no more Bukat on the Baleh.

In the meantime, around 1860–1870, the Belatei also left their land, heading for the upper Kapuas by the footpath over Mount Cemuki (see Molengraaff 1902:192) or by that of the Kenalau. They made their home on the Sivo, a tributary of the Tahum, as Lumholtz confirms (1920:218), and were therefore known as Bukat Sivo. There, in the mountains between the Sivo (Kapuas) and the former Bukat territory of the Halunge, these Bukat harried the Aoheng (the subgroup known as Long Apari), who were then, around 1870, living at Data Noha. Identifying them with other Bukat (the Helevusu') who were at that time living on the Levuhi, and who had contacts with the Aoheng of the Huvung (below), the Aoheng Long Apari called these Bukat Sivo by the name of Levusu'. The Aoheng attacked the Bukat in retaliation for their raids, killing two Bukat, first Bayung and then Lemase. At this the Bukat moved down to the Bovasang (renamed Levusu'), and made peace with the Aoheng, who were at that time (1880) living

at Aring Opung. As a result of this alliance between the groups, there
is a Levusu' descent group among the Aoheng Long Apari.

Possibly at the request of the Aoheng, the Bukat went to live on the
Seke, on the left bank of the Mahakam, farther upstream. From this
position they patrolled the region of the headwaters. On occasion,
they killed a few Iban who had come over without permission to collect damar resin on Aoheng land. It is entirely likely that Aoheng and
Bukat acted together to organize raids against the Iban collectors; the
Bukat undoubtedly wanted revenge upon the Iban, and both they and
the Aoheng had reputations as fierce headhunters (Nieuwenhuis
1900a:293). In 1885 a large group of Aoheng accompanied by some
Bukat appeared in Kapit on the Rejang to trade and to pay a fine
imposed upon them by the Sarawak government for killings such as
these (SG 1885:31). But even on their journey home some of the more
uncontrolled among the Aoheng and Bukat warriors, meeting Iban
collectors along the way, committed fresh homicides (Sellato 1986b).

The result, in the summer of 1885, was a great Iban expedition
against the Mahakam, involving some thousands of fighters. Initially
meant as a punitive action against the upriver Aoheng and the Bukat,
this war soon lost all semblance of order: mobs of Iban warriors
burned all the villages of the Aoheng and also one Kayan village (for
details, see Sellato 1986b; also Elshout 1926:265). Aoheng and Bukat
took refuge in the upper Serata. There, the Bukat mingled even more
closely with the Aoheng, and also with the Punan Kuhi (or Kohi) who
had been living there for some time. It was there, tradition has it, that
these Bukat had their first experience with agriculture. During this
time Kayan and Aoheng chiefs from the Mahakam made their way to
Kapit (SG 1887:74), no doubt to negotiate a peace settlement and ask
for damages (see SG 1890:52; 1891:73).

After the Iban war and a temporary rally downriver (at Long Okap:
see Nieuwenhuis 1904:273–274),around 1900 the Aoheng of the
Long Apari subgroup went back upriver to Long Kacu. The Bukat
group broke up: some families stayed on the Serata, mingling with the
Aoheng Tiong Bu'u, while others followed the Aoheng Long Apari
upriver. From this time onward the upper Mahakam was to be under
Dutch administration, and these Bukat were officially considered to be
settled in fixed villages.

We return now to the Bukat of the Helevusu', in the upper Kapuas.
Toward 1850, some families of this group came to live on the left bank

of the Kapuas, in the region of the Tanyan. From there they made contact with the Aoheng subgroup living on the Huvung, and one of them asked for the hand in marriage of Sung, daughter of an Aoheng chief. According to Aoheng Huvung oral tradition, these people, who had long been sedentary farmers, looked down upon the nomads and rejected their offer. There followed a state of feud between the Aoheng Huvung and these Bukat (whom the Huvung called Levusu', after the river Helevusu'). This episode gave rise to a Huvung epic recounting the tale of Sung and her people and their conflicts with the Bukat.

An alliance was finally established (around 1860), with the marriage of a Bukat man named Sagong to Kuat, an Aoheng Huvung woman. The Bukat then went to live on the upper Levuhi (a tributary of the Apari), in the mountains (Diang Mokat and Diang Cangpalang), maintaining a regular trading relationship with the Huvung. Nieuwenhuis, a little later, described the Bukat as living in family groups in the forest, migrating from one valley to the next in search of wild game, fruits, and sago. They avoided contact with sedentary peoples except at the harvest season, when they temporarily joined up with one tribe or another (such as the Huvung) to trade forest products for rice, salt, cloth, and beads (1904–1907:255; see also 1900b: 198–199). These ties with the Aoheng Huvung were to last for the next half-century.

Although they had good relations with the Aoheng Huvung, the Bukat, from their base on the Levuhi, readily raided the Aoheng led by Irang Ubung, living at Doang Hakong (the subgroup later to be called Cihan). Tradition has it, in particular, that they took the head of a child. After this killing, a settlement brought hostilities to an end (around 1870), possibly through the mediation of the Huvung. Tehujei, the killer, paid a fine of one gong, and the Bukat gave one of their women (Dayun, the daughter of a leader variously called Tising or Pahang by different informants) to be married to Kuay, son of Irang. This is what the Aoheng call *ori totong hocong* (making a barrier against hostilities), a marriage of alliance (in Bukat, *petutung*).

In 1885 the great Iban expedition descended the Mahakam. The Huvung took refuge on the Penane, making a temporary village at Long Iri, where they spent some years. The Bukat, hereditary enemies of the Iban, scattered before their army. Some followed the Huvung to Long Iri, and others fled toward the Bungan (in the upper Kapuas). Once the danger was past, Sung, now the chief of the Aoheng Huvung, soon returned to the river Huvung with her people and settled in a new village at Levohon, along with some Bukat families. Her brother Kaya, for his part, stayed on the Penane and settled at Long Mecai, not far from a Seputan settlement, and a few Bukat stayed with him.

Tromp, in the first reference to Bukat on the Mahakam, reported three villages on the Kaso (Kacu): one village of "Penhing" (the Aoheng led by Kaya) of some seventy-five people downriver; then a Seputan village of about three hundred people; and finally, farthest upriver, a small settlement of about fifty "Penhing-Bahungan" (1889: 291). Actually, the three villages were on the Penane, a tributary of the Kacu, at Long Mecai, and so close as to touch each other along the river. The Penhing-Bahungan were the Bukat who went with Kaya. Bahungan is a misspelling of Bohongan (the Seputan name for the river Bungan), and refers to the origin of these Bukat, in the upper Kapuas (which itself is sometimes called Kapuas-Bohong, a name also derived from the Bungan). Nieuwenhuis reported Kaya's village in 1896–1897 (1900a:305). Those Bukat who took refuge on the Bungan stayed there for some time. Molengraaff, in 1893–1894, found them still encamped there, apparently near the mouth of the Bulit (1900:213; 1902:204). They later rejoined the others on the Penane.

In 1898–1899, Nieuwenhuis visited the Aoheng Huvung village of Levohon, which he calls Amun Lirung, from the teknonym of its chief, Bang, husband of Sung; he notes the presence of some Bukat huts nearby (1900a:295; 1900b:198–199, 201; 1904–1907:255). Nieuwenhuis also reports the slaughter of two Seputan by these same Bukat living with the Huvung. As he tells it, Lirung (actually Dirung), daughter of Sung, sent these Bukat after a certain Si Hebar, a "Malay"; since they were unable to catch him and bring his head back to Dirung, they killed two Seputan as a proof of their prowess (1904–1907:375). It should be noted that these are Seputan of the upper Kacu, not those of the Penane, who were allied with the Huvung. Aside from this, it is possible that this Si Hebar is in fact the well-known Raden Sahidal (whom the Aoheng called Sehidan), a trader from the Barito who traveled widely in the region. This episode of the killing of the two Seputan is also reported by Lumholtz (1920:253). It may be on the basis of these killings, for one thing, and the earlier skirmishes between upriver Bukat and Aoheng Long Apari, for another, that Lumholtz (1920:252) mistakenly refers to "wars" among Aoheng, Seputan, Kereho, and Bukat at this time.

The establishment of little groups of Bukat on the Huvung, the Bungan, or the Penane, in settlements already less impermanent than those prior to the Iban incursion, does not necessarily preclude the existence of families still living as nomads at that time in the Müller mountains, away from any villages; but nothing is known about them. It should, however, be noted that Sung (called by the teknonym Hinan Lirung, "mother of Lirung," actually, in Aoheng, Inon Dirung) ordered back to Sarawak some Batang Lupar Iban come to collect forest products on the territory of "her" Bukat (Nieuwenhuis 1904–1907:384), which suggests that some Bukat had gone back to nomadic living in the upriver forests. These Bukat Helevusu', with their ties to the Aoheng Huvung, like their cousins the Bukat Sivo with their own ties to the Aoheng Long Apari and the Aoheng Tiong Bu'u, were considered officially settled by the beginning of the twentieth century.

We return now to the other Helevusu', whom we left on the upper Kapuas around 1850. They continued to live in the region of the Oseai and the Helevusu' for several decades, as far as is known. Around 1880, these Bukat of the Helevusu' began to harry their Hovongan neighbors to the south. These Hovongan were a cluster of small groups, still partly nomadic, formed from the mingling of a portion of the Semukung and the Kereho of the Bungan. It is possible that, as tradition recounts, other Bukat (from the Mendalam, fleeing Iban raids) joined the Helevusu' to attack the Hovongan, and that these raids may have been instigated and backed by the Kayan of the Mendalam.

One of the first attacks was made on the Hovongan subgroup of the Bulit, the Hovorit, living at Maang Lo. Isolated farms were stormed, and five people killed. The Hovongan say that the Bukat lost their leader, Nuka, and five other warriors in that attack. A second attack took place against another Hovongan subgroup at Diang Kaung, in which a woman was abducted. At this some Hovongan moved off to live farther south, on the Belatung, while others rallied where they were. Tradition says that the woman who had been kidnapped managed to escape and rejoin her people at Diang Kaung, bringing with her two black Bukat dogs. The Hovongan who had stayed counterattacked: a score of warriors went up the Kapuas and confronted the Bukat far upriver at Baraharung, to which they had withdrawn after their raids. Taken by surprise, many of the Bukat were killed (between fifteen and thirty, according to Hovongan informants, but this is probably an exaggeration). The others fled to the upper Helevusu', or farther still to the upper Hakat; those from the Mendalam went back where they had come from.

This episode is not mentioned by Bukat informants. For them, there was never a real war against Hovongan or Kereho, "just a few heads taken," a bit of a squabble. Nevertheless, though the "Punan" (Hovongan and Kereho) and the "Mankettan" (Bukitan and Bukat) may have all been allied with the Kayan against the Taman (Veth 1854:II, 372), it does not necessarily follow that they were allied with each other. We may recall the skirmishes mentioned earlier (Lumholtz 1920:252), the mention of a war between Bukitan and Punan around 1890 by King (1975a), and the fact that the Bukat are described as headhunters more dedicated even than the Punan (Enthoven 1903:90). Finally, Wariso (1971:15) confirms the hostility between Punan and Bukat.

Even if the above accounts are not entirely to be relied upon, with regard either to dates given or to the groups in question (for what is known of the nomads comes almost entirely at second hand, from other ethnic groups), it is certain that at the end of the nineteenth century there was fighting among the nomad groups of the right bank of the Kapuas and the nomadic or partly settled groups of the left bank. Gemala, the old Bukat leader, recounts that after these "few heads" were taken, the Bukat made peace *(petutung)* with the Kereho, cementing their alliance with a ceremony of blood-brotherhood. In similar fashion, the hostilities with the Hovongan were ended with an alliance by marriage (around 1890), when the Bukat gave two women, Nyoripun and Nyata, to be married respectively to two Hovongan men, Suo and Da'a.

Shortly afterward, Hovongan and Bukat began to associate to some extent with each other. At the time of the very first Dutch expedition in this region (1893–1894), Molengraaff, as has been said, reported meeting several Bukat on the Bungan (Helevusu' in flight from the Mahakam), and other Bukat a little above the mouth of the Gung (again, these were Helevusu'); and he mentions the existence of other nomadic Bukat higher up the Kapuas (on the Helevusu' itself; 1902: 187; 1900:177). Evidently then, by the last decade of the nineteenth century, some families of Bukat in the upper Kapuas had already begun to build, if not truly permanent settlements, at least small riverbank villages.

We now turn once more to the Mendalam region, whose story was interrupted around 1850. The half-century that followed was a troubled one. The pressure of the Iban and their Beketan confederates on the Mendalam groups gradually became much stronger, as the raids of the headhunters became more frequent and more lethal. The Bukat bands of the upper river, Soa Kalöp, Tain Kiat, and Koyan, along with the groups of the Metevulu who had come back from the Baleh, were scattered and driven downstream, closer and closer to the Kayan. Nanga Hovat became a regrouping point for the Bukat in their disorderly retreat. Some families, around 1880, may have joined their cousins on the Helevusu'. Only the band known as Belatung, in the headwaters of the Mendalam, held firmly to its lands.

The headhunters' attacks were aimed not only at the Bukat, but also at the Taman (see King 1985) and the Kayan. Aoheng tradition mentions in particular a savage raid carried out around 1875 by Iban and Beketan on Nanga Tukung (also known as Urin Batu), a mixed Kayan-Aoheng village on the Kapuas. The village was burned, and the Kayan Uma' Pagung (newcomers to the region, who may have come from the Balui after the great expedition of 1863 against the Kayan), along with the Aoheng led by Nyagang, sought refuge with the Kayan of the river Mendalam. There they suffered another Iban raid, which, Aoheng tradition has it, took place, the year of the eruption of the volcano Krakatau (1883).

Nevertheless, on the whole, the situation in the region was quieter after 1880, the year the colonial government first placed a representative at Putussibau. The unrest among the Iban groups eventually subsided (Enthoven 1903:56), and relations between the Kayan Mendalam and the Iban also improved (SG 1886:93–94). In 1887 and 1888 peace treaties were made among the larger ethnic groups of the area, Iban, Maloh, Kantu', and no doubt Kayan as well, and from 1888 till the mid-1890s conditions were more or less stable (King 1976:103), due in particular to the installation of the Dutch Resident, Tromp, who lived there after 1893–1894 (Enthoven 1903:57). However, the situation was to worsen again with the Iban rebellions of the last years of the century (see Pringle 1970).

Even in 1894, though, Nieuwenhuis noted that the insecurity of conditions in the Mendalam led the Bukat to draw closer to the Kayan (1900a:73). A dozen Bukat were killed by the Iban (Anonymous 1894:5–2, paragraph 13), possibly in the upper Mendalam. Enthoven reported a significant gathering of Bukat in the 1890s on the upper Samus, between Mendalam and Sibau (1903:24, 87). The number he gives of 150 families is certainly exaggerated, as King notes (1979b:

93), given the area of the Samus river basin even including the surrounding mountains; nevertheless, it is possible that the colonial
administration had brought together there some of the Bukat who
were in flight from the headwaters.

However, no Bukat informant mentions the Samus as a dwelling-
place. It might be that this location was no more than a site for barter
trade, set up by the authorities for Bukat ranging farther to the north
or, for the sake of safety, more toward the east. Enthoven notes that
these Bukat (like other nomads) traded without direct contact with
their farmer neighbors (1903:88), the common practice among
nomads who had not yet established formal relations with their trading partners. This would suggest that these Bukat of the Samus would
indeed have been refugees from the headwaters rather than Bukat of
the Hovat, who were already well accustomed to trading with the
Kayan.

Whatever may have been the case with these people of the Samus,
this period of regroupment downriver (1870–1900) is in general one
of close contacts and marriage alliances between Bukat and Kayan
(Nieuwenhuis 1900a:217). Although the Kayan, who like the Taman
were stratified farmers, looked on the nomads with a certain contempt, economic motives prevailed (family ties facilitating trade in forest products), and King notes that marriages took place between well-
respected nomad leaders and Kayan women (1979b:95).

The situation in this troubled second half of the nineteenth century
must have been even more difficult for the Bukat of the Sibau than for
those of the Mendalam. Tradition has it that these Bukat Hovut were
half-annihilated by Bukitan and Iban raids, and that those who
escaped fled, most certainly toward the east. These would no doubt
have been among the Bukat reported by Enthoven on the Samus in
the 1890s (1903:24, 87). However, Nieuwenhuis (1900a:267) and
Enthoven (1903:86) both mention the presence of suspect "Punan" on
the upper Sibau. By the end of the century, according to Enthoven
(1903:66) and King (1975b), the majority of Bukitan had moved to
Sarawak, for the most part to the river Gaat, where other Bukitan (or
Beketan) may have already been living. A group of no more than
about sixty of them stayed on the Embaloh, where they were absorbed
into the Maloh, until by 1913 there was no longer a distinct Bukitan
community (King 1975a:3; 1985:53). These "Punan," unlikely therefore to be Bukitan, and still less likely to be Kereho from the left bank
of the Kapuas, may well have been Bukat. This makes it possible to

believe that a few brave Bukat Hovut families might have held their ground in the upper Sibau in spite of the raids.

A survey of the status of the Bukat around 1900 shows that there were then virtually no Bukat left in the Baleh: after having stubbornly resisted the Iban advance (King 1975a; Freeman 1970:134), they had finally left the region. There were several Bukat communities on the Mahakam, some of which lived part of the time in small villages. Similarly, more or less permanent hamlets existed on the upper Kapuas, and that of Nanga Hovat, on the Mendalam, was to serve as a central site for the future settlement of bands as yet still living a nomadic life upriver. Fully nomadic bands persisted as well in the headwaters of the Mahakam and the Kapuas. The twentieth century was to see an increasing degree of interference in the lives of the Bukat by the colonial and subsequently the Indonesian governments, and notable changes in the means of subsistence of these nomadic groups.

1900–1980 (Maps 8.3 and 8.4, Chronologies I and II)

I shall begin with the Bukat Hovut, of whom little is known. Whether or not some of them did stay in the upper Sibau during the time of the Iban and Bukitan headhunting raids, or others of them took refuge in the Samus, the Bukat Hovut seem to have reemerged into the light of history after these hostilities were over. The old leader Gemala told me that, under pressure from the authorities and after the peace treaties were made among the larger ethnic groups, Bukitan and Bukat made with each other a peace that endured, at least in regions close to administrative centers. After this the situation was more stable on the middle Sibau, as on the Mendalam. In any case, after 1910 there were few Bukitan left on the Embaloh. The Bukat Hovut consequently settled themselves once more in the Sibau, probably close to the local Taman. These people, still in the market for forest products, must have convinced "their" Bukat to stay and keep on supplying them, rather than going back to join the Bukat of the Mendalam, as the authorities wanted them to do.

Not having had the chance to visit these Bukat, I have no firsthand information on their recent history. Baling (1961) notes the presence of Bukat, whom he calls Punan Ukit, at Nanga Putan, above the mouth of the Sawei, on the upper Sibau. According to Bücher (1970), Nanga Putan was situated some four hours' paddling above the last Taman village. In 1977 there were reported to be five houses at Nanga

Putan (or Kutan: see Ding 1977:126). In 1987, Nanga Putan, an isolated village of five houses, was administratively assimilated to its nearest Taman neighbor (Guerreiro, personal communication). Indeed, an official map shows the name of no community (*desa*, the smallest discrete administrative unit) above the last Taman villages, which are known as Sibau Hulu I through V. Some of my informants indicate that there are Bukat living in the midst of one of these Taman villages. It is therefore possible that since 1970 a certain number of Bukat Hovut have joined a Taman village, while some stubbornly independent families still keep to themselves as a small settlement farther upriver. Whatever the case, it may be supposed that the conditions of existence of these Bukat have undergone the same transformations as those of their Bukat neighbors of the Mendalam, to whom we now turn.

Under the economic influence of the little town of Putussibau, also the local center of administration, Bukat trade became more and more important over this period, not only with Taman and Kayan but also with Malay petty traders (King 1979b:94–95). Bukat and Punan understand the Kayan language and the local Malay dialect, Senganan (Anonymous 1901:577). Gradually, as trade relations intensified, the Bukat came under the control of the colonial government. Around 1910 these authorities began a campaign to sedentarize these Bukat and convert them to agriculture (Bouman 1952:56; 1924:175). The Belatung, perhaps the last Bukat band to hold out in the upper Mendalam, came down to Nanga Hovat around this time, undoubtedly in response to government demands; but they stayed there no more than three years before going off to join the group led by Sekudan on the Kapuas. Under pressure, then, from the Dutch (and the Kayan), the Bukat began to farm. Bouman mentions two villages, Nanga Selua' and Nanga Hovat (1924:175), totaling 206 people (1924:192), and notes that the Bukat had replaced the simple shelters of their nomad camps with longhouses in the Kayan style (1924:175). One may stress, as Bouman does, the interesting fact that the men of the group kept up the nomadic life, ranging in search of forest products, while the women stayed at home to farm the group's swidden fields (1924:175).

As has been described, the Bukat leader Sekudan, after his flight from the Baleh, went to live in the headwaters of the Mahakam. Around 1910 he came back to the Kapuas, leaving behind in the

Mahakam a few families that had followed him, and settled alone or almost alone at Nanga Ira', near a group of Semukung. He went to fetch some of his relatives from Nanga Hovat and with them formed a group of two households on the Kapuas at Nanga Kerien, just above Nanga Ira'. They stayed there for two years, then the Belatung, who in the meantime had come down to Nanga Hovat, came to join him. Sekudan, his people, and the Belatung then moved to Nanga Balang, farther upriver, where they spent another two years. The Dutch placed confidence in Sekudan, so tradition reports, and encouraged his vision of bringing together all the Bukat in a truly Bukat village. With their approval this group moved a little farther upriver, to Nanga Keriau, around 1915.

Sekudan gradually persuaded some thirty families who were living as nomads on the Hangai to come and settle at Nanga Keriau. These Bukat of the Hangai were the remains of the former Mendalam bands Soa Kalöp, Koyan, and Tain Kiat, who were, so it is said, on their way back to the Mendalam after ranging the northern part of the Müller mountains. Their leaders were Bahun, Majai, Nahanye', Koeng, and Lejiu (note that the last two names are Kayan). Not much is known of what happened at this time to the last Helevusu'. It is possible that those who were still living on the Helevusu' ended by joining their cousins on the Mahakam. Those whom Molengraaff met above the mouth of the Gung probably followed Sekudan.

Around 1920, therefore, there were three Bukat villages: Nanga Selua' and Nanga Hovat in the Mendalam (Bouman 1924:175) and Nanga Keriau on the upper Kapuas. There may no longer have been any fully nomadic Bukat bands in the upper Mendalam, even though Bukat men continued to roam and work in the forest. On the other hand, the thirty families of the Hangai (a total of 150 to 200 persons, if the figure is not an exaggeration) were still nomads, as Bouman confirms (1924:175). They were probably not included in the 244 Bukat counted in the region of the upper Kapuas in 1927 (Tillema 1939:230, citing van Kempen Valk). It would be another decade before these families joined the group at Nanga Keriau.

In 1924 a general peace was made in Kapit among all the ethnic groups of the region, and from then on the situation on the Kapuas was calm. By 1930, all the Bukat were officially considered settled. The first phase of the program of sedentarization initiated by the Dutch around 1910 (see Bouman 1924, 1952; King 1979b:95) had been completed; there remained the matter of converting the nomads to agriculture. This happened only very slowly. Bouman noted that the men continued to make their living as nomads (1924:175), but, optimistically, he reported that the Bukat were eating an increasing amount of rice (1952:56).

In his map of 1961, Baling reported two Bukat villages on the Mendalam, Nanga Obat (Hovat) and Nanga Selirong; Bücher confirmed this in 1970 (Nanga Howat and Nanga Selirung). King gave a population of eighty persons for Nanga Hovat (1974:39). For this same village Ding Ngo estimated twenty households in 1977. My own data in 1980, from local statistics, give eighty-six inhabitants in ten households for the *desa* of Nanga Hovat. It is probable that the Nanga Selirung of Baling and Bücher was in fact no more than a hamlet only a little way upstream from the main community of Nanga Hovat, and forming part of it. In 1987, Nanga Hovat, as an autonomous *desa,* included eighteen houses for about 110 people, under the leadership of Jugah (Guerreiro, personal communication).

We return now to Nanga Keriau, where the old leader Sekudan died around 1940. Jaruk (the uncle of my informant Gemala), who replaced him, moved the village during the time of the Japanese occupation farther upriver, to Nanga Menilei (also known as Nanga Menjuei). Wariso, who visited the Bukat around 1967, records the name of the former village as Nanga Menjuei (1971:23). Narok, the son of Sekudan, and Gemala (son of Nyeparin) later brought the whole group down to Metelunai, where they live today. According to Bücher (1970), they established themselves there in 1963. The village, however, is noted by Baling in 1961. The move must have taken some years, extending over the decade of the 1960s. By 1967 Metelunai had 198 inhabitants, with a longhouse, a school (probably the one started by Bücher), and a community headman bearing the important title of *temanggung,* Gemala (Wariso 1971:5, 12, 14).

In the early sixties, Sawing, one of Gemala's sons, moved down the Kapuas and settled at Nanga Balang with two or three families. Baling (1961) notes the presence of "Temenggong Jemala" at Liu Daru ("long island," that is, the long island at the mouth of the river Balang). In reality Gemala, who may then have been visiting Nanga Balang, lived at Metelunai. From that time on, Bukat began to make swidden farms on the lower Keriau (in Kereho territory: see Wariso 1971:24), and Bukat and Kereho, old enemies, began to live together. Nanga Balang saw the arrival of a few Kereho families. Ding Ngo reports from 1977 that there were only five houses in Nanga Balang (125). According to King, the combined population of Metelunai and Nanga Balang reached a total of 200 persons (1974:39). King states that Nanga Balang is primarily inhabited by Punan (Kereho), while Ding Ngo seems to consider it as a Bukat village. The latter mentions also a small Bukat settlement far upriver, at Nanga Mensikei (1977:7), and counts a score of houses at Metelunai (1977:125). It seems, therefore, that between the visits of Wariso and Ding Ngo the longhouse was replaced by separate family houses.

Around 1975, a serious disagreement divided Metelunai, opposing Gemala and his other son Janen to another family head, Lahat. The first chose to leave the village, moving downstream with their families to settle at Nanga Tepai. My own data for Metelunai give 156 inhabitants in 1980 (local statistics). Supposedly included in this number, besides the village of Metelunai proper (about twenty-five houses), were the three households led by Gemala at Nanga Tepai, four families at Riam Pelahi at the mouth of the Gung, and four others at Sempolok. At Nanga Balang in 1981 there were six houses, two of them Bukat, three Kereho, and one Senganan (a group of upper Kapuas Moslems).

Officially, Nanga Balang was part of the *desa* or administrative unit of Metelunai, and therefore its population should be included among the 156 inhabitants of this *desa*. Note that there were also some Bukat individuals living at Nanga Ira', among the Semukung (or Uheng), and at Nanga Enap, among the Aoheng. It may be this emigration downriver that was responsible for the absolute drop in the population of the *desa* of Metelunai. Nevertheless, it is a more likely assumption that in fact only the Bukat families of Nanga Balang were included in the total official figure for Metelunai.

A few notes on certain aspects of modern political and economic life in these Bukat settlements: Each *desa* like Metelunai has a village headman or political representative (*kepala desa,* Lahat at Metelunai) and a headman in charge of applying traditional customary law, *adat* (*kepala adat).* For the latter type of leader there is a complex hierarchy. The title of *temanggung,* borne by Gemala and still used by his son Janen, would in principle make him the leader of all the Bukat of West Kalimantan, as the Bukat of the Mahakam confirm. The modern equivalent of this title seems to be *kepala kampong kompleks* (headman of several neighboring villages of the same ethnic group: see A.Y.H. 1980:21). Above this would be the title of *kepala persekutuan*

adat (headman of a cluster of several ethnic groups). Thus Janen
might officially be the leader of the Bukat and the Kereho together, a
possibility which the latter reject out of hand (Wariso 1971:15). It is
probable that the local government, in the context of its attempt to
bring together the nomadic groups in large downriver settlements, has
tried to impose a political restructuring that is opposed by those
groups who would lose their autonomy within it. This question of a
multiethnic leadership position may be pending at the present time; at
any rate, it was unclear in the minds of my informants, of whatever
ethnic group.

At the time of my most recent visits there were small shops in both
Nanga Balang and Metelunai, and another had recently been established in the Hovongan village of Nanga Bungan. Janen was raising a
few cows at Nanga Tepai; and timber companies with camps at Nanga
Ira' and farther downriver employed a few Bukat. Forest products
were exported downstream, including a small amount of damar resin
(prices are low), gold obtained by panning the gravel of the riverbed,
rotan floated down in bundles, and most of all illipe nut in season
(*tengkawang: Shorea macrophylla,* Dipterocarpaceae).

I return now to the Bukat of the Mahakam, last seen as they were in
1900. There were then four groups of these people, all with close ties
to Aoheng groups and living in their villages: one with the Aoheng
Huvung of the river Huvung, a second with the Aoheng Huvung of the
Penane, a third with the Tiong Bu'u, and the last with the Long Apari.
Besides these, there was still a group of completely nomadic Metevulu
in the headwaters of the Mahakam, the people Sekudan had left
behind when he moved back to the Kapuas.

The Aoheng of the Long Apari subgroup, under their hot-blooded
young chief Tingang Kuhi, had settled, along with several Bukat families, at Long Kacu. Tingang wanted to return to the lands they had
come from, and dreamed of taking revenge on the Iban. But the
powerful Kayan group downriver, anxious to keep the peace, forced
him to go back down to Noha Silat around 1905. Some of the Bukat
followed him there, but others, led by Toneng, went off to settle for
the first time by themselves at Noha Boan.

At the turn of the century, the Aoheng Huvung led by Kaya went
down the Penane and built a village at Donu Pao, on the Kacu. Tradition reports that some Bukat followed Kaya. This is confirmed by
Stolk, who in 1905 visited Donu Pao (which he calls Ranu Pahu) and

there met people he calls "Punan Habungku" (another mistranscription of Hovongan or Bungan). According to Stolk, these people referred to themselves as *orang bukit* (mountain people), came from the upper Mahakam, and wandered sometimes toward the Penhing (Aoheng), sometimes toward the Kapuas-Bohong (the Bungan); they had learned Malay as a lingua franca in West Kalimantan (1907:18). There can be no doubt that these *orang bukit* were Bukat.

The Bukat of the Huvung, like those of the Penane-Kacu, had, as a result of their inevitable intermarriages with the Aoheng, begun to farm for themselves, at the same time as or alternately with their traditional activities in the forest. When all the Huvung gathered together around 1910 at Temeriting (in the lower Kacu, below the Toron Tingang rapids), the Bukat of the Huvung and those of Donu Pao went to live at Noha Boan, the first real Bukat village in the Mahakam, where other Bukat were already settled. It is probable that the colonial authorities had something to do with this regrouping. Indeed, the upper Mahakam had been under direct rule by the colonial government since 1907 (Eisenberger 1936:85–88).

The band of Metevulu from the Baleh were still living in the headwaters of the Mahakam. Probably under the influence of the colonial administration, mediated by the Aoheng, those who had not wanted to follow Sekudan to the Kapuas gathered at Noha Boan around 1910. A fact that may have some connection with this is that the Baleh had been officially reopened to Iban settlement in 1905 (Freeman 1970:137). But strife with the Iban was not at an end. The Aoheng chief Tingang Kuhi rejected both Kayan overlordship and Dutch interference, preferring to negotiate with the authorities in Sarawak about settling his group on the Baleh. His followers, who formed only a portion of the Long Apari subgroup, went back up the Mahakam to Noha Maci', where they made a temporary camp before setting out for Sarawak. The Bukat of Noha Boan were supposed to participate in this migration. But, tradition recounts, "they spent some time looking for food in the forest, and came late to Noha Maci'." By the time they arrived, the Iban (in spite of previous peace treaties) had attacked the Aoheng and massacred most of them (including the family of Tingang Kuhi, who himself had gone to Kuching to talk with the rajah). The survivors rallied at Noha Silat (1912), where a few Bukat were reported to be living in 1916 (Lumholtz 1920:216: his "Nunci Lao" is clearly Noha Silat). These consisted of only a few individuals, married to Aoheng.

Whether the Bukat associated with the Aoheng Tiong Bu'u joined their cousins in Noha Boan is not entirely clear. However, the great majority of the Bukat of the region gathered in that settlement after the Noha Maci' episode. A new peace treaty was negotiated in Kapit (possibly in 1922) before the general peace was made in 1924. The occupation of the site of Noha Boan must have lasted for at least twenty-five years. Lumholtz reported the village in 1916 (1920:216; see also Klausen's maps of the area, 1957:78). Vorstman, writing in 1927, also reported it and gave the name of its leader, Uwang Ubung (1952:210). Von Kuehlewein provided a figure of 124 inhabitants for Noha Boan in 1929 (1930:114). It was during this period that the Bukat began serious farming. Lumholtz reported that in 1916 they still grew only a little rice, depending primarily upon wild sago, and that they were as yet unable to make boats for themselves (1920:216, 218–219).

Around 1930, the Aoheng moved from Noha Silat upriver to Sungai Tohop, and the Bukat community of Noha Boan split apart. The Bukat Metevulu (who had come down from the headwaters of the Mahakam), with the addition of some families of Bukat Sivo, left for Sarawak. They crossed the river Baleh and went overland to settle at Nanga Be on the Balui, where they lived for about ten years before moving on to Sungai Aya'.

According to Gemala, the old Bukat leader of the Kapuas, around 1980 there were some dozen households at Batu Aya' (Sungai Aya', or Long Aya'), led by Gasei, a Bukat Metevulu. Since their move, the Bukat of the Kapuas called them Buköt Rajang. Rousseau reported this hamlet, inhabited by 125 people in 1971, in the district of Belaga (1975:34, 40; see also Harrisson 1965:339, n. 73). Rousseau specified elsewhere that the hamlet included ten households and that its headman was Gase (or Gasai Butek, in Rousseau's MS 1971). The return of those Bukat from Noha Boan to Sarawak was confirmed by Ding (1977). These Bukat (or Ukit) of the upper Balui were visited by Barclay (1980:70) and also by O'Hanlon (in 1983). The latter indicates that they had not yet wholly abandoned their hunting-gathering economy, and that they cultivated only a little rice; they still made rattan mats and blowpipes (1985:174, 178; 174–175).

The other Bukat of Noha Boan stayed on the Mahakam, but a portion of them went to live at Linga Lea, on the Apari. The small settlement of Noha Boan, including Linga Lea, was officially recorded as having a population of 124 people in 1938 (Israel 1938). This partial retreat toward the headwaters is something my informants could not explain. It could be that the Bukat, like the Aoheng of Sungai Tohop, wanted to keep their children out of school. The first mission school in the upper Mahakam was opened in 1929 at Batu Ura, and the Dutch tried to make the Aoheng, in particular the chiefs of the group, send their children there. The Aoheng admit that they were not at all enthusiastic about schooling. This possible reason for the retreat upriver may also help to explain the emigration of the Bukat Metevulu into Sarawak.

Later, around 1950, when the Aoheng had already been settled at Long Apari for a long time (they had settled there around 1935 and still live there today), the Bukat made themselves a village at Noha Tivap (called Naha Tiwap by the local authorities, Linga Tibab by Bücher:1970). In 1977, according to Ding Ngo, it had a population of 120 inhabitants. Strangely, Whittier seems to have overlooked the Bukat in his list of "Punan" groups of East Kalimantan (1974).

In 1980, Noha Tivap had a population of 147 people living in fifteen houses. The headman *(kepala kampung)* was Berikum Ubai (son or nephew of Toneng), who had held the post for a very long time, and the *kepala adat* was Diam Da'o. Administratively, the village belonged to the district *(kecamatan)* of Long Apari, whose main settlement is Tiong Ohang, and for matters of customary law it came under an Aoheng *kepala adat* at the district level. The school was at Long Apari, about twenty minutes' walk away, but the educational situation had been recently called into question by the government's plan of gathering all the population of the district's villages into the vicinity of Tiong Ohang. The Aoheng, and with them the Bukat of Long Apari, having refused to move, coercive measures had been taken, including the withdrawal of local teachers. The closest small dispensary *(poliklinik)* was at Tiong Ohang.

Trade with areas downriver was very limited in 1980. Even the most vital trade goods rarely reached Long Apari, and prices might be twenty times those of the coast. Few forest products were exported: the drop in the world price of damar resin meant that almost none was collected, swifts' nests were gathered but production was low, a little rattan was floated downriver, and some gold was panned in the streams of the upper Mahakam. There was no market for illipe nuts on the Mahakam, as there was on the Kapuas; so the Bukat went to the Kapuas to collect the nuts whenever the trees bore fruit, an irregular and unpredictable event. There was no logging on the upper

Mahakam above the rapids, whether by timber companies or by unregulated felling (*banjir kap,* prohibited by the authorities). No salaried jobs were available in the district, except for local officials or the woodworkers occasionally called upon to construct public buildings. This trade and labor situation was in large part due to the presence of the great rapids that isolate the upriver plains of the upper Mahakam and the two districts that include them. The Bukat of Noha Tivap cultivated swidden rice, but still depended heavily on wild sago and cassava, as was sometimes (but rarely) the case with the Aoheng.

Demographic Survey

To conclude as my informant Gemala did, we may summarize what remains today of the original Bukat subgroups. Of the downriver Bukat (Buköt Alung) nothing remains, all of them having been assimilated by the Kayan. I was unable, in the course of my brief visit to the Mendalam, to determine whether there are Kayan families that still recall their distant Bukat ancestry. Of the Hovut, as has been seen, there remain only a few families living on the Sibau. The Soa Kalöp and the Tain Kiat apparently make up the majority of the people of Metelunai. Of the Koyan, only a few scattered individuals remain (one being Janen's wife). Of the Tayung, nothing remains. The Tovaliu form the majority of the group at Nanga Hovat. The Mekajo, Temoan, and Höloi have disappeared as such, to reappear under the ethnonyms of Belatung, Belatei, and Metevulu, which bring together the survivors of the original groups. The Belatung, of whom Gemala is one, live at Metelunai (Nanga Tepai). The Belatei are on the Mahakam, along with a major part of the Metevulu. The rest of the Metevulu, and some Belatei as well, are in Sarawak, on the upper Balui. Of the Metevulu who descend from Sekudan and his people, there remains only Jenahang at Metelunai.

If one attempts to put a number to all these remnants, one comes up with an optimistic total of some three hundred persons for the Bukat of West Kalimantan. This figure is reached by taking the "hard" statistics (if they can be so called) for the populations of Nanga Hovat and Metelunai, and adding to them estimates of twenty to twenty-five Bukat at most for Nanga Balang, barely more for Nanga Putan, and several scattered families or individuals at Nanga Ira', Nanga Enap, and around the various timber camps.

For 1920 the estimated total is 400 people, which implies an absolute drop in population from 1920 to 1980 that is quite striking. It is possible that, like the estimate of 150 families on the Samus given by Enthoven, the figure of thirty families on the Hangai provided by my informants is an exaggeration. The marked reduction in population on the Mendalam may without risk be attributed to the type of marriages made by Bukat with the Kayan, for whom postmarital residence is strictly uxorilocal. Bukat husbands would always move in with the families of their Kayan wives; however, Kayan husbands would not want to go to live among nomads, whom they thought of as savages. This would lead to a movement of population in one direction only. It is probable, however, that the most important factor in this demographic decline is the departure for Sarawak of a group of Bukat (possibly from the Mendalam) around 1964–1965 (Harrisson 1965:339, n. 73). This group apparently settled first along the Baleh, then was made by the administration to move down toward the lower Rejang.

As for the population of the Mahakam, we may compare the figures of 124 inhabitants in 1929 and 120 inhabitants in 1977. There was an early drop in population in the 1930s, when the Bukat Metevulu left for Sarawak. Subsequently, the stagnation in population may reasonably be attributed to a combination of individual emigrations to the Kapuas and intermarriages with the Aoheng.

Changes

This half of the chapter takes a thematic approach, returning to various elements met with in the course of the preceding historical reconstruction and introducing others that seem pertinent to Bukat history, in order to reconstruct, in diachronic perspective, a number of processes pertaining to the changes undergone or initiated by the Bukat over this period of more than a century and a half. Among the matters examined will be the relationship of ethnicity to the process of acculturation, the economic relationships of nomads and farmers, transformations in the subsistence economy, modifications in material culture, and finally, social and religious changes.

Ethnicity and Cultural Assimilation

As many writers have pointed out, Bukat and Bukitan groups display similarities, particularly regarding language. Related to both, again, were the Sru (who became the Lisum and Lugat). In the eighteenth century and up to the arrival of the Kayan, this group of nomadic peoples probably ranged over the whole of the mountainous

region that borders present-day Sarawak, including a part of the
Baleh, if not all of it, and part of the Balui and the middle Rejang.
These peoples no doubt came into conflict at times, though fully
appreciating that they were akin.

The penetration of Sarawak territory at the end of the century by
Kayan coming from East Kalimantan gave rise to profound changes in
the ethnographic map, in particular through the gradual assimilation
of certain groups (those who were to become the Kajang, for example)
and the expulsion of others toward the south and west. In the early
years of the next century, the intrusion of Iban coming from the southwest was to bring further changes in the distribution of nomad groups.
Some of these were absorbed (the Tanyung, for instance, and some of
the Sru) while others were driven toward the east. The Iban advance
toward the east pressed hard upon the Bukitan. Those who survived
eventually allied themselves with the Iban, joining in their attacks on
groups farther to the east, Taman, Kayan, and Bukat. The Bukat of
this period lived in many small scattered bands, which at times skir-
mished with each other. When Iban hungry for virgin forest sought to
enter their lands, the Bukat, unlike the Bukitan, made stubborn and
persistent efforts to force them back; even when the struggle proved
hopeless, the Bukat never became Iban allies. After 1900, when they
were no longer able to hold out in the Baleh, they moved back to
Kalimantan.

In the Kapuas river basin the situation was different. The physical
boundary between lowlands and mountains is quite distinct on the
Mendalam and the Sibau, and so therefore are the limits of the territories of Bukat on the one side and Kayan and Taman on the other, each
occupying a well-defined geomorphological domain. The Kayan and
the Taman are both agricultural peoples with a stratified social system
who like to farm good, flat land (see King 1985) rather than clearing
primary forests on the mountainsides, as the Iban of the Rejang like to
do (see Morgan 1968; Freeman 1970; Padoch 1982). Before the
arrival of the Kayan, a relationship had established itself between
Bukat and Taman, no doubt to be recreated by the Kayan on their
own account, beginning with the first years of the nineteenth century.

What type of relationship might this have been? From their mountains, the nomads harassed neighboring farmers who hunted or collected forest products on the fringes of their territory, and whom they
resented as intruders. This they did in the case of three separate
subgroups of Aoheng in the second half of the nineteenth century,

and probably also much earlier in the case of the Kayan. It would therefore have been necessary to make a formal alliance to put an end to hostilities.

Two types of alliance (*petutung* in Bukat) have been customary in the interior of Borneo: alliance by blood-brotherhood (fictive kinship created by an exchange of blood between two individuals, who cut their own arms then place the wounds together or suck the other's blood: Bukat *kuman da'*), and alliance by marriage (Bukat *pasoo*). As soon as an alliance had taken place, the farming village was in principle safe from attack by the band to which it was allied, though not necessarily from attack by another band. From the other side the alliance was equally specific: Bukat allied to the Aoheng of the Huvung nevertheless attacked the Aoheng of another village (with whom they would also subsequently make an alliance). It is notable that in alliances at this early stage women moved from the Bukat to the farmers, rather than the reverse. Relations remained fairly distant, even after an alliance had been made. The general contempt that farmers felt for nomads has often been noted (see also Nieuwenhuis, 1904–1907:255; King 1979a:19). The nomads themselves were reluctant to make direct contact with the farmers, to the point that the two groups often traded without meeting each other.

Little by little, however, along with their intermarriages, nomads and farmers developed a form of association that has been characterized by certain authors as symbiotic, but which is so only in part. A corollary of their alliance is that the nomad band took the side of its farming allies in regional politics. Thus the Kayan possibly involved the Bukat in Liju Aya' 's expedition to the Kapuas, and certainly brought them into their wars against the Taman. The Bukat were used as trackers and scouts, sometimes even as hired henchmen, as when the Bukat of the Huvung were sent by an Aoheng chief to hunt down Si Hebar. The Bukat also served as border guards, to warn of enemy attacks coming from upriver; and they provided the farmers with severed heads and slaves. In exchange, the farmers gave the nomads a certain amount of protection. In case of need (war or famine), the Bukat drew closer to their Kayan allies (Nieuwenhuis 1900a:27). The Huvung protected the territory of "their" Bukat against Iban collectors of forest products (Nieuwenhuis 1904–1907:384). This did not necessarily keep the farmers from exploiting nomad bands other than their own, on occasion, as sources of fresh heads or slaves (see King 1979b: 95), which makes it easier to understand the nomads' reluctance to have direct contacts with them. During the colonial period, when Iban, Taman, and Kayan made peace, each of these major ethnic groups pledging itself also in the name of its nomads, Bukat and Bukitan of the Kapuas also made peace with each other.

Another corollary of the alliance between farmers and nomads, and an essential factor in the eagerness of the farmers to make such alliances, was the establishment, at the limit of their territories, of points of commercial contact. The farmers provided the nomad collectors of forest products with an outlet for their products and, in their position as intermediaries, exploited the nomads shamelessly. The limits of the "symbiotic" aspect of these relations are already evident.

The groups may have engaged in trade without direct contact (also called "silent trade") before they became allies, but after that they traded face to face. In the early days of the relationship, the nomads periodically came down from their mountains to visit the farmers' village, where they stayed from a few days to several weeks, or as long as it took to bring their transactions to a conclusion. This is what happened on the Huvung whenever the Bukat came down from the Levuhi. Such a foray into farmer territory often involved only men, who left their families in the security of the forest, establishing a little camp close to the farmers' village. In later days, the nomads would put up a few huts at a short distance from the farmers' village, no doubt on the farmers' initiative, as with the Huvung on the Penane. This little hamlet would stand empty most of the time, the nomads coming there periodically to trade.

The Mendalam provides an example of another possibility: a camp or a small hamlet would be built, by Kayan or Bukat, at the boundary of Bukat territory, to serve as a trading center, as Nanga Hovat was for the downriver Bukat after Liju's invasion, and again after 1880 for the upriver Bukat. Few if any people would live there permanently, but Kayan and Bukat would meet there regularly in order to trade.

When intermarriage between a given band and a farmer village had created sufficiently close relationships, some Bukat families from the band that traded at this center (Nanga Hovat) would come to live there more permanently, while others might go on downstream to live in or close to the village of their Kayan trading partners. These Bukat would then act as middlemen between the Kayan and other nomad bands with which the farmers were not allied. Thus, in the first half of the nineteenth century, the downriver Bukat probably passed on to the

Kayan the forest products collected by the upriver Bukat. In any case,
the agricultural peoples took care to keep open and improve this prof-
itable channel of trade, and to keep it exclusively for themselves.

As intermarriage increased, the Bukat communities that were
nearest or most closely linked to the Kayan village ultimately became
part of that village, taking to agriculture under the pressure of those
around them, and becoming Kayan in custom and language. This is
what happened with the downriver Bukat (Buköt Alung), who quite
simply ceased to exist as a separate group. So did the Bukitan of the
Embaloh, who became Maloh; and the same thing is currently happening to the Bukat of the Sibau, with the Taman, and to some extent
to the Bukat of Noha Tivap, with the Aoheng of Long Apari.

I shall return later to these questions of trade, conversion to agriculture, and sociocultural change, considering them in more detail. For
now, let us go back to the question of territory. It is extremely important to stress here that nomad and farmer concepts of territory were
quite different: for the farmers a territory was the basin of a river
bounded by the watersheds that fed it, while for the nomads a territory was a mountain massif bounded by the main rivers into which its
waters drained. Thus it appears that Bukat territory was historically
bounded by four rivers, the Kapuas (whose left bank belonged to the
Semukung, Hovongan, and Kereho), the Mahakam (whose right bank
belonged to the groups later called Aoheng), perhaps the Sibau (whose
right tributaries were occupied by Bukitan), and the Baleh. It follows
that while for farmers the main routes of communication were rivers,
for the nomads they were mountain ridges and passes. One may note
that the Bukat came close to the banks of the Kapuas, below its
headwaters, only fairly late in their history; and they have only
recently begun to make use of the dugout canoe as a means of trans-
portation.

In subsequent years, when the major farming groups made the
region's political decisions for themselves and, as overlords, on behalf
of their nomads, the latter's territories were modified accordingly,
tending to be reduced to the upstream portion of the river basin that
was the territory of the farming group with which the nomads were
allied: in other words, their territory became modeled on that of the
farmers. Later still, when the Bukat were officially settled as farmers
themselves, the government allocated a tract of land to each village;
but Bukat practice took no heed of this.

In written sources, the Bukat have always been characterized as intrepid warriors. They did indeed fight against the Iban to hold onto their lands in the Baleh, until the last hero of this forlorn struggle, Sekudan, retreated to Kalimantan. They managed to hold their original homeland in the Mendalam, in spite of the intensity of the raids made on them. In reality, however, the Bukat are not a people prone to all-out war; they say they have never waged a real war. Their strategy has been one of harassment—night attacks on isolated houses, the ambushing of hunters in the forest. For example, the Bukat deny ever having been at war with the Hovongan: they say the hostilities were no more than a matter of a few heads taken.

In fact, rather than warriors, the Bukat are excellent hunters, and they won their fame for their talents in a special form of hunting, that of human game. Their conflicts with the Aoheng of the Mahakam, with the Hovongan, the Kereho, and the Seputan, were confined for the most part to a few casualties on each side; in any case, the matter usually ended with an alliance. But the rearguard guerrilla actions of the Bukat of the upper Mahakam against the Iban gave rise to the full-scale war of 1885 and may also have led to the smaller war of 1912. The Bukat took care to stay out of both.

It may seem surprising that nomad groups like the Bukitan and Bukat should have been dedicated headhunters. In fact, the heads they took were of no use to them, as no ritual of theirs required a head; nor did they have any use for slaves, there being no place for slaves in their society. They killed their enemies or intruders into their territory, in general, from a distance with a poisoned blowpipe dart, and immediately fled. The heads they took, like their captives, were intended for their allies and backers in the stratified farming groups (Iban, Kayan, or Aoheng, and possibly Taman), who needed both for the proper ritual and social functioning of their societies.

What sense the Bukat themselves have of their ethnic identity is a question easier to ask than to answer. Still recently nomadic, probably to this day not very good at farming, and viewed by the agricultural peoples with a certain paternalistic contempt, they picked up a variety of exonyms (most of them toponyms), in particular on the Baleh and the Mahakam, and adopted some of them for their own local use. Even the Aoheng, in part former nomads themselves, condescendingly call the Bukat *arung tana* (inlanders: living only on sago), including in this category the Hovongan and the Kereho (and sometimes even the Seputan), while they call themselves *arung pora* (people who collect only now and then, for instance when short of rice). The Hovongan, for their part, set up a similar hierarchy based on diet: they have accepted the exonym of Punan Bungan, this corresponding in their minds to their own economic situation, living as they do partly on rice and partly on sago, and call the Bukat "Pu'unan," meaning real nomads "living in caves"—this in spite of the fact that the Hovongan lived like the Bukat in the past, and the Bukat today live like the Hovongan.

The Bukat today still undoubtedly preserve a sense of common origin, the knowledge of their common homeland on the river Buköt whose name they bear. Moreover, the Bukat language of the Kapuas and the Mahakam is still identical, with very minor exceptions (and one major one: the vocabulary relating to rice). It must, however, be stressed that the Bukat groups have always remained in contact with each other across the mountain ranges. Traditionally, though, the Bukat were divided into many bands, which sometimes entered into conflict with each other. Each band, a descent group, was an autonomous political and economic entity. The Bukat seem always to have identified with the band, that is, with the family in the broadest sense, rather than with the ethnic group. Indeed, there has apparently never been a Bukat coalition against an enemy, never any policy or action involving more than one band, never any concerted migratory movements, and therefore never any form of political organization above the level of the band, up to recent times. Each leader of a band managed his people as he liked (or rather, as they liked).

The history of the Bukat, as is clear from the account of it given above, is actually the history of Bukat bands, each one deciding its movements for itself, joining another band or parting from it on the basis of criteria specific to each. Political decisions might indeed be made below band level: from a single band (the Halunge) one family head made an alliance with the Amue, another with the Acue, at a time when Amue and Acue were enemies. Sekudan himself, the progressive leader whose goal was to gather his people to live together, charismatic though he was, began his campaign with his own family. Even in 1975, the withdrawal of Gemala and his family (of the old Belatung band) from the village of Metelunai showed that the autonomy of the extended family was still a factor to be reckoned with, counteracting the collective interests of the village community.

Moreover, the Bukat, who quite commonly speak five or six languages, see nothing problematic about settling in the village of another

ethnic group if marriage ties exist or they find it advantageous to do
so, as has been seen in the case of the Bukat of the Kapuas. Nor do
they seem to consider it a problem that their children should become
something other than Bukat.

Economic Relations

Writers since the middle of the nineteenth century have
reported that the nomads (Beketan and others) lived off the produce of
the forest (Burns 1849:141–142; Veth 1854:II, 366). However, these
societies should not be envisioned as living, at least in historical times,
an entirely self-sufficient existence. Although these nomads could
indeed feed themselves from forest products alone, some bands at the
fringes of a territory, like the downriver Bukat, had long been in contact with their neighbors, whoever they might be (Taman or Kayan),
and had trade relations with them. Similarly, bands deep inside their
territory, like the Bukat of the headwaters of the Mendalam, though
they themselves had no contact with farming peoples, still might trade
to some extent with the more peripheral bands. Even if these nomads
did, as Gerlach assumed (1881:304), "live in trees, eating roots, leaves
and fruits," the possibility of a thin but far-spreading stream of
imported objects cannot be excluded a priori. This subject will be further discussed below.

What do the nomads have to trade? First, there are the forest products, which many writers fail to specify; I shall try to provide an inventory of them here. There are resins (damar, *Agathis dammara; jelu-
tong bukit, Dyera costulata,* gutta-percha, *Palaquium* spp.); wild
honey and beeswax (important in trade but often unreported); aro-
matic resin from incense wood *(gaharu, Aquilaria microcarpa);* camphor (found in the fissures of *Dryobalanops aromaticus*); several types
of rotan or cane (*Calamus rotan* and other species); poison for blowpipe darts (one source is *ipoh* or *ipu:* see Nieuwenhuis 1900a:137);
the antlers of deer (the sambar, *Cervus unicolor*); rhinoceros horn (see
Tillema 1939:142); pharmacologically valuable bezoar stones (con-
cretions formed in the intestines and gallbladder of the gibbon, *Sem-
nopithecus,* and in the wounds of porcupines, *Hestrix crassispinus*);
birds' nests, the edible nests of swifts (*Collocalia* spp.); the heads and
feathers of two species of hornbills *(Buceros rhinoceros, Rhinoplax
vigil);* and various hides (clouded leopards, bears, and other animals).
King also lists illipe nuts *(tengkawang, Shorea macrophylla)* and gold
dust (1974:41), but the demand for these may be more recent.

Another common type of product is meat and fish, dried or smoked, that the hunting nomads provide to farmers whose lands are less rich in game (see Seitz 1981:293).

The nomads also deal in manufactured goods. They have long made high-quality blowpipes and rotan mats, two crafts at which Lumholtz reported they were expert (1920:218–219, 246). Rotan baskets, too, have often been mentioned. One may for that matter consider plant poisons as manufactured products, since they are subject to special preparation.

A third category includes the products of human game, severed heads and captives. Burns said of the Beketan that they were the region's slave merchants, capturing the members of one ethnic group to sell them to another (1849:141–142). According to Veth (1854:I, 57) the principal occupation of the Mankettan was kidnapping children to sell them to the Pari (the Kayan; see also Nieuwenhuis 1904: 59). The Ukit of Sarawak delivered heads to their Kayan patrons (Brooke 1866:II, 250). The relationships of the nomads with the Pari were already very close at that time, as we have seen (von Kessel 1849: 187). These captives turned over to the farmers would be sold downriver, kept as slaves or concubines, or sacrificed in the course of major religious festivals (see King's account of Bukitan captured by the Maloh, 1985:53; and von Kessel 1857:397, quoted by Hildebrand 1982:203). The heads themselves were used in rituals (particularly funeral rites). It is probable that the Kayan would put in a special order with the Bukat at the death of an important chief (see also Brooke 1866:II, 250).

What did the Bukat get in exchange? First, let us consider the case of salt. Although one author supposes that the nomads ate no salt (Enthoven 1903:87), most other Dutch authors give salt a prominent place among trade goods. Many saline springs exist in this region, and the nomads might have made use of them, as the farmers did. However, modern authors, among the best specialists in nomad studies, concur with Enthoven's opinion (Harrisson 1949:139–140; Urquhart 1951:513).

Other articles of trade were tobacco, iron, cloth, rings, and glass beads (Gerlach 1881:304; Nieuwenhuis 1904–1907:255; Enthoven 1903:88; King 1985:52). The nomads were passionately fond of tobacco (Molengraaff 1900:197). Iron was important, for axe blades to fell the sago palms, and even more for the rod used to bore blowpipes (von Kessel, however, states that blowpipes themselves were obtained from the farmers, 1857:408; Lumholtz, on the contrary, says that the Bukat provided the farmers with them, 1920:246). The rest were luxury items.

On some occasions the nomads were able to procure valuable objects, gongs and ceramic jars (King 1979b:95) or items in copper or brass (Enthoven 1903:88). These objects, which they were unable to carry along with them in their travels, were hidden in caves or buried in the forest (some Bukat hid objects of this sort in caves on the Menjuei; Harrisson 1965:328). These objects of value could be saved, passed on, or spent: with them, it became possible for some of the nomad leaders to engage in prestige-enhancing strategies, for instance, to make the marriage gift that permitted them to marry a Kayan woman. These objects might also be used to pay fines, as when the Bukat of the Mahakam presented a gong to the Aoheng in compensation for a killing before making an alliance with them, or when the Punan paid a certain number of gongs to the colonial authorities (Molengraaff 1902:80). They were also valuable simply for the status that accompanied the possession of objects of prestige, gaining the nomads the respect of their farmer neighbors.

On the Kapuas, the nomads traded with the Kayan and the Taman, or even at times with petty Malay traders (Enthoven 1903:88; King 1979b:94–95). In the particular case of the Bukat, the Kayan placed themselves in the position of middlemen between the nomads and the Malay and Chinese traders downriver, as the Taman did with the Bukitan (King 1985:52). As has been said, the farmers made a considerable profit from this trade and tried to keep it to themselves. Noble families in particular kept "their" Bukat bonded to them for this reason. On the Mahakam, the situation with the Aoheng was similar. Generally speaking, the nomads were cheated of a considerable portion of the value of their products in these trading operations (Enthoven 1903:89; King 1979b:95). It is probable that the colonial authorities subsequently tried, without great success, to make these exchanges fairer.

A point that needs clarification is the degree of interest the nomads had in the farmers' rice. According to Nieuwenhuis (1900b:198–199; 1904–1907:255), the Bukat of the Huvung coveted Aoheng rice and traded for it, and with that in mind came to camp near the Aoheng at harvesttime. There is a similar mention in Gerlach (1881:304). Nevertheless, up to the present day the Bukat do not particularly care for the

taste of rice. Brooke in Sarawak states that the Ukit obtained from the
Kayan, in exchange for heads, not just rice but also sago (1866:II,
250). This last point suggests that in times of insecurity, when the
nomads dared not risk themselves too far from their protectors and
the supplies of wild sago in the neighborhood were exhausted, they
might have taken an interest in the farmers' foods. Besides this, when
the nomads came to trade, they no doubt seized the opportunity to live
at the expense of their patrons.

The ways in which exchanges were carried out have been mentioned
above. There was trade without direct contact, in which the nomads
deposited their goods at an agreed-upon location, then withdrew;
their trading partners then set down the goods they offered in
exchange, and withdrew in their turn, and so on, until both parties
were satisfied (more complete descriptions of this type of trade among
the Ot of the Barito can be found in Hartmann 1864 and Perelaer
1870; see also Gerlach 1881). Direct trade took place at a focal site or
trading center where nomads and farmers met face-to-face, in farmers'
villages, and with Malay traders who probably came to the villages.

It should be noted that if the nomads were dissatisfied with the way
in which trade was carried out, or with what they were given in
exchange for their produce, they could look for other customers. This
may be why the Bukat Hovut found (or went back to) another outlet
for their goods, an alternative to the Mendalam, in dealing with the
Taman of the Sibau. Similarly, they could take an item of trade to any
river basin where a market for this product existed. Thus the present-
day Bukat of the Mahakam prefer to go to Sarawak to sell (to the Chinese, covertly) products such as deer antlers or the casques of helmeted hornbills.

The colonial authorities made efforts at various periods to establish
direct commercial relations with the Bukat, for reasons primarily
administrative and humanitarian. The concentration of Bukat on the
Samus may have in part originated in the desire of the Dutch to gain
direct access to the Bukat living in the north, in the mountains, thus
cutting out Kayan and Taman middlemen in the Mendalam and Sibau.

Among products recently or currently exported by the Bukat may
be mentioned several varieties of rotan (*serutup* and *segah* in particular), wood (in the event of unregulated private felling and rafting),
gold, illipe nuts, and some resins.

From Sago to Rice: The Conversion to Agriculture

As described above, the downriver Bukat (Buköt Alung), who had come into contact with the Kayan at the start of the nineteenth century, might already have begun to practice agriculture before Liju Aya' of the Mahakam came to make war against the Taman of the Kapuas. These Bukat later became Kayan farmers, whose descendants may or may not remember their Bukat ancestors.

After 1880 the process of acculturation gained a new impetus when the upriver Bukat occupied the site of Nanga Hovat, where the downriver Bukat had lived before them. In fact, the process should be viewed as one of constant flux, nomadic Bukat moving down from the headwaters at the same time as the so-called downriver Bukat settled and became Kayanized. Around 1880, though, the pressure exerted by Iban and Bukitan became harsher, driving the upriver Bukat downriver in greater numbers.

By 1880, all the Bukat living in the region of Nanga Hovat were still hunter-gatherers. As Molengraaff described, they lived on fruits, roots, and meat (1900:196; 1902:187). Even those married to Kayan women spent most of their time in the woods rather than the fields, feeding their families on the yield of the hunt (Nieuwenhuis 1904–1907:I, 197). The views of the Dutch on this state of affairs are revealed by their (symbolic) gathering together of the Bukat on the Samus between 1890 and 1900: they wanted to convince the nomads to settle down and clear little rice fields (King 1979b:95).

Around 1900, at Nanga Hovat and around it, the Bukat (in particular the Tovaliu, as Gemala reported) still lived in lean-tos or rudimentary huts *(lapo)*, rather than the more elaborate huts or houses they built later *(lavu')*. They still ate sago, and, though they planted fruit trees and no doubt also cassava and banana trees, they did not yet plant rice. In fact, they lived on wild sago and game until about 1910 (Bouman 1952:56), and on the produce of their gardens. It was at this time that pressure from the authorities at last succeeded in setting the Bukat to cultivating rice.

Nevertheless, the Bukat remained reluctant farmers. The swidden clearings *(umö)* they made were at first very small, and people did not give them the time and care they required: hence a very poor harvest. Families left the freshly sown field to take care of itself and went off to look for sago *(allo)* in the forest. What Enthoven said of the Bukitan (1903:66) holds true for the Bukat: they learned to farm, but a high percentage of them still relied on sago and wild game. It may be noted in passing that Enthoven's mention of nomads storing sago at a particular site for their next visit there (1903:87) appears somewhat strange: the best way to store sago may well be to leave it in the palm tree. The Bukat of the right bank of the Kapuas seemed less strongly motivated to farm than the Punan of the left bank (some of whom, like the Hovongan, had long been part-time farmers). Bouman noted that the Bukat found it harder to adjust to sedentary life than did the Punan, Bukat men continuing to roam and gather forest products while the women farmed (1924:125).

This last point should be stressed, for two reasons: first, it seems to mark a noteworthy intensification in the sexual division of labor in subsistence activities, as will be further discussed below; second, it helps to explain the dual economic orientation—toward both sago and rice—which prevailed during this phase of Bukat sedentarization. The two types of subsistence activity, agriculture and the gathering of wild sago, thus coexisted within a single nuclear family: a cleavage was evident between the man who gathered and the woman who farmed. But it should not be forgotten that within a single extended family or a single band there might also coexist, at one and the same time, some nuclear families entirely committed to agriculture and others still totally integrated into the economic system of hunting and gathering. Thus, to stay within the context of the Mendalam between 1910 and 1920, while some families were making swidden farms at Nanga Hovat and Nanga Selua', others continued to roam as nomads in the headwaters.

As pressure from the authorities continued, so did the phenomenon of a constant flow of movement from the headwaters downstream, as nuclear or extended families little by little shifted from the nomadic way of life to that of part-time farmers, gradually increasing their dietary dependence on rice at the expense of sago. This gradual transition from one economic system to another, from the headwaters of the Mendalam to Nanga Hovat, was paralleled by a transition from one sociocultural system to another, as Bukat families allied themselves to the Kayan and were subject to their influence in social and religious matters. Thus, in 1922, Bouman reported that Punan and Bukat were eating more and more rice (1952:56). As far as the Bukat were concerned, this finding held true only for the Bukat of the Mendalam and of Nanga Keriau. It should not be forgotten that there were still many nomadic families in the headwaters of the Kapuas, on the Hangai.

These would be brought together and officially settled only around 1930, at Nanga Keriau.

On the Mahakam, in a different ethnic environment, the same type of contact was established between Bukat and the various Aoheng subgroups. At around the same time (1885) and in the same context of retreat before the Iban, the Bukat of the Mahakam came to live with the Aoheng on the Serata and the Penane, after some years of sporadic commercial contacts. There they had their first experience of agriculture, between 1890 and 1900; but the only Bukat who seem to have taken a real interest in it were the ones who had already married into the Aoheng communities of these two rivers. Just as on the Kapuas, and at about the same time (1910), the Bukat were made to build themselves a settlement (Noha Boan) and to begin swidden farming. Again as on the Kapuas, there were some who did actually do some farming, and other families which preferred to keep on eating wild sago even though they were officially settled at Noha Boan. It should be noted that this process of partial conversion to farming probably slowed between 1930 (with the rejection of schooling and withdrawal inland) and 1945 (the end of the Japanese occupation), but picked up speed again in the fifties, as the Bukat returned to the banks of the main river.

As suggested above, the introduction of the Bukat to agriculture undoubtedly happened quite independently on the Mendalam and the Mahakam, as is shown by the difference in rice-related vocabularies. The Bukat of the Kapuas borrowed from the Kayan the terms *baha* (hulled rice) and *kanen* (cooked rice, food in general), whereas the Bukat of the Mahakam, like the Hovongan and the Kereho, use the expression *luang pare* ("inside of the rice") for hulled rice, and *aku'* for cooked rice or food in general (*okun* in Kereho, Hovongan, Seputan, and Aoheng). The Bukat of Sarawak also borrowed the term *baha,* possibly from the Kayan of the Balui. In 1912 the Bukat of Noha Boan, who would be joining in the emigration of the Aoheng Long Apari to Sarawak, still lived on wild sago. And in 1916, Lumholtz noted that these nomads who had recently converted to agriculture still in fact grew very little rice, depending upon wild sago for the major part of their diet (1920:216).

The situation has not changed much since then. King reports (1979a:19) that at the start of the seventies, although the majority of the former nomads of the Kapuas were now settled in semipermanent villages and spent "at least some time" cultivating rice, they were still significantly involved in nomadic pursuits such as collecting wild sago and forest products and hunting. This generalization does not apply to the Aoheng of Nanga Enap, who have been farmers since they came to the Kapuas, nor for the most part to the Hovongan, who have long been part-time farmers. It is true that the Bukat, compared to other "Punans," may be the most dedicated of all to the nomadic way of life. They certainly are not totally dependent upon rice, and are not likely to be so any time soon, simply because they do not want to be, so long as there is a continuing commercial demand from downriver markets for forest products. They will keep on spending a certain amount of their time in the forest *(ngerarang),* and while there they will continue to live on sago.

My own investigations in 1980–1981 among the Bukat of the Kapuas (at Metelunai, Nanga Tepai, and Nanga Balang), though fairly superficial where this subject is concerned, suggest that dependence upon rice was clearly greater than 50 percent, perhaps indeed as high as 60 or 70 percent. At Metelunai as at Noha Tivap, whole families did periodically leave the village—sometimes during the period between harvesting their rice and the clearing of new fields, but more often between sowing and harvest—in order to live in the forest and exploit its resources, on Bukat land or elsewhere, basing their diet on wild sago. Certain families of Noha Tivap also made prolonged visits (of several months, or indeed several years) to their relatives in the Kapuas, and spent considerable time in West Kalimantan when there were illipe nuts to harvest (once in three to four years, according to I. Nicolaisen 1984:34; once in two to nine years, according to T.A.D. 1981:32). In such circumstances it is extremely difficult to estimate the average proportion of rice and sago in the Bukat diet. It is true, however, that certain families, like those of Gemala and Janen at Nanga Tepai, were almost exclusively farmers. As mentioned, Janen even kept a few cows, for sale or sacrifice.

We may recall the goals recently promulgated by the local authorities: on the Kapuas, to bring together all the formerly nomadic peoples in big downriver villages, and to promote the cultivation of cash crops and the raising of livestock; and, on the Mahakam, to resettle all the upriver people (*Resetelmen Penduduk* or *Respen*) around Tiong Ohang, head settlement of the district (a project which the Bukat, along with the upriver Aoheng, have to this day stubbornly resisted). These programs do not take into account the need of the Bukat for a

residence close to an extensive range of virgin forest, from which they
draw the main part of their commercial revenue. On the upper Balui in
Sarawak, it appears that the Bukat (or Ukit) have maintained their
forest way of life at least in part up to the present day, no doubt for the
same commercial reasons. (Ideological factors will be further discussed below.)

Material Culture

From the literature, it would seem that the material culture of
the Bukat at the time when they were entirely nomadic hardly differed
from that of the still nomadic Punan groups of Sarawak. Hunter-gatherers' possessions are necessarily fairly limited in number and type,
since portability is a prime consideration. Without going into detail, a
distinction may be made between those objects made by the Bukat
themselves (mats, baskets, blowpipes, garments of beaten bark, different types of bamboo container, items made of wood or deer antler)
and objects obtained by trading with sedentary groups (metal for tools
or weapons and for making blowpipes, cloth, and eventually cooking
utensils). Later we shall take a closer look at some of the elements of
Bukat material culture.

First, though, a brief note on Bukat appearance and its cultural
modifications. Molengraaff described the Bukat as magnificent human specimens, tall in stature and well-muscled (1900:196; 1902:
187). Unlike the "Punan" groups of the left bank of the Kapuas but
like the Bukitan, Bukat men in the past acquired numerous tattoos, as
many writers of the time reported (among others, Veth 1854:II, 393;
Nieuwenhuis 1900a:235; Molengraaff 1900:197, and 1902:188;
Enthoven 1903:87; Haddon 1905:113). Men's bodies might be completely covered with complex designs, including in particular a tattoo
on the lower jaw. Women apparently were not tattooed (Molengraaff
1902:188 n.). These tattoos were all the more striking as the Bukat
have very light, almost white, skin (Molengraaff 1900:197 and 1902:
196; Enthoven 1903:87).

Bukat tattoos seem traditionally to have differed from those of the
Iban (see, in particular, the photograph of a Bukat from the Samus in
Nieuwenhuis 1900a:I, 26). Iban tattoos, however, have been widely
influential; many old Hovongan, among others, bear Iban-style tattoos, souvenirs of their travels, and young Bukat may still get Iban
throat tattoos. Like Iban women, Bukat women generally were not

tattooed (or very little); this in any case sharply distinguished Bukat tattoos from those of the Kayan, among whom only women normally wear them. However, tattooing among the Bukat would appear to have been women's business, with women tattooing men (Haddon 1905:113). The filing of the incisors to an even line, a Kayan and Busang custom apparently limited to the Mahakam region, has been optional among the Bukat, as among Aoheng and the other groups of the Müller mountains (Lumholtz 1920:434).

Hunting *(kanup)* has been mentioned above. It may be stated that the Bukat have no food taboos. An exception is mentioned by Lumholtz, that of the sambar deer *(Cervus unicolor)*, whose meat was apparently forbidden to the Bukat of the Mahakam; but this may be a prohibition borrowed from Kayan and Busang, among whom it has been customary.

Bukat have traditionally hunted with their blowpipes *(supit)*, using darts tipped with plant poison. However, one of the oldest written sources, von Kessel (1857:408), stated that the original arms of the nomads of the Kapuas were clubs and wooden spears, and that they obtained their blowpipes from their farming neighbors (this thorny issue will be reviewed below, in the section on hunting in Chapter 4). It appears that the Bukat began quite early to keep dogs, probably around 1880 (when they were raiding the Hovongan), and perhaps even before then, since Gemala claims that the Bukat have always had dogs. Hunting with dogs was done with the metal-bladed spear, or at least with the fire-hardened wooden spear, not with the blowpipe (again, see Chapter 4 for a further discussion). These two methods of hunting have probably coexisted for a long time, as they continue to do today. Each has its specific aim: the blowpipe is used primarily for birds, monkeys, and small animals, while spears and hunting dogs are used for big terrestrial game. An important point is that among the Bukat, as among other groups of the Müller mountains, women hunt just as men do, even taking a spear to big game, and they also fish.

It is not easy to estimate the role of fish in the Bukat diet. For Nieuwenhuis, hunting and fishing are both significant (1902:189). However, two factors argue against ascribing great importance to fishing. The first is natural: along the spines of the mountain ranges, where the sago palms grow, streams are small and fish are few. The second factor is technological: the nomadic Bukat had no nets, and apparently no fish traps. It is probable that from time to time they came downhill to larger streams, built barriers across them, and stunned the fish with a plant poison extracted by pounding up wild roots of up to ten different species.

Bukat groups traveled by mountain routes from one valley to the next, moving on as soon as local resources were depleted, on the track of herds of wild pigs, from one grove of sago palms to the next, or following the ripening of wild fruits. Enthoven noted that they rarely stayed more than three months in any one place (1903:87). In fact, it seems that the average stay was between half a month and a month, depending primarily on the size of the sago grove they were harvesting. In the course of their wanderings the Bukat constructed temporary camps of small huts, most often simple lean-tos with roofs of leaves. According to Enthoven, it was women who made these shelters, called *lapo* (1903:87).

This type of shelter continued to be made over a long period. When they moved into trading sites like Nanga Hovat, the Bukat built huts on posts, slightly more elaborate, with walls made of sheets of bark (*lavu'*: houses). Only around 1920 did they begin to build a single home for the whole community, a longhouse (*titing lavu'*: row of houses), as Bouman reports (1924:175). This custom was borrowed from the Kayan of the Mendalam. At present, government policy opposing longhouses has led the Bukat to return to building separate houses. Of course, the forest lean-to is still used by people traveling to gather forest products, and small huts are still built alongside swidden ricefields.

Mention should be made of the use of caves, especially as dwelling-places, a practice mentioned in the literature (Nieuwenhuis 1900a: 280; Enthoven 1903:87–88; King 1979b:94). These are either real caves (in limestone country) or simple shelters under a rock ledge. I have seen many such caves and rock shelters, and all the dry ones show traces of human occupation. According to Harrisson, nomad culture on the Kapuas cannot be understood without taking into account this relationship with caves (1965:347, n. 155). Caves could be defended in case of attack, and they served as hiding places for the valuable objects (jars and gongs) that some Bukat leaders obtained by trade (Enthoven 1903:88; Harrisson 1965:328; see also the discussions of ownership and social organization in Chapter 5).

The Bukat lived in the mountains, then, only rarely coming down to the shores of the main rivers. Only after they had begun to live close to the sedentary ethnic groups, Kayan or Aoheng, did they dare to try river travel, especially dangerous in the headwaters where rivers are steep and rapids common. It is in part because of the nomads' fear of the rivers that the Aoheng call them *arung tana* (inlanders, land people), while they view themselves more as people of the rivers.

When the Bukat have to cross a stream, if they find no natural bridge (a fallen tree), they stretch a length of rattan between the banks and shinny across hanging under it, holding on with their legs and arms. If the river is too wide, they make a raft. The rare mentions of bark canoes in the Borneo literature apparently do not refer to the Bukat. At Noha Boan in 1916, the Bukat had not yet learned to make dugout canoes (Lumholtz 1920:218–219). Bukat tradition says that the last among them to live on the Baleh sometimes used boats, but as this same tradition states elsewhere that they were still nomadic, what they probably used were rafts. To this day, the boats (*halur,* a term similar to both the Kayan *haruk* and the Aoheng *arut*) made by the Bukat of the Mahakam are of poor quality.

The local form of the machete or multipurpose bush knife is not part of the nomads' traditional tool kit. It appears that the Bukat of the Mahakam, before they came to that river, had borrowed or at least learned about this tool from the Kayan of the Mendalam, as these Bukat refer to it by the Kayan term *malat* rather than the Aoheng term *olok*. But the Bukat of the Balui, who passed through and lived on the Mahakam, have both terms: *tiolok* for the bush knife and *malat* for the more elaborate war sword.

Terms for domestic animals also suggest their origins. The chicken (*sio* in Bukat, related to Hovongan *sio* and Aoheng *siu*) may have been acquired on parallel occasions in the Mahakam and Kapuas, but not from the Kayan (who call it *hnyap*), unless perhaps in the case of the Mendalam Bukat. For the domestic pig the Bukat have two terms, *ukot* and *uting,* the first from Hovongan (related to the Aoheng *okot*), the second from Kayan, both of which are used, it would appear, quite interchangeably.

When trying to use lexical relationships as a key to possible cultural borrowings, it is important to bear in mind that these Bukat were in contact with three separate major ethnic groups in three different regions: in the Mendalam with the Kayan, in the high headwaters of the Kapuas with the Hovongan (and to a lesser degree the Kereho), and in the Mahakam with the Aoheng (and to a lesser degree the Seputan). The groups in these last two regions of contact had themselves undergone considerable cultural and linguistic influence from Kayan groups (of the Mahakam and the Kapuas), and from the Long Gelat. It is therefore at times a matter of some difficulty to determine the precise origin of a borrowing. Moreover, one must take into account the earlier contacts of Bukat with Taman, and certain contacts, old or recent, with the groups of the Balui. It may be noted that the Bukat of the Mahakam call their river the Köhean, after the Aoheng Kehan, rather than Mekam, its name among the Bukat of the Kapuas, who follow in this the Kayan of the Mahakam and Kapuas, and the Busang of the Mahakam.

A few further details from the literature before we turn to Bukat social organization. The Bukat very much appreciate tobacco (Molengraaff 1900:197; Enthoven 1903:87). Indeed, like all the nomads, the Bukat quickly developed a most intemperate taste for tobacco, to the point that this became as coveted an article of trade as salt or metal. Bukat women carry their babies in a sort of sling, according to Molengraaff (1902:204), not in a baby-carrier made of wood, like Kayan and Aoheng women. A little later, Lumholtz (1920:433–434) notes that the Bukat have taken to using the Aoheng baby-carrier *(boning).*

Finally, it should certainly be said, in agreement with Molengraaff (who definitely became very fond of them), that the Bukat are likeable, pleasant, agreeable people (1902:188), despite all that had been said of them by earlier authors, who held them to be cowardly, cruel, and warlike, and who had never met them.

Bukat Society

Bukat bands were generally made up of families related by blood (see Bouman 1924:175). The number of these families (in this case, nuclear families, consisting of parents and children) varied between four and ten (Enthoven 1903:87), which permits an estimate of band size of between twenty and fifty individuals. The term for the nuclear family *(kajan)* is related to the Maloh *kaiyan* (King 1985: 103), and probably also to the term *kevian* used by the groups of the Müller mountains (including Aoheng, Seputan, Hovongan, and Kereho: Wurm and Hattori 1983). One might also note the Iban term *kaban,* meaning a cognatic kindred.

The extended family is known as *puhu',* also meaning descent group, or local group: in other words, that entity here for simplicity's sake called "the band" (the term may also stretch to cover the entire ethnic group; it is a cognate of the Kayan term *puhuu'*, defined in Ding Ngo 1977:142). This local group, the band, is totally autonomous in its movements and decisions. It may join up with another *puhu'*, perhaps allied to it by marriage, to create a temporary band of greater size. But the number of individuals in a band is always limited by the food resources of their forest neighborhood. As soon as people find it necessary to move in search of food supplies more frequently than they like, the band will split up.

The leader of the band is the oldest person in the family group, often the person from whom the majority of its members is descended (Bouman 1924:175). The leader is in fact one of the elders *(lino tangön)* of the band, a mature and experienced individual. If there is only one extended family in the band, it is probable that the leader will be the senior member of the family, sometimes a woman. Succession to the position will pass to the leader's brother, son, nephew, or son-in-law or the female equivalent, chosen for his or her personal qualities, knowledge of the territory, wisdom, and experience. Given the autonomy of the nuclear families within the band, a person whose leadership is repudiated by the band will simply be replaced, or indeed deserted.

Bukat society acknowledges no rank system, no stratification of any kind. Their hunting-gathering economy, the close blood relationships within the band, the absence of a residential focus or ancestral "house" —all these things act to oppose the development of aristocratic lines of descent. Moreover, the ideology explicitly expressed by the Bukat rejects such a differentiation. "We don't want distinctions," says the old leader Gemala (the former *temanggung,* who, given this title, might have been expected to take a different view). "Among other people the nobles lie around and the common people work; with us, everybody works." A term for aristocrat or noble, *sipoi,* does however exist, the Bukat version of the Kayan word *hipui* or the Aoheng *supi;* but it has no referent in Bukat society, even today. It is used to comment on the situation in other ethnic groups or in cases when a leader chosen by common accord is criticized for behaving like an aristocrat.

During the process of sedentarization, there must indeed have been some temptation for leaders to establish their own line of descent as the aristocratic one of the community, at the expense of others. Dutch policy furthermore encouraged the impulse, in particular through the granting of titles such as *temanggung,* the equivalent of "tribal chief." But such temptations were always opposed by the Bukat community, above all by the *lino tangön,* the elders, leaders, or notables of the different bands or family groups that lived together in the villages where they were settling down.

The position of leader of the village may be assumed alternately by elders of different lines of descent. Sekudan, the old leader of Nanga Keriau, who first led a band of Metevulu and then brought together so many of his fellows, was succeeded by Jaruk, a Belatung. Jaruk was succeeded by Narok, son of Sekudan, and Narok in his turn by Gemala, nephew of Jaruk. The leaders of the community of Metelunai have therefore been, alternately, elders of the two original bands, Metevulu and Belatung. It appears that Lahat, present *kepala desa* of Metelunai, is a descendant of the Bukat who lived on the Hangai. It may well be that the withdrawal of Janen and Gemala from the community was due to a power struggle between descent groups, though they do not care to talk about it.

It must, however, be admitted that, although the idea of one aristocratic descent line of hereditary leaders is unacceptable to the Bukat, they find rather more acceptable the idea of one prominent descent group, or several, from which leaders may be chosen. Clearly, by virtue of his situation, the son of a leader is more likely to become familiar with essential leadership skills such as decision-making processes, dealing with the authorities and administrative procedures, and the art of oratory. The Bukat of the Balui say that they have a four-tiered system of social stratification, like their Kayan and Kenyah neighbors (Rousseau 1974:23), but it may be that they claim this only in the presence of these neighbors, so as not to seem inferior (Rousseau personal communication 1986).

The sexual division of labor among the Bukat is an interesting subject, but one on which there exists little historical information. As among all the nomads of the area, women hunt and fish just as men do, though less often. They carry burdens just as men do, according to their individual ability, when the group travels. They are also in charge of building a shelter and gathering firewood (Enthoven 1903: 87). The heavy work of extracting sago, such as felling, cutting up, and splitting the sago palms, is usually done by men, but women participate actively in the subsequent phases of the extraction and the preparation of sago flour.

When the Bukat began to farm on the Mendalam, as already mentioned, Bouman reports the significant fact that it was women who took care of farm work, while men continued to hunt and gather forest products (1924:175). On the other hand, it may have been men who built the village huts at that time. Among the Kayan, the different phases of agricultural work are divided among men and women according to physical aptitude, on the one hand, and ritual criteria, on the other. This new type of sexual division of labor, permitting a dual orientation of effort toward field and forest, made it possible for Bukat men to invest more time in the collection of forest products for commercial purposes. Even if the harvest of their farms was poor, field size being small and these new farmers relatively unskilled, it had to feed only women, young children, and old people, since the men were living on wild sago. And as the band's women and children were settled on the Mendalam, the Kayan (and later the Dutch) were assured of continuity in the supply of forest products from the men of Bukat families.

The Bukat system of kinship terminology has been given in Kinship Chart I. Kinship is reckoned bilaterally, and the system of kinship terminology, as often in nomad societies, does not distinguish order of birth or gender among consanguines (except for parents and parents' siblings). On the other hand, a distinction is made, based on the sex of the speaker and that of the person addressed or referred to, in the category of affines of Ego's generation. It may also be noted that the terms for husband and wife (H, W) are words meaning "man" and "woman." Two terms for child (C) coexist, one *(kelavi)* being the Bukat term, the other a borrowing; similarly, of the two terms for child's spouse (CSp) *anak boson* seems to be borrowed from Hovongan and Kereho, while *kajan* seems to be the original Bukat term (it is interesting to note that this is the same term that designates the nuclear family). Of the two terms for co-parent-in-law (CSpP), *isan* is borrowed from the Malay *bisan,* while *ave'* shows a relationship to the languages of the people of the Müller mountains.

Marriage *(pasoo,* to get married: intransitive) is strictly monogamous among Punan and Bukat, according to Lumholtz (1920:216–217). However, since I know of several cases of polygamy (polygyny) among the Hovongan, I would not be quite so ready as Lumholtz to claim a total absence of polygamy among the Bukat. Similarly, one may express reservations about Lumholtz's assumption that premarital sexual relations are permitted but adultery very severely punished (1920:216–217).

Postmarital residence in the nomadic band was always neolocal, the newly married couple immediately making themselves a separate shelter. Nevertheless, one may distinguish two cases. If the young couple belonged to the same band (what is here called band endogamy, though this must be understood to be a practice rather than a rule), they would live neolocally but remain within the band, which in no way prevented this new autonomous entity from leaving it later. When the two belonged to separate bands, postmarital residence was in practice utrolocal, the couple choosing to live with one band or the other, a choice which could afterwards be altered.

Cases of band endogamy were frequent, and so (in consequence) were marriages between blood relations; first cousins were allowed to marry. At present, however, it is possible that this type of marriage is no longer practiced, due to the influence of neighboring farmer groups: the regional norm is that first cousins may never marry; second cousins, only upon payment of a fine (van Naerssen 1951–1952: 139–140). This new rule was the more readily put into practice because of the concentration of dispersed bands in villages averaging a hundred or so inhabitants, which widened the range of potential partners and the increasing normality of marriages between different ethnic groups.

These interethnic marriages, as has been seen, became common from the time that Bukat bands began to live in close proximity to other ethnic groups (Kayan or Aoheng). Previous to this the Bukat had very few contacts, and those extremely wary, with the farmers who were their trading partners; they were almost exclusively endogamous within the ethnic group and showed a preference for band endogamy. Marriages between nomads and settled farmers followed a particular pattern that conformed neither to the customs of the farmers nor to those of the nomads, and that led to a demographic deficit on the part of the nomads, as noted above: the farmers used their rule of uxorilocality to make Bukat husbands move in with their new wives, while men from the farming groups who married Bukat wives were unwilling (or unable) to go live as nomads. The Bukat thus gave up, not just their men, but their women as well to the farmers (especially in formal alliances). Nevertheless, some farmer men did settle with their Bukat wives at a trading site and made a notable contribution to the sedentarization of the bands and the introduction of agriculture. Some elements of the *adat* (customary law) of the sedentary uxorilocal groups strongly influenced the nomads as they settled, and the practice of uxorilocal residence is common in present-day marriages between different formerly nomadic peoples. Thus marriages between Hovongan and Bukat show a fairly clear tendency to uxorilocality.

It is unclear whether the custom of bridewealth, a marriage gift to be made by the groom, existed among the Bukat before the Kayan influenced them. It is sometimes mentioned that the bride-to-be had to give her future husband a blowpipe (probably made by her father). Apparently the marriage of the two young people was confirmed by community recognition, without further formality. With the increasing influence of the sedentary groups, the principle of a marriage gift or payment became more general. This payment *(ahu')*, made by the groom's family, consists (among the Bukat of the Kapuas) of gongs whose size (measured in handspans) is set by custom. The marriage payment properly speaking *(bureng)* is a gong six handspans in circumference, with a supplement *(siring oset)* in the form of a gong of five handspans if the girl is a virgin (or rather, if this is her first marriage). There is a later payment *(usit)* of one or more larger gongs if the husband wants to "take the bride away" *(pusit doro)* to live with his own parents *(ngivan)*. Among Kayan and Aoheng, the marriage payment varies with the social rank of the family, and in the case of noble girls it is very high. One can understand why Bukat leaders ambitious to buy themselves higher status by marrying into an aristocratic farming family would collect gongs in secret caves.

Bukat traditional religion, as far as can be judged today, acknowledges a married couple of creator deities, Kito and her husband Minang. These two are also known to the Hovongan and the Kereho. Above these gods reigns an all-powerful divinity, unique and aloof, Amön Tingai, who is the Amun Tingai of the peoples of the Müller mountains (Aoheng and others), who may be equivalent to the Kayan supreme being, Tipang Tanangaan or Tinge. Besides these, several categories of spirits exist *(atu,* a term related to the Kayan *to'* and the Aoheng *otu).*

The Bukat of the Kapuas believe in a single soul *(bujön)*, of the living or of the dead. Lumholtz notes that the Bukat of the Mahakam say that they have five souls, and he suggests that this belief may be a borrowing from the Aoheng (1920:433–434). The soul of the dead *(bujön lino kavo)* travels toward Leang Apang (or Tehinan: these names suggest a Kayan origin), its final home. Written sources indicate that Bukat funerary ritual was extremely minimal or even nonexistent altogether. The Bukat abandoned the dying person and the camp (Bouman 1924:175–176). When a person died, everyone else fled, leaving the corpse behind (Lumholtz 1920:219). Bukat informants said that their forefathers ran from the dead, leaving them lying on the earth or buried. Interment may be a more recent practice than simple abandonment. This marks a difference from the Hovongan, who, reports Bouman, left their dead in a coffin, in a cave, or under a tree (1924:175–176).

Present-day Bukat bury their dead and may practice a ritual in which the soul is escorted to the afterworld. This ritual *(lematang)* is probably borrowed from the people of the Müller mountains (*lomatang* in Hovongan; *nemotang* in Aoheng).

For cases of serious illness, the Bukat have a choice of two types of ritual healing, one in which the illness is symbolically extracted *(pövayu)*, the other in which a specialist makes a spiritual journey *(musui)* in search of the straying soul. In the latter case, the healer is assisted by special spirit helpers *(atu busui)*. Lumholtz reports that the Bukat of the Mahakam have healers (which he calls by the regional name of *belian,* here inappropriate), of whom some are women (1920:216). He notes elsewhere that the ideas of the Bukat with regard to these *"belian"* and to illness and its treatment are identical to those of the Aoheng and possibly are derived from them (1920:434).

As for rituals associated with agriculture, they have been borrowed, like farming techniques themselves, from neighboring ethnic groups (van Naerssen 1951–1952:150). But as far as I have been able to judge, the Bukat only rarely practice them. Bukat food prohibitions as Lumholtz describes them, including the taboo on deer meat (1920: 216) and others followed by pregnant women (1920:433–434), are also borrowings.

CHAPTER 3
THE KEREHO OF THE BUSANG RIVER

THE KEREHO are a small group of former nomadic hunter-gatherers living in the southern part of the Müller mountains. The Kereho subgroup living along the Busang in Central Kalimantan refers to itself as Kereho Busang, in contrast to the subgroup of the Kapuas river basin in West Kalimantan, which is called Kereho Uheng (Uheng being the Punan name for the Kapuas). The Kereho Busang are better known by the exonyms Penyabung, Penyawong, or Punan Penyabung; they were formerly included in the term Olo Ot (upriver people). The Kereho of the Kapuas are called Punan Keriau.

In the Busang river basin, of which they are the sole inhabitants, the Kereho are distributed among five isolated hamlets. They are widely dispersed over the lands they occupy: even these little hamlets do not account for the entire population, since certain families live permanently in isolated houses. From the headwaters downstream, these are the settlements as they existed in 1980: Tamalue (eight families, only five of which live in the village); Ketipun or Tipun (about fifteen families, only four of which live in the village); Parit (three to five families); Jojang (eight to ten families); and Parahau' (three to four families).

On the upper Busang—that is, along the part of the river upstream from the notoriously dangerous rapids called Riam Duabelas—the first four villages comprise around 270 people. At Parahau', where several hundred people still lived a decade ago, not many now are left. Recent emigrations have been directed toward the towns downstream, in particular Tumbang Juloi, but also Teluk Jolo, Tumbang Konyi, and Purukcahu. Tamalue, the only village I was able to visit as I crossed the mountains from the Mahakam in East Kalimantan, has an official population of a hundred or so, but about thirty of its inhabitants are living temporarily in West Kalimantan.

This region of the Busang is part of the district *(kecamatan)* of Sumber Barito, whose main town is Tumbang Konyi; this district is itself part of the *kabupaten* Barito Utara (or Murung Raya), whose main town is Muara Teweh. The district of Sumber Barito counted 7,358 inhabitants in 1977 (*Monografi Kalimantan Tengah,* 1979). Apparently the official record lists only one administrative community *(desa)* for the entire Busang river basin, this being Parit.

The Kereho Busang, at least those of Tamalue, cultivate swidden rice, but frequently resort to cassava and wild sago.

Historical Reconstruction

Written Sources

This group has been the subject of no formal study and has been visited only very rarely. Nevertheless, it has been mentioned by a few authors. The first of these seems to have been Becker (cited in Hildebrand 1982:111), who referred to the group by the name of Olo Ot Nyawong. He described these people as nomads, living "like wild creatures in the woods" (1849a:427), with no set territory, though they possessed a gathering place to the north of Mount Kaminting (Keminting) in the headwaters of the Sintang (the Melawi; 1849a: 326). Schwaner, a little later, mentioned a people known as Ot Punan or Nyawong (1853:II, 67), of whom some three thousand were supposed to be living at that time close to the headwaters of the "Rungan" (1853:II, 116). This river Rungan is probably the Bungan of West Kalimantan, in which case Schwaner, like Becker, would be referring generally to all the forest-dwelling groups of the Müller mountains. This is the case with other authors as well, in particular those who traveled in Central Kalimantan, who referred to all the nomads of the northern part of this region by the generic term of Olo Ot (upriver people). Some of these writers (Meyners d'Estrey 1891, after Perelaer 1881) made a vague distinction among subgroups, like the Olo Ot Pangan (probably Kereho) or the Olo Ott Bohong (more likely to be Hovongan).

Schwaner, moreover, mentions a Mount Nyawong in this region (1853:II, 95). Molengraaff for his part refers to a Mount Piyabung (a mistranscription of Penyabung) in the Müller mountains (1893–1894: 465). Enthoven (1903:22) mentions Tebeluwai as the home of blood-thirsty Punan related to the Punan Keriau (the Kereho of the Kapuas); Tebeluwai is in fact the river Tamalue, right tributary of the Busang.

The first writer to visit the Kereho Busang was Stolk, who made contact with the village of Doan Kabo (actually Doan Kavo') and the temporary settlement of Sabaoi (actually Sovaoe) in 1905, when he traversed the region on his way to the Mahakam. After him Lumholtz, Mallinckrodt, and Tillema provided some data on the Kereho Busang. Whereas Mallinckrodt (1927:590) and Tillema (1939:230) continued to refer to them by variants of exonyms, Penyabung or Ot Panyawung, Lumholtz was the first to mention the name Kereho, applied to this group by the Seputan and the Bukat (1920:429). Kereho is the autonym (in fact, a toponym), though almost no one uses it either in the literature or in the regional administration. More common are the many variants of the exonym: Punan Nyawong, Ot Nyawong, Olo Ot Nyawong, Punan Ot Nyawong (see Hildebrand 1982:111), Punan Penyabung, or Kenyabung (Hildebrand 1982:116; Anonymous 1920: 72). These variants persist even in the most recent literature, for example LeBar (1972:176) and Salzner (1960), while Avé (in LeBar 1972:185) seems to consider the Panyawung and the Punan Kareho as distinct groups. Bücher for his part calls the inhabitants of the Keriau River basin Punan Penyawung (1970).

The language of the Kereho Busang was the subject of a vocabulary survey in 1916 (Holle's *Woordenlijst*, no. 145), a list that was reprinted in the *Daftar Kata-2* of 1957. I myself compiled an extensive vocabulary list at Tamalue in 1980.

Origins of the Kereho (Maps 9–12, Chronology III)

Kereho Busang oral tradition reports that this group came from the Belatung, an upper tributary of the Keriau (or Kereho) of West Kalimantan. The Kereho Uheng are still living on the Kereho at the present day, and they say that a group led by four heads of families, Pinang, Ireng, Savung, and Tingang Luhan, left the upper Kereho to forage on the upper Tamalue. They settled on top of Diang Bonong (Mount Bonong), where they made a camp; according to certain informants, they lived there in caves. This migration may be dated to around 1880. From this time on, the Kereho were apparently at peace with the Seputan of the Kacu (or Kaso, on the Mahakam in East Kalimantan), after the marriage of Pinang's sister to a Seputan man. The existence of these good relations is confirmed by Lumholtz (1920: 431–432).

The Busang River was evidently occupied at that time. Stolk reports in 1905 that there had in the past been a Malay village (Bekumpai, or perhaps Ot Danum) where the Tamalue flows into the Busang. Juba', the Hovongan (or Punan Bungan) leader of the village of Belatung, states that the Ot Danum were in possession of the entire Busang River basin and had many villages there: Dare and Uhai (locations unknown), Danum Buro, Tamalue, Sovaoe, and Ketipun. Indeed, many of the tributaries of the Busang, up to the high headwaters, still bear the names the Ot Danum gave them.

Why did the Kereho come to live in the Busang River basin? The Kereho of West Kalimantan have a long history of hostile interactions, first with the Ot Danum (those of the Melawi and those who settled the upper Mandai) and later, after they had made an alliance with the Ot Danum of the Mandai, with the Mbau, as they call the Malays (locally referred to as Membau; cf. the town of Selimbau). The Kereho often attacked and destroyed isolated Mbau hamlets and massacred groups of collectors who ventured into the upper Mandai; they were sometimes incited to do this by other ethnic groups (see von Kessel 1857:403). The Mbau, on their part, carried out retaliatory raids against the Kereho and killed their leaders Berujung and Bayan.

After the arrival of the Dutch in the area, with their determination to put local affairs in order, the Kereho withdrew farther up the Keriau (to the camps of Kulong Keloha' and Data Ohop), curbing their sorties to the Mandai and to downriver regions in general. It was at this time that one or more bands left West Kalimantan for the Busang River basin. A little later, by the time of Molengraaff's geological expedition on the Mandai in 1893, it appears that the colonial authorities had already gained some influence over the Kereho, as they were able to make them pay a fine for killing a porter (Molengraaff 1902:80). The Kereho were subsequently "settled" at Nanga Talai, on the lower Keriau.

The Kereho conquered the upper Busang, according to Juba', and the Aoheng and the Seputan confirm his statement. Juba' relates that the name Penyabung, from the Malay root *sabung* (meaning "to fight"), was applied by the Bekumpai (Islamicized Dayaks, Malay in culture, of the middle Barito) and in general by the people of Central Kalimantan to all the forest-dwellers of the Müller mountains, because of their combative nature. All these groups did indeed form an alliance to attack the Ot Danum, whom they hated, calling them (as the Aoheng did) "vile beasts" (literally, bad animals: *kanon ca'at*).

This reputation for aggressiveness is nothing new: as early as 1853 Schwaner had reported that the peoples of the Müller mountains were

savage and warlike (1853:I, 230), and that the upper Kahayan was
emptied of its inhabitants in the first half of the nineteenth century as a
result of sneak attacks by the Nyawong, who killed or enslaved the
people they ambushed (1853:II, 67).

A French traveler, Adolphe Combanaire, writing around 1900,
mentions these Nyawong or Kereho, whom he calls "Pounan." "The
Orang Pounan, terror of the Dayaks, live in the great central mountain range, frequently changing their place of residence. They have no
villages, taking refuge at night in trees. They know nothing of fire.
Constantly sheltered from the sun, their skin is almost white, and their
backs are bent. The Orang Mourong [a reference to the river Murung,
located east of the Busang] dwell in the mountains that divide the
basin of the Kapuas River from the basin of the Kotei [Mahakam].
Utterly wild, probably cannibalistic, their way of life is unknown,
since they carefully avoid all contact with what they perceive to be
humans more advanced than themselves" (355). Combanaire reports
elsewhere "men as wild as monkeys, whose vertebral column termi-
nates in a tail" (281), a familiar theme in the early writings on Borneo.
Perelaer (1881, in Meyners d'Estrey 1891:306) says of these unfortu-
nate nomads (here called Olo Ott) that, "cowardly and treacherous,
they love to behead their fellow humans and eat their bodies, without
salt if they have none," and that "they sleep in nests in the trees, in
whose branches they travel with monkey-like agility." Enthoven views
the Kereho as bloodthirsty warriors (1903:22). They raided the Duhoi
or Dohoi (the Ot Danum; Lumholtz 1920:325); the Ot Danum and
the Kahayan greatly feared these Ot Panyawung (Tillema 1939:230).

All accounts confirm that the forest groups of the Müller mountains
and the Aoheng and Seputan (themselves, in part, former forest people) made alliances against the Ot Danum. The Aoheng say that they
launched expeditions against the Mengiri (as they call the Ot Danum,
their sworn enemies), bringing together Seputan and Kereho to join
their raids. Similarly, Seputan informants mention significant alliances
among Aoheng, Seputan, Kereho, and Hovongan against the Mengiri
(those of Central Kalimantan and of the Melawi, and even of the
Mandai in the Kapuas River basin) and against the Tebidah of the
Melawi (see Sellato 1986a). The involvement of the Seputan in long-
distance raids on the Melawi and the Murung is confirmed by
Lumholtz (1920:256).

Enthoven also reports this enmity between the "Punan" of the Müller mountains and the Ot Danum of the Melawi (1903:418, 420,

422), citing attacks against the Pangin (1903:419) and the Ot Danum of the Gilang (1903:418). Besides this, informants note a major raid by the Seputan chief Urang against Tumbang Naan, an Ot Danum village of the Juloi. Thus the Kereho of West Kalimantan boast of having "conquered" the upper Juloi, meaning in this case that they drove out its inhabitants.

The Kereho, along with their Aoheng and Seputan allies, also attacked the Punan Murung. With the support of allied groups (Aoheng, Seputan, Hovongan) to the northeast and northwest, therefore, the Kereho controlled the interior of their mountain range, the southern part of the Müller mountains, and the northeastern part of the Schwaner mountains, and from this stronghold they raided the upper basins of rivers to the west, the south, and the east. They must have pressed their attacks fairly far to the southeast, since the Ot Danum of the Melawi report their presence on the upper Jengonoi, in the Lekawai-Tonduk River basin and even as far as Bukit Raja, the highest peak in Indonesian Borneo. Molengraaff also notes that "Punan" were believed to roam the mountains of the upper Lekawai (1893–1894:350; see Map 9).

Present-day Ot Danum refer to the nomads of this area by the names Punan Uut, Uut Sio, Punan Sio (or Mesio); on a wider, more regional scale they are called Punan Kaki Merah (Punan with red legs). This last name refers to their habit of plastering their lower legs with clay for protection against leeches (as the Ot Danum explain it), while *sio* or *mesio* designates a red-legged bird that hops instead of walking, also like the Punan, who move through the forests at a kind of running walk in which their heels never touch the ground. I saw such footprints in 1985 near the headwaters of the Lekawai, without knowing who had made them. Avé (personal communication) identifies the Punan Kaki Merah with the "Ot Siau," and reports that the Ot Danum locate them in the region of Mount Mendap, south of the headwaters of the Ambalau.

Map 9 gives an indication of the range of Kereho activity at the end of the last century: they controlled the highlands for 300 kilometers from west to east and 200 kilometers from north to south, keeping the farming peoples locked into their lowland plains. It should be noted that other small groups of nomads may have existed before the turn of the century in the Schwaner mountains to the southeast of the Kereho (possibly Molengraaff's "Punan"). An Aoheng informant reports that the Kereho pioneers on the upper Busang were attacked by the "Abe."

These Abe (named probably after a leader) lived in caves between Juloi and Melawi. It would only have been after driving them from that region (possibly toward the southwest) that the Kereho would have dared to settle for good on the upper Busang. Local mentions of the Punan Sio may have been due to the presence of these Abe.

Conquest of the Busang River Basin
(Maps 11 and 12)

The Kereho began their "war of conquest," as shown in the above description, with repeated raids from their traditional home territory, the Kereho River in West Kalimantan. Subsequently they established a frontline base on Diang Bonong; from there, according to their own prideful claim, they conquered the Busang. These elusive nomads with their blowpipes, entrenched among the peaks of the upper Tamalue, certainly had the power to make the situation of the Ot Danum untenable. As the Kereho describe it, they waged a guerrilla war of constant harassment, causing so pervasive an insecurity that work in the fields could not be carried out and the Ot Danum were threatened with famine. This no doubt is just what had happened earlier on the upper Kahayan.

After a series of such skirmishes, a few more substantial expeditions by Kereho, Hovongan, Seputan, and Aoheng together, with the strength to attack and burn Ot Danum villages, would have been enough to provoke a mass exodus of Ot Danum toward regions farther down the Busang. *"Busang tana aho"* (the Busang is conquered land, or, land taken over), say the Kereho. We may, however, note that it is entirely possible that all this "conquest," from the first harassment of the farmers, was undertaken at the instigation of the Aoheng and/or of the Seputan, silent partners, as the Kayan of the Kapuas may also have been, in the hunt for human trophies.

After the expulsion of the Ot Danum from the high headwaters of the Busang, a group of Seputan came there to establish a pioneer settlement on the Deringei. These Seputan had already begun to farm. Some Kereho married Seputan and went to live among them on the Deringei. A few years after their move to Diang Bonong, some Kereho Busang made a camp at Diang Apot, on a little plateau near the Apot caves, near the headwaters of the Dehipui. Intermarriage with the Seputan continued. No doubt it was under Seputan influence that the Kereho came down from their mountaintops, the situation now seeming more secure, to establish themselves in open country. One may nevertheless note that they still chose a site close to caves, which offered potential refuge in case of attack.

We have now reached 1890. The leaders of Diang Apot at that time were two brothers, Daring and Bu'. Kereho tradition recounts that the camp at Diang Apot, with its inhabitants, was "petrified" (*huvon:* a supernatural sanction in which houses and persons turn to stone due to the transgression of a prohibition; actual disasters are often given this mythical dimension). Daring was able to make his escape and join the Seputan; some of the Kereho went back to the basin of the Kapuas. In fact, the destruction of the camp of Diang Apot may well have been the result of a retaliatory raid by the Ot Danum. Indeed, Molengraaff reported that six "Punan" were killed by the Ot Danum of the Juloi and that the rest of the "Punan" withdrew to the mountains between Central and West Kalimantan (1893–1894:350). The Seputan of the Deringei, moreover, moved around that time far up the Busang, to a place called Baang Tutung. It is possible that the Ot Danum chased them that far and destroyed their village, because *baang tutung* means "burnt house." After this the Seputan left for the Kacu in the Maha-kam river basin.

The Kereho who remained (in hiding or among the Seputan, or having come back from West Kalimantan) went to live at Ihi, on the Doan Kavo', a stream not far from Diang Apot, probably around 1898. Stolk, who visited this village in 1905, reported that it had already been in existence for seven years (1907:23). The regional situation must have stabilized, and the Kereho must have curbed their raiding, in consequence of the Ot Danum attack and, no doubt, as a result of the increasing influence of the Dutch authorities and their native representatives, in particular the famous Temanggung Silam, chief of the Siang at Purukcahu. The Ot Danum had withdrawn to the lower Busang. The Seputan were no longer on the Busang, but their territory still extended to the south as far as Deringei, including all the high headwaters of the Busang and the Bekohu.

At Ihi (which Stolk called Doan Kabo), the Kereho, under the influence of the Seputan who had come to live with them, built a little longhouse that in 1905 sheltered some sixty people, under the leadership of Kerasut (whom Stolk called Klasut; 1907:23). The Kereho were still living on wild sago, but the Seputan living at Ihi probably farmed; Stolk indeed hinted at the presence of Seputan at Ihi (1907: 25). Lipa Pisa of Tamalue said in 1980 that "When all the sago of the area was exhausted, the Kereho asked the Seputan of the Kacu for seed rice" to start their own fields. Tradition reports, at Ihi and in the neighborhood, other heads of families, Pinang and Deleng (or Dereng; this might be the Daring mentioned above).

In 1905, then, Stolk visited the longhouse of Kerasut, leader of Ihi, and also Sovaoe (which he called Sabaoi), a little camp of three huts on the river Sovaoe (1907:25). Tradition in fact reports five families at Sovaoe, living on sago *(oa')* under their leader, Uvang, while fewer than ten families lived at Ihi with Kerasut. The description that Stolk gave of the longhouse at Ihi (1907:23) was fairly derogatory: it was dirty, falling apart, built of soft wood with walls of sheets of bark and a roof of leaves, almost without interior partitions. The inhabitants, on the other hand, aside from a few with scabies, seemed to him to be in good health. Among them, of course, was the old white-haired leader Kerasut, who, Stolk reported, was said to have to his credit more than a hundred and fifty severed heads! At Savaoe, the nomad camp, Stolk found the situation even more deplorably primitive.

Beginnings of Sedentarization (Chronology III)

In 1905, then, we find, on the one hand, a little longhouse and the beginnings of agriculture under the influence of a few Seputan and, on the other, a more traditional camp whose inhabitants were living on wild sago, less than a day's journey apart. Kereho Busang oral tradition continues the story. Some years later, the people of Sovaoe and some of those who lived at Ihi moved to live together at the junction of the Sovaoe and the Tamalue, at Tumbang Sovaoe, with their leaders, Uvang and Dani. This change of site was undoubtedly the result of instructions from Stolk and from the headmen of the Siang and other groups who accompanied him, in the context of the official policy promoting the concentration in downriver areas of the unstable population of the headwaters. The teacher Sengek, of Ukai (on the river Jengonoi, in the district of Nanga Ambalau, Melawi), reports that his father, Arip, an Ot Danum of Ukai, married a Kereho Busang woman of Tumbang Sovaoe and took part in the making of the group's first swidden clearings.

Settling at Tumbang Sovaoe was only a first step; Stolk wanted to see all the Kereho gathered on the banks of the Busang. At that time, alliances (via blood brotherhood or marriage) were made with the Siang and the Ot Danum, at the instigation of the Dutch, to consolidate the peace that then existed. Swidden agriculture spread at Tumbang Sovaoe, where fruit trees and traces of secondary forest can still be seen. Also around this time, according to Kereho sources, the Kereho began to practice the traditional religion *(adat)* of the Ot Danum, or at least those aspects of it that concerned funerary rites; indeed, the remains of *torai* (funeral posts, *toras* in the original Ot Danum) are still visible on this site.

It is possible that as soon as the Kereho were considered to be settled and harmless, Bekumpai and Siang traders set up a trading center at the mouth of the Tamalue, at the location called Telusan, to channel forest products out of the upriver area and so to introduce the Kereho into commercial networks of trade on the Barito. Prior to this, it is likely that the Kereho Busang traded in part with the Kapuas River basin (and the Kayan Mendalam) through the Kereho Uheng of the Keriau, and in part with the Mahakam through the Seputan of the Kacu.

A little later, most probably around 1915, a portion of the population of Tumbang Sovaoe and Ihi settled at Telusan. Lumholtz mentioned two villages, Sabaoi (Sovaoe) and Tamaloe (Telusan), inhabited by a total of seventy people. Their leaders were Pisa (whom Lumholtz called Pisha) and Nijung or Lijung (1920:I, 173–174). Apparently Nijung, "brother" (that is, blood brother) of Temanggung Silam, was himself given the title of *temanggung,* leader of all the Kereho Busang. According to the Kereho of West Kalimantan, this Nijung seems in fact to have been a Seputan who married into the group.

There were said to be thirteen families at Telusan. As Lumholtz did not mention Ihi, one may suppose that not many people still remained at that location. Telusan became the main Kereho village. A visitor named Massey confirmed that in the year 1918 Tamalue-Telusan was the most important village of the Busang (cited in Hildebrand 1982: 116). Intermarriage with the Seputan continued, to the point where Lumholtz could report that the culture and rituals of the Kereho were borrowed from the Seputan (1920:174). This is a view that needs to be balanced, as we will see below. At that time, indeed, the cultural influence of the Seputan must have begun to give way to the influence of the Barito groups.

Tamalue-Telusan was growing, and other heads of families came to settle there, among whom two are remembered, named Bok and Tusin. It was at this time that the population of the upper Busang must have undergone a demographic explosion, relatively speaking, with the arrival of numerous families from West Kalimantan or from the borderland between the two provinces, in relation to the opening and development of this locally important commercial outlet for forest products.

Other population movements began to be perceptible around 1920–1925. While there were still Kereho of the headwaters who had not yet made their way down to Telusan, other Kereho were already leaving that settlement to move farther down the Busang. Around 1925, according to Mallinckrodt (1927:590), there were Kereho not only at Telusan (Tamalue), with some few still at Tumbang Savaoe, but also at Liut Mulung (actually Liut Murung), Tumbang Pusu (location unknown), and Muara Katipu Langangui (in the region of present-day Ketipun). The teacher Sengek, for his part, states that at that time Kereho had settled at Tumbang Angoi and at Jojang, but notes that Ketipun and Liut Murung were Ot Danum villages. It may be that these Ot Danum either had not left the middle Busang or had returned there; in any case, it may be concluded that even at that time a merging of Kereho families into the nearest Ot Danum villages had already begun.

Moving in the opposite direction, more and more Bekumpai and Siang traders came to settle in Telusan. As well as the classic trade in such things as rotan and forest resins, some commerce in gold and diamonds on the upper Busang was reported by one traveler (Miller 1946).

Let us summarize the situation of the Kereho around 1925. They had been brought together for political reasons (stabilization of the area, census-taking, administrative control), while at the same time they were being integrated into a network of trade which imposed upon them the demand that they exploit forest products—in other words, that they redisperse. This indeed is what happened: before the Kereho had completed the process of assembling at Tamalue-Telusan, which in fact never became more than a nominal settlement occupied full-time only by traders, they had scattered again into at least five widely separated hamlets. Ihi and Tumbang Sovaoe, upriver, were apparently inhabited as late as 1930–1935, using Telusan as their outlet for forest products. The Kereho groups that had settled downriver opened new areas for forest collecting, some of which were in Ot Danum territory; at the same time, they made it possible to cut out the middlemen of Telusan by trading directly and more profitably farther downriver.

It is not hard to visualize the possible effects of this economic situation on Kereho agriculture. The Kereho were constantly prompted to gather forest products by the system of revolving credit practiced by the traders (*utang,* meaning debt; discussed in the next section); as a result they spent very little time cultivating rice. Massey (cited in Hildebrand 1982:116) found the village of Telusan virtually empty when he visited it in 1918. During this period, then, one can observe the early stages of development of a type of economy that still prevails today.

Regrouping and Recent History

Around 1930, it appears that the Ot Danum villagers of Ketipun and Liut Murung (and perhaps also of Jojang) moved down below the great rapids of Riam Duabelas to settle at Parahau', taking along a certain number of Kereho families, among them the people of the hamlet of Tumbang Angoi. This is the beginning of the major Kereho dispersal downriver to regions below the rapids. Around 1935, however, an unexpected outside element intervened. A group of six Iban, coming from the region of Kapit in Sarawak for an unknown reason (no doubt on *bejalai,* traveling to seek their fortunes), came to settle in Telusan. An Aoheng informant calls them Iban-Beketan, and they may well have actually been Beketan from the Kapit region. The leader of these newcomers, Kuling, married a local woman and set out to establish order among the unstable and relatively disorganized Kereho people. Possibly with Dutch support, he became the leader of all the Kereho and managed to bring together almost the whole group at Telusan. The people of Ihi and Tumbang Sovaoe came down from the Tamalue, while some of those who had scattered downstream came back up. But here, once again, political will had not the weight to overcome economic reality for long. Some years later, in any case undoubtedly after the Japanese occupation, a new dispersal took place, including more people and spreading into regions even farther downstream, triggered by the reopening of commercial networks of trade downriver, which created a new demand for forest products.

At this time, families from Telusan went to live in the more or less abandoned villages of Liut Murung, Ketipun, and perhaps others. When the old Iban leader Kuling was replaced by Kevang, a Kereho, the Seputan-style longhouse of Telusan split apart, and at least two-thirds of its Kereho inhabitants emigrated downriver. Apparently Indonesia's national independence had no impact on the life of the Kereho, aside from the abandonment of the title of *temanggung,* the creation of the community *(desa)* of Parit, and the naming of a village headman *(pembakal,* the local equivalent of *kepala desa)* and a headman responsible for customary law *(kepala adat)* to live in it. This suggests that, at that time, Parit must have been the largest of the Kereho villages. The Kereho dispersal was not limited to the downriver regions. Around 1947, a group of Kereho from Parahau' left for the Melawi, to settle with the young teacher Sengek at Ukai, where they still live today.

Around 1954, a Seputan chief named Hujang Nani' led a group of six or seven families to settle at the mouth of the Bekohu, which marked the downriver limit of Seputan territory. They stayed there four years, then moved farther upstream to the mouth of the Danum Buro ("river of gold"), where they stayed for nine years. Toward 1965 this group moved back again, a few at a time, to the Kacu. In those years the Seputan living at Long Berane on the upper Kacu, who had maintained a monopoly of the collection of forest products on the upper Busang (including the Bekohu), moved away down the Kacu, turning over to the Kereho their rights to collect forest products on the upper Busang, keeping for themselves only their rights over birds' nests in the caves of the Bekaang. This factor probably played a role in keeping some of the population of Telusan from leaving the upper Busang.

Around 1960, the people of Telusan moved to the site of the present village known by the name of Tamalue, which is now no more than a little hamlet. The tendency to move downriver was consolidated by increasingly intense emigration to Parahau', below the rapids, then by the outflow of population that emptied Parahau' in its turn for the benefit of the Barito towns.

In 1980, there were about three hundred Kereho Busang living in the Busang, and perhaps another two hundred scattered down the Barito. A good half of the first group undoubtedly lived in isolated houses rather than in hamlets. Moreover, certain families officially living in one or another of the hamlets of the Busang were actually living elsewhere, like the nine *kepala keluarga* (heads of nuclear families) of Tamalue who had been spending two and a half years on the Bungan in West Kalimantan, gathering rotan and illipe nuts and making ironwood shingles for sale in the Kapuas markets. Of these nine nuclear families, it is said that six recently went back to the Busang.

The village of Parit, the main settlement of the administrative unit *(desa)* of Parit, was the seat of a *kepala kampung* or *pembakal* (village headman) and a *kepala adat;* other hamlets were led by a deputy *pembakal* and a deputy *kepala adat.* Thus the deputy *pembakal* of Tamalue, Dani, took his orders from the *pembakal* of Parit, Kujat (who also happened to be his father); and Hunyan, *kepala adat* for all the Kereho Busang, who lived at Parit, had as deputies Baka at Ketipun, Lipa at Tamalue, and others.

As has been seen, the upper Busang region, above the river's many dangerous rapids, was extremely isolated from the towns of the Barito. The closest school was at Tumbang Juloi; the center of trade and the timber companies were at Teluk Jolo, farther downriver; the closest medical dispensary and the administrative center were at Tumbang Konyi, still farther downstream. It took four days of paddling to travel down from Tamalue to Teluk Jolo, with another day to reach Tumbang Konyi, and eight days to paddle back up from Tumbang Konyi to Tamalue.

At Tamalue, in 1980, there were only two or three people who could read, and no available medicines at all. Despite its isolation, the village economy was oriented downriver, in particular toward Teluk Jolo. This town is located at the point in the river's course at which cargo carried in big river barges must be transferred to longboats and serves as a center of trade for the river basins of the Juloi, the Murung, and the Busang. At Tamalue, the principal forest products were timber and rotan, with a little gold. Felling of forest trees was unregulated; trees felled were marked with the owner's initials and left to the mercy of periodic floods, which might or might not carry them downstream. The drifting logs would collect of their own accord in a natural pool at Teluk Jolo, where one or more timber companies would fish them out and credit the number of logs to the woodman's account. This is the system called *banjir kap,* long forbidden (as wasteful and dangerous to boats) in other areas of Kalimantan. Rotan was bound into rafts and guided down to Teluk Jolo.

The commercial unit for timber was the *kepeng* (a plank of four, six, or eight meters in length; the number of planks that could be obtained from a single log was estimated by eye), which was worth about 150 rupiah in 1980. Rotan was cut into *bintir,* six-meter lengths, of which the hundredweight (100 kilos) was worth 20,000 to 25,000 rupiah in 1980. Transactions between traders and upriver people, however, were carried out without recourse to cash money, by the system of revolving credit or *utang,* mentioned above. A running account kept by the trader obliged a client in debt to bring in more timber or rotan or, if he had a credit balance, enabled him to take the goods he wanted; but since he could usually be persuaded to take more than he had goods to pay for, the pressure on him to keep collecting was virtually constant. The least that can be said about this system, which persists today, is that it is not usually to the upriver peoples' advantage.

In 1980 the majority of families in Tamalue were already short of rice by the end of July (the harvest having taken place around February). Apparently, despite the fertility of the lands around it, Tamalue normally could live no more than half a year on the product of its annual rice harvest. Cultivated cassava and wild sago enabled people to make their dietary ends meet. Families who had run out of rice went into the forest to live off sago, a practice called *pano peraran.* This confirms the data of Avé (1977:28). Coffee bushes were grown here and there, though the beans were apparently not roasted, or indeed harvested. Similarly, sugarcane was eaten raw, and there was no extraction of juice to make molasses. There were chickens in the village, dogs, some pigs, and a few cats. Asked about the reasons for the inadequacy of rice production, family heads gave as most important a general lack of discipline in cooperative work and the great number of "enemies of the rice" (birds, deer, and so on).

The houses of Tamalue had posts and frames of ironwood, front walls and floors of softwood, and side and rear walls of bark. Shingles were tied on with rotan, more rarely nailed. These were single-family houses, quite close together. The eight households included, respectively, three, four, seven, eight, eight, ten, eleven, and sixteen persons, spanning from two to four generations. In certain houses stacks of gongs and a few jars were stored in a corner; otherwise tools, weapons, and utensils were few in number. Other aspects of the culture will be discussed below.

In the direction of the headwaters, communications with other river basins over the watershed of the Busang were relatively rare. The footpath via the Bekaang to the Kacu was rarely used except by Seputan or Aoheng looking for wage labor on the Barito; the path over the upper Sovaoe to the Melawi was no longer in use, but a branch of this path leading from the upper Sovaoe to the upper Kereho (the village of Belatung) and to the Bungan was used once or twice a year.

Changes

In the light of the history outlined above, we may now try to describe Kereho Busang society and culture as they traditionally existed, and as they appear to have changed.

Material Culture

There can be no doubt that, ethnically and linguistically, the Kereho Busang belong to the Kereho group of the Kapuas, itself related to the Hovongan (or Punan Bungan) and to certain ethnic elements that contributed to the formation of the Seputan and Aoheng groups of East Kalimantan. This set of peoples form what I have elsewhere called the Punan complex of the Müller mountains (Sellato 1981b). The provisional results of research in progress permit the conclusion that the nomad bands of the southern half of the Müller mountains were all Kereho speakers, and that some of them formed the Hovongan through admixture with the Semukung, while others contributed to the formation of the Seputan. The Kereho-Hovongan together (grouped here because the other peoples referred to were subject at an earlier period to the cultural influence of the Kayan groups of the Kapuas and the Mahakam) covered, as they still do, the mountain ranges between the upper basins of the Busang, the Melawi, the Kapuas, and the Mahakam. Major neighboring cultures, from the east to the southwest (on the rivers Mandai, Melawi, Juloi, and Busang), the Ot Danum; to the east and the west (on the Mahakam and Kapuas) the Kayan groups, and to a lesser extent the Taman; and farther to the north the Iban.

As has been seen, the Kereho of the Kapuas were most closely associated with the Kayan of the Kapuas, and, through the Seputan and the Aoheng, with the Kayan and Long Gelat of the Mahakam. Subsequently the Ot Danum, their deadly enemies, also became their allies. In the case of the Kereho Busang, the major cultural influence came from the Mahakam by way of the Seputan, with whom the Kereho Busang had long been intimately associated. Then the times changed, and the Kereho Busang found themselves oriented toward the Barito; their former enemies the Ot Danum became both their trading partners and their political overlords, since the chiefs of the Barito were the representatives of the colonial government.

Thus, though the first seed rice (pari) may have been given to the Kereho Busang by the Seputan, their subsequent regrouping and sedentarization took place under the patronage of the ethnic groups of the Barito. It is notable, however, that Kereho Busang vocabulary relating to agriculture is on the whole taken from the Seputan. This introduction to agriculture occurred after a period of intermarriages with the Seputan, who had built a little longhouse at Ihi and begun to cultivate rice. Families who were not "Seputanized" by marriage were eventually, when local sago had been used up, faced with the choice between moving on to find more wild sago (as the Sovaoe group did) and starting to clear their own fields after obtaining sufficient seed grain from the Seputan of the Kacu. Given the importance of cassava in current Kereho subsistence, it is probable that this tuber played a decisive role at this stage of their sedentarization. That most of the Seputan themselves at this time relied on a combination of cassava, rice, and (to some extent) wild sago would tend to confirm this hypothesis. Thus, from the very beginning of agriculture among the Kereho Busang, a certain tension developed between those who favored change (like Kerasut, leader of Ihi) and those who held to the old ways (like Uvang of Sovaoe).

It is worth noting that the Kereho Busang word for longhouse (*baang*) is the Seputan and Aoheng term, while the Kereho of the Kapuas adopted the term *lovu* from the Ot Danum of the Mandai.

Aside from agriculture and the longhouse, it is hard to distinguish in the material culture of the Kereho Busang of today what was originally their own from what they borrowed from the ethnic groups of the Kapuas (the Kayan) while they were still living in the Kapuas River basin, and from what they subsequently borrowed from the ethnic groups of the Mahakam (Kayan and Long Gelat) by way of the Seputan.

Among those cultural elements coming from the Mahakam are women's tattoos (a band tattooed around the ankle), a type of triangular winnowing basket, the mouth organ, and perhaps a form of mouth harp (these instruments being in any case nearly extinct). Stolk (1907: 23, 24) notes that although the Kereho Busang use bead ornaments and weapons like those of the Seputan, the style of women's skirts differs. In fact, even though they use the specific term of the Müller mountain groups, *kotip,* they follow the style of the Kayan of the Kapuas, in which the wraparound skirt overlaps over the right thigh rather than in the rear, the style in the Mahakam. In 1981 this skirt had been replaced by a Malay sarong or a printed dress, and the loincloth *(ovi)* formerly worn by men was worn in Tamalue only by one old man, Lipa, son of the leader Pisa.

With regard to hunting *(nganup),* it may be noted that, as with all the groups of the Müller mountains, women hunt just as men do (Lumholtz 1920:253). Lumholtz also noted that blowpipes were bought from the Seputan (1920:174). At present older people continue to prefer hunting with the blowpipe *(soput),* while the young like to hunt with spears *(doha')* and dogs. This distinction is primarily a function of the kind of game sought, but it is sometimes also a matter of personal preference. It may also be noted that though the bush knife *(olok)* and the spear are referred to by their Punan names, the term that designates the shield *(kelibit)* is of Kayan origin.

The question of the dugout canoe must doubtless remain unanswered. In the highlands, as at Ihi, boats are useless. At Tumbang Sovaoe they become a necessity. The Kereho recognize that they traditionally had no skill in boat-making (and by the look of the boats of Tamalue, they are still not expert); but it is not possible to determine whether they learned what they now know from the Seputan when this group lived on the upper Busang, or from the Siang and the Ot Danum at the time when the Kereho were assembled at Telusan. It is all the more difficult to resolve the problem since the term for canoe or dugout boat, *'out* (close to the Hovongan *'aut)* is as closely related to the *arut* of the Seputan as it is to the *arut* of the Ot Danum, but not at all to the *jukkung* of the Siang. Other terms relating to the boat and its accessories are, in any case, the same as in Seputan.

The domestic pig *(okot)* and the chicken *(siu),* to judge by their Aoheng or Seputan names, were certainly introduced from the upper Mahakam.

In the sphere of music and dance, the influence of the Barito ethnic groups is very clear. The *gambus* (a kind of three-stringed lute) is almost the only instrument still used in the practice of the musical and dance genres *deder, tasai,* and *kerungut.*

Kereho Society

Kereho Busang society was first subjected to outside influence through contact with the Seputan. The Seputan of the Kacu had already adopted, with some reluctance, the type of stratified society that prevails in all the upper Mahakam, entailing in particular a major opposition between *supi* and *kovi* (nobles and commoners, respectively, in the Aoheng and Seputan languages). At Tamalue it was not possible for me to confirm this opposition. The words used there to designate these categories are Seputan terms, and everybody claims to be *supi* or the descendant of *supi,* citing such and such an ancestor said to have been the leader of all the Kereho. When asked what has happened to all the commoners, they answer that all of them are dead or else that they all migrated downstream.

It is not impossible that the families of well-known leaders might have tried to establish a system of hereditary nobility, and that other families might have preferred, rather than yielding, to go seek their fortunes elsewhere. Indeed, Stolk (1907:25) reports a distinction in the value of the marriage payment between the families of "tribal chiefs" and those of the commoners. However, as this was the situation at Doan Kavo', at which (stratified) Seputan were living, it is most probable that this was a borrowed custom, which would not persist. It seems more reasonable to envisage an egalitarian society within which one person particularly esteemed among the elders *(dino tohokan)* is considered to be the informal leader (like Kerasut at Ihi), which would not prevent another family head with different views from leaving to make his camp elsewhere (like Uvang at Sovaoe). Moreover, in the third generation in a group of sixty to a hundred persons every member of the group might well call himself or herself a descendant (direct or collateral, one or both always being the case) of Kerasut or Uvang. And this in fact is what happened: Dani, the young deputy *pembakal* of Tamalue, is the son of Kujat, *kepala kampung* (head of the *desa*) of Parit, who himself is the "son" of Dani senior (see below), who was the leader of Tumbang Sovaoe, himself the son of Kerasut, leader of Ihi; similarly, Lavung, minor leader at Parahau', is the son of Nijung; and so at Tamalue, everyone descends from either Kerasut, Uvang, or Nijung. We should note in passing that the term for "son" just as often designates a nephew or a distant cousin as it does a real son. At Tamalue, nothing appears to distinguish one family from another with regard to social status.

Although it would be premature to conclude on the basis of investigations in a single hamlet that stratification is absent in Kereho Busang society, even in the minimal form of a weak opposition between noble lines of descent and commoners, it is nevertheless evident that in the absence of strong pressure from the administrative authorities the Kereho show very little group cohesion and that family groups (nuclear or extended families) have a high degree of autonomy with regard to their movements and their choice of a way of life. As we

have seen, three out of eight families at Tamalue and eleven out of fifteen at Ketipun have chosen to live outside the hamlet; and many families have left to travel outside the territory for years on end, coming
back only to leave again. The family *(kevian)*, then, though it
acknowledges its membership in a larger community (*puhu'*, the family in a very broad sense, or the band, descending from a common
forebear), remains an autonomous entity. The affiliation of the *kevian*
to a given community (band or hamlet) is therefore extremely unstable, and it is highly uncertain how long any given community itself
will last. This very marked tendency to family-group autonomy naturally acts to counter the establishment of large villages.

Although social stratification has apparently left no mark on
Kereho Busang society, such is not the case with the system of postmarital residence. At Tamalue, the five houses of the hamlet are all
owned by women. In seven couples out of eight, the man lives in the
house of his wife or his wife's parents. The word for this, *ngevan* (to
live with the spouse's parents), is the term used by the ethnic groups of
the Mahakam (as also by the Kayan of the Kapuas). As part of the
marriage rites (*adet pevosaa,* from *bosaa,* to get married), the man
makes a marriage payment (*buleng,* the bridewealth properly speaking, and *ketumat,* for a girl previously unmarried) in the form of
gongs, and adds to this another hefty payment if he wants to "take the
woman away" *(pusit dora),* that is, if he wants her to come live with
him or his own parents. This uxorilocality, at once the ideal rule
and the common practice, is the norm among Kayan and Busang
groups; but it may be noted that the Ot Danum also have an ideal of
uxorilocality.

Stolk (1907:25) reports that the marriage payment consists of several gongs for the families of "tribal chiefs" and a bush knife, a blowpipe, or a spear for common people. The only informant at Tamalue
who mentioned such a distinction to me was a very old Seputan
woman, the wife of Lipa. Stolk, moreover, does not specify in which
direction this payment is made. We may recall that Schwaner (in a
mention that predates the arrival of Kereho on the Busang but concerns the Ot in general and therefore probably includes the Kereho of
the Juloi: in Roth 1968: CXCVII) reports that it is the woman who
chooses the man and makes him a gift of weapons. It is possible, therefore, that at the time of Stolk's visit two practices coexisted, a mar-

riage gift in the form of weaponry from the woman to the man (which might be the traditional system) and a gift in the form of gongs from the man to the bride's father, a custom borrowed from the Seputan. Only the latter practice would have survived. We may also note, as Stolk did, that this payment was apparently unaccompanied by any celebration or any particular ritual, the betrothed couple simply being declared to be married.

Marriage between second cousins is common, and marriage between first cousins (of which several cases exist at Tamalue) is possible after a rite of purification involving the sacrifice of a pig. This ritual, like pigs themselves, was probably introduced by the Seputan, among whom it is customary.

Kinship terminology (see Kinship Chart II) is very similar to that of the Seputan, and therefore very different from that of the Ot Danum, the Siang, and other ethnic groups of the Barito. Like Seputan terminology, it shows some borrowings from the Kayan. Unlike the Kayan, though (and like the Bukat, see Kinship Chart I), it provides a system of three terms for affines of Ego's generation, based on the sex of the speaker and that of the person addressed or referred to, a feature common to the languages of many nomad groups and similar to that of certain Barito languages and some languages of Sarawak (see Sellato 1983b). Kereho Busang kinship terminology is very close to that of the Kereho Uheng of West Kalimantan. Differences between the two terminologies are noted in Kinship Chart II.

Aside from this, there exists at Tamalue a system of some twenty necronyms, names adopted by individuals on the occasion of the death of particular relatives, similar to the system used by the Seputan and the Aoheng. This system of necronyms seems to be specific to the nomad groups of the Müller mountains.

According to Lumholtz (1920:174), the sexual division of labor among nomadic Kereho Busang is as follows: women are responsible for the construction of the house, the collection of rotan, gathering plant foods, fetching water and firewood, cooking, carrying goods and children when the group moves, and hunting with dogs and spears. Men are responsible for hunting with the blowpipe, but they bring back only the news of their success: women have to find and fetch home the game the men have killed. Men, however, are also responsible for the band's protection and defense. Lumholtz says

nothing about the work involved in the extraction of sago, but it is
probable that the job of felling the palm and extracting the pith, at any
rate, is done by men.

Rituals and Religion

With regard to matters of religion, Tamalue in 1980 included
one nominal Catholic and no Muslims, with the rest of its inhabitants
stating that they followed a traditional religion that differed from the
religion known as Kaharingan, practiced by most of the un-Islami-
cized groups of the Barito. Among Kereho Busang living farther
downriver, the proportion of Muslims is probably higher, but I have
no data on this point.

According to this traditional religion, a sister and brother, Kito and
Minang, created the universe and the human race, then "departed"
and are no longer invoked. This pair of creator deities is found in near
identical form among the Seputan, the Hovongan, and the Aoheng.
(See also the discussion of Bukat religion in Chapter 2.) The god that
people pray to, who supervises humans and assists them, is Amun
Tingai, present as well among Aoheng and Seputan, who corresponds
to Tinge or Tingai of the Kayan and Busang. Spirits, both good and
evil, are called *kerengoa,* a term found also among the Hovongan.

Shamanistic healing rituals are of three types: *tosop, habai,* and
penyangon, which serve to cure the sick, plus a rite of purification for
places and people, *nyari.* All these rituals are present among the other
groups of the Müller mountains, and Lumholtz seemed to believe that
the Kereho, who had no such rituals, must have borrowed them from
the Seputan (1920:174). The esoteric and metaphorical language used
in Kereho rituals is often Hovongan daily speech. Certain prohibitions
(toheng) may be noted in passing: a prohibition on eating deer meat
for those who are carrying out healing rituals and a general prohibition on speaking one's own name.

It appears, therefore, that a significant proportion of Kereho
Busang religious practice and belief belongs to the religious system of
the Punan of the Müller mountains, common also to Hovongan, Seputan, and Aoheng, with some additional touches borrowed by the
Kereho from the Kayan and the Long Gelat. It is probable that this
system derives in part from the religion of the Pin, former inhabitants
of the upper Mahakam. But the Kereho, more isolated than the Hovongan and the Seputan, no doubt inherited Pin tradition only after it

had been well blended among the Seputan with borrowings from the Long Gelat and the Kayan.

The Kereho believe that human beings have one soul *(beruon)*, which after death becomes a spirit *(kerengoa* or *otun kovo)*. This spirit must be accompanied to its last home by appropriate rituals. Present-day death rites have been borrowed from the Barito groups (Siang, Ot Danum, and others). There are two stages of funeral ceremony, one immediate and one delayed. First the body is buried, and on the grave people erect a small wooden structure in the shape of a T *(misan)*, and plant a leafy bough *(tabe')* leaning to the west. Sometimes they add a small superstructure in the form of a roof *(lopu)* over the grave. A prohibition *(bureng)* is then placed upon a specific area of the forest territory, a stream basin where the dead person used to live, forbidding survivors to use its produce or even to walk through it. The family then gets together supplies for the second ceremony, the *daro'*, which centers on the erection of a funerary post *(torai)* enabling the soul to climb to the world above *(havun)*.

In fact, the Kereho *daro'* does not actually correspond to the rite the Ot Danum call *daro'* (secondary funeral rites), but rather, involving as it does the erection of the *torai*, to the ritual they call *nesirip*. The Ot Danum *daro'* entails the making of a statue in the image of the dead person and the sacrifice of a cow or a water buffalo, but since it is probable that no member of either species has ever yet made it past the rapids to Tamalue, there people manage with a pig. However, there are statues at Tamalue. So the Kereho have adapted Ot Danum rituals in their own fashion. For that matter, it appears, from the account of Avé (in LeBar 1972:194), that the Ot Danum of Central Kalimantan, neighbors of the Kereho, themselves no longer practice the secondary funeral rites still in effect among the Ot Danum of the Melawi. In any case, the Kereho seem to believe that their religion is not Kaharingan (for more on the Kaharingan religion, see Sarwoto 1963).

The *daro'* ceremony, as the Kereho practice it, is the occasion for great festivity, in which relatives near and distant and the whole village are summoned to share. The necessity to raise funds and supplies for the feast and assemble the kin group means that it is often impossible to hold the *daro'* until several years after the death. At Tamalue, for example, after the death in 1979 of Uting, a well-respected elderly man, family members were still waiting in July of 1980 for relatives then living temporarily on the Bungan to return to the village.

A few remarks may be added on the history of the introduction of Barito-type funerary rituals among the Kereho Busang. According to the elder Lipa Pisa, who once lived at Ihi, the first *torai* were made while the Kereho were living at Tumbang Sovaoe. It is probable that at that time ceremonies of blood brotherhood (like that which may have taken place between Temanggung Silam of the Siang and the Kereho leader Nijung) and intermarriages with the Siang and the Ot Danum led a certain number of individuals from the Barito ethnic groups to settle at Tumbang Sovaoe. Lipa states that there definitely was no *adat torai* (the name for the funerary rite) when the Kereho lived at Ihi.

At Ihi, according to Lipa, people buried their dead in coffins, with *misan* structures erected on the graves. Stolk, however, reported that the body was placed on a flat stone, at which the family sacrificed an animal, adding at a later date a jawbone or some other part of a human body, the fruit of a headhunting expedition (1907:25). Lumholtz for his part mentioned a coffin made from a single hollowed-out log that was left without ceremony on a platform in the forest (1920: 174). Another form of interment was attributed at an earlier date to the Ot Nyawong: "they cremate the body, gather up ashes and bones in a piece of cloth and stuff the bundle into the trunk of a tree . . . the opening then being closed with resin, the trunk heals over it" (Perelaer 1881, in Meyners d'Estrey 1891:320).

Whatever type of interment may have been practiced in the nineteenth century, it is certain that later, at Telusan, the erection of *torai* became a common practice; however, these posts are no longer visible, having recently been lost with the river's erosion of the bank on which they stood.

In conclusion, one may envision a minimal religious substratum of Kereho tradition, or rather more generally of Punan tradition, from this region of the Müller mountains, including, no doubt, significant borrowings from the Pin by way of the Seputan. The pantheon seems specific to the Punan, but the healing rituals of purification may have a variety of origins (the *penyangon* of the Kereho is lexically related to the *pesangen* of the Barito groups, a term that itself probably derives from *sanghyang* (the ancient Sanskrit and modern Ngaju term for spiritual beings). Besides this, there were some borrowings from the Busang and Kayan groups.

The recent and rapid adoption of enormously expensive Barito-group funeral festivals by the Kereho soon after their sedentarization suggests that, in the context of their traditional nomad culture, death was not the occasion for much ritual activity. Even today, after more than fifty years of contact, the Kereho take many liberties with these borrowed rituals. It may also be noted that features of Kereho Busang *adat*, or customary law, collected by Dormeier (1952) seem to have been borrowed from the Barito groups.

Conclusions

A few general conclusions may be suggested relative to the transformations in Kereho Busang life between 1880 and 1980. The Kereho Busang, belonging culturally and linguistically to the "Punan complex" of the Müller mountains, established themselves in the upper basin of the Busang River and, alone or with the help of allied groups, drove the Ot Danum from this region. It follows that nomadic hunter-gatherer groups are not always fated, as some writers seem to think, to be forced gradually back by the farming groups into inaccessible mountains: they may be able not only to defend the integrity of the territories over which they range, but also, though no doubt at the initiative of outsiders and with their help, to conquer new lands.

Subsequently, thanks to the general shift of the farming populations downriver, the Kereho became the sole inhabitants of the Busang River basin, down to its junction with the Barito. Moreover, after the Seputan abandoned their rights over the headwaters of the Busang, it was the Kereho who made use of the region's resources. Thus they currently have available to them an immense territory in which they exploit forest resources, forming the economic niche (in the sense of a specialized economic activity) that they have been able to keep for their own.

From forest nomads, the Kereho became part-time farmers under the influence, first of the Seputan, then of the administration and the Barito groups. This political demand for sedentarization and the practice of farming being incompatible with the commercial demand for forest products, the Kereho have been induced to develop a mixed subsistence economy combining rice, cultivated cassava, and wild sago, and to engage in intensive commercial collecting. This same incompatibility of demands has led to a particular type of residence pattern, combining village cores, isolated houses, and mobile forest camps, and including the option of travel outside the group territory for commercial reasons. Consequently, Kereho society has remained fundamentally egalitarian, despite possible local tendencies toward the establishment of noble lines of descent under the influence of the Seputan. The near absolute autonomy of family groups, subject only to the authority of heads of families, has been maintained.

From ethnic groups with whom the Kereho were in contact, they borrowed, adapted, and more or less integrated only those cultural features that seemed able to fill a need or provide a practical improvement in their lives (dugout canoes, for example), to permit certain families to gain prestige (funeral rituals, tattoos, perhaps the marriage gift), or simply to bring pleasure (rice beer, betelnut, tobacco)—features, moreover, that could do these things without disrupting the dynamic balance between life on the farm and life in the forest, and the autonomy and mobility of family groups. Other cultural elements such as social stratification and a strong central authority, which were viewed as endangering their chosen way of life, were rejected. An element such as uxorilocality, introduced from the Mahakam by the Seputan (and strongly reinforced by the Barito groups), may have been seen as a "neutral" factor, having no direct impact on economic choices. The Kereho, then, may be envisioned as acting with a certain pragmatism, in which the practical realities of the economic sphere are combined with the will to maintain a particular way of life centered on family autonomy and mobility.

Above: A Punan territory: volcanic highlands in the headwaters of the Belayan (East Kalimantan).

Left: Rapids barring the route to the upriver lands (Mahakam, East Kalimantan).

Above: Morut, an isolated Punan settlement in the headwaters of the Murung (Central Kalimantan), seen from the air. Note the cassava gardens and the banana trees behind the houses.

Below: A view of the Bukat hamlet of Noha Tivap (East Kalimantan).

Top left: A forest shelter, a simple platform with lean-to roof (Bukat, East Kalimantan).

Above: A hut in the Hovongan hamlet of Nanga Bulit (West Kalimantan), with bark walls and a roof of palm leaves.

Left: A house in the Bukat hamlet of Noha Tivap (East Kalimantan), with board walls and roof of shingles.

Left: A Hovongan hut on the river Bungan (West Kalimantan), surrounded by cassava, banana trees, and other fruit trees.

Below: The "modern" Lisum village of Long Top, on the Uhu', in the headwaters of the Boh (East Kalimantan).

Return of a successful hunter to the Hovongan
(Punan Bungan) village of Bo'ung, in the
upper Kapuas River basin, West Kalimantan.
(Photo by Jean Subra, O.M.I.)

Above: A sago palm *(Eugeissona),* left unfelled on the edge of a swidden clearing.

Below: Rotan or cane, an important article of trade, ready to be taken downriver.

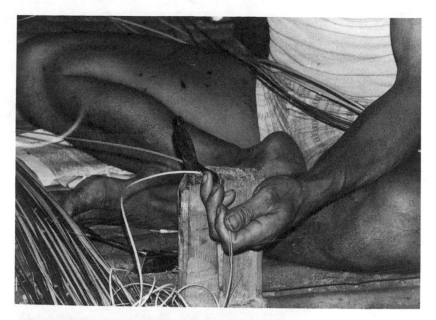

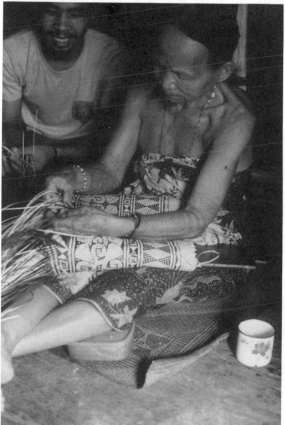

Above: Paring lengths of rotan between two fixed blades to produce narrow strips for use in weaving mats or baskets.

Left: A Lisum woman of Muara Belinau (upper Belayan, East Kalimantan), tattooed in Kenyah style, making a fine rotan basket.

left: Collectors of damar resin store their goods in a forest shelter before carrying them on downriver (Bukat of the Mahakam, East Kalimantan).

below left: A rare item of trade, casques of helmeted hornbills (*Rhinoplax vigil*) slain by blowpipe. Used by the farming peoples to make ornaments; by the Chinese, for medicine.

right: An arcane alchemy: the making of poison to tip blowpipe darts. Various ingredients, including tobacco juice, are blended with toxic tree sap on a wooden board.

below: Beside the bamboo quiver filled with darts already fitted with their light pith stabilizers, new darts are coated with poison. Grooves made near the tip of the dart ensure that the point will break off in the wound.

Left: Making the blow-pipe. The hardwood shaft to be bored is fixed between the uprights of a framework built for the purpose, above the platform on which the maker sits.

Below: A long rod of iron is slowly forced through the wood from bottom to top, its chisel point being driven in and then rotated to hollow out the barrel: a lengthy and painstaking process.

Above: Recording an interview in the office of the headman of the Bukat village of Noha Tivap (East Kalimantan).

Right: A Beketan of Tubo' (upper Belayan, East Kalimantan) playing the *sape'* (similar to the lute). Note that his brows have been completely depilated, in the traditional style.

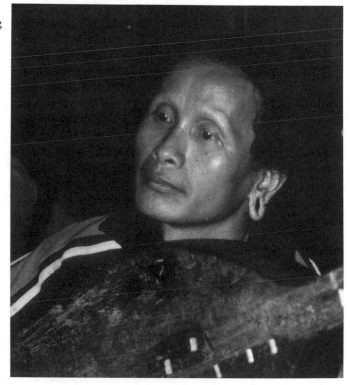

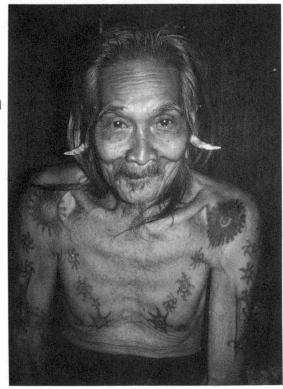

Above: Beketan mother and son from Tubo' (East Kalimantan). Note the weight of the rings that elongate her earlobes, her gold-capped teeth, and depilated brows: these are all fashions borrowed from neighboring Kenyah.

Right: Old Hovongan man from the Langau in West Kalimantan, covered with tattoos and wearing clouded leopard fangs in his earlobes. (Photo by Jean Subra, O.M.I.)

PART TWO

TRADITIONS AND CHANGES

Origins of the Punan

This second part of the book deals at a more general level than the first with Punan culture and cultural change. A description of the traditional culture of the nomadic hunter-gatherers will be followed by a discussion of the transformations undergone by this culture, from the nomads' earliest contacts with farming groups up to the stage at which sedentarization may take place.

Over the past few decades, the question of the origin of Borneo's nomadic hunter-gatherers has been a topic of contention among the supporters of three general lines of argument. The first, represented by Hose and McDougall (1912), Kennedy (1935), Urquhart (1959), and Stöhr (1959), views these nomads as cultural vestiges, remnant groups left over from a process of evolution leading to the farming peoples. On the basis of similarities of culture and close relationships between certain nomad and farming groups, these writers conclude that a general evolutionary process of conversion to agriculture has affected all the peoples of Borneo, and that the nomads are those groups that this process has left behind.

A second line of argument is based upon the idea that hunter-gatherer culture is independent of the culture of the farmers. Supported by Vrocklage (1936), Heine-Geldern (1946), and more recently by J. Nicolaisen (1976a, 1976b), this view is founded upon the existence of incompatible traits in the culture and social organization of hunter-gatherers and farmers.

Finally, the third line of argument (Harrisson 1949; Seitz 1981; Hoffman 1983) maintains that the culture of the hunter-gatherers is a "secondary primitivism," the result of devolution. Some of the grounds for this argument are technological (see the discussion of hunting weaponry in Chapter 4); others are linguistic, making the assumption that the nomads descend from Austronesian-speaking groups who, when they reached Borneo, had already mastered the cultivation of rice (Blust 1976; it is, however, debatable whether the nomads here discussed were among those groups). Thus, according to this theory, the hunter-gatherers would be the descendants of farmers who went off to live in the primary forest for reasons that might be political (warfare) or economic (specialization in the exploitation of the forest environment).

Certain reservations about these theories must be expressed. First, our knowledge of the nomads of Borneo is still extremely fragmentary (no serious and complete inventory of these groups has yet been made). Furthermore, our knowledge is biased in having been almost exclusively drawn from just one region, Sarawak, and one relatively recent span of time. It clearly lacks breadth and depth of perspective, geographic and diachronic.

Another reservation concerns the general validity of these theories and their tendency to contradict one another. In the present state of our understanding, it seems impossible to prove any single theory, much less ascribe to it the value of a general model. Moreover, nothing by definition prohibits the coexistence in different parts of the island, or the succession within a single region, of two or more of the processes described above. Supposing an autonomous culture of hunter-gatherer groups to have existed, some of these groups have undeniably converted to farming, in which case those who remain nomadic might indeed be described as vestiges or remnants left behind by evolutionary change; and there may also have been specific instances of devolution.

A flaw intrinsic to all these theories is, in my opinion, the opposition of nomad to farmer (more precisely, rice farmer), as if they were mutually exclusive, which leads certain writers to describe the conversion from one type of culture to the other in terms of an "evolutionary necessity" with "intermediate stages" in an obligatory order. I intend to show, on the contrary, that nomad is not the opposite of farmer, and that these two apparent alternatives may in fact be combined to characterize a variety of economic systems that, rather than being intermediate stages in a unidirectional evolutionary process, are stable in themselves and possess their own attractions.

As will be seen below, my conclusions, based upon my field data as outlined in preceding chapters and supplemented by data relating to other groups of former nomads that I have had the opportunity of studying (such as the Punan Murung and the Aoheng; see, in particular, Sellato 1986b), along with further data from the literature, support the concept of an autonomous original culture of nomadic hunter-gatherers.

With regard to the question of an evolutionary process, I will say only that within a setting bounded by constraints both geographical (the central part of Borneo) and temporal (the past two centuries) we are indeed dealing with a process of sedentarization of nomads that may be called an "evolutionary tendency," within this particular setting. This implies no prejudgment of what may have happened in earlier centuries or millennia, or of what may have been happening outside this geographical area. That the nomads are settling down is an undeniable fact. This does not necessarily mean that they convert completely to agriculture, much less to rice farming. But it is true that rice is gaining ground, and not only in Borneo. As Avé says (1977:28), it is striking that throughout insular Southeast Asia sago-eating peoples are shifting to rice.

The reconstructions presented in Chapters 2 and 3 in general confirm, over two centuries of history, the results of recent studies on the sedentarization of nomad groups (the Penan) in Sarawak, though with this major exception: as will be seen below, the practice of rice farming is very clearly not the inevitable end of the nomads' sedentarization.

In what follows, Chapter 4 will present an outline of the traditional culture of the nomadic hunter-gatherers; Chapter 5 will deal with those socioeconomic processes which, along with the intensification of commercial contacts, sedentarization, and the practice of certain forms of agriculture, have acted to change this culture. As well as providing a description of the mechanics of this process, I will attempt an explanation of its deeper causes; and I will argue that the nomads have elaborated new economic systems compatible with their underlying traditional ideology.

CHAPTER 4
TRADITIONAL NOMAD CULTURE

As WILL BE SHOWN in the following pages, a comparison of the available data on the nomadic (or formerly nomadic) groups of Borneo brings out many common sociocultural features. These groups will be collectively referred to here as Punan.

There is no need to review here all aspects of the culture of the nomadic Punan, their material culture in particular. This nomad culture will be described in the form it took after contact with farming groups and before the beginnings of sedentarization; some features that may have existed earlier than this stage will be discussed (see the section on hunting), but no special mention will be made of features that may persist among semisettled or settled Punan. Of this traditional culture, only those aspects will be described which for various reasons seem to me to be particularly relevant or characteristic: the subsistence economy (strategies relative to the exploitation of sago, special techniques of hunting and fishing); the concept of territory (its occupation, its defense); social organization (egalitarianism, collectivism, the practice of band endogamy); and *adat* (customary law, rituals, the domain of the sacred). This review confirms that each of these groups resembles any other known Punan group much more than it does its own nearest neighbor among the rice farmers, and that this holds true over a geographical area of very wide extent.

The Forest Environment and the Nomads' Domain

The nomadic hunter-gatherers occupied, as their descendants still do, a vast portion of the interior of Borneo, made up of hills and mountains covered with primary forest (see Maps 3 and 4). This territory is defined not so much by its elevation as by the presence of pri-

118

mary forest. It is made up of several distinct ecological zones, dependent upon altitude: the lowland forest (up to 500 meters), called the Dipterocarp forest; the mountain forest (above 1,000 meters), which has a completely different species composition; and, between 500 and 1,000 meters, a forest of intermediate composition. The present limits of this forest domain are set by human activity—more precisely, by the exploitation of the primary forest by groups of swidden farmers. Generally it is the lowland forest that is affected, though the high interior plateaus have also been settled by some farming groups. A secondary forest, of a different species composition, grows on deforested land. When the soil loses its fertility through overuse, treeless grasslands develop.

The primary forest, in particular the lowland and intermediate forest, constitutes what I will call an economic niche, rich in animal and plant resources. It is this niche that the nomadic hunter-gatherers occupy. Its limits are dynamic and fluctuating; its location is always beyond the world of the farmers, farther upstream. This niche is exploited not only by the nomadic hunter-gatherers (the Punan), but also by those farming populations who live on the outlying fringes of the agricultural world (the Iban are a good example) and by professional collectors of commercial forest products (the Islamicized Bekumpai of the Barito, the Malays and Chinese of the Kapuas, the Bugis of the Mahakam).

But only the Punan are permanently dependent upon the forest for their daily subsistence. Most writers have stated that the Punan live exclusively off the produce of the forest, which permits them total autonomy as far as diet is concerned; and this is confirmed by the most recent serious studies on the Penan of Sarawak (Brosius 1992).

If the realm of the nomads appears to be limited toward regions downstream only by the extent of the primary forest and the presence of neighboring farmers, its upward limits appear to be set by altitude, since the principal species of sago palm does not grow above 1,000 meters (Anderson et al. 1982:118). It is therefore likely that the Punan tend to avoid the high mountain regions, unless they need to travel through them.

It is typical of the Punan domain to be surrounded on all sides by the lands of the farming peoples. The Punan region is therefore a territorial enclave, and the Punan are enclave hunter-gatherers (the expression is from Testart 1981). The territory of a Punan group is typically a high river basin upstream from the region occupied by farmers.

From the mountainous area in which the river has its headwaters, the territory opens into other high basins from which other rivers flow, with the lands of other farmers lying downstream. This state of affairs, which may seem too obvious to require comment, is actually a factor of the greatest importance.

The territory of a given Punan group will indeed be bounded by its various interfaces or zones of contact with the world of the farmers. Similarly, the group's history will be shaped by the history of the political and economic relations that occur in these contact zones. According to the physical shifts of these zones over time, the Punan territory may be reduced in area (as swidden farmers gnaw away at the primary forest) or, on the contrary, expanded (by the general tendency of farmers in certain regions to migrate downstream).

The lands of the nomads are also traversed by the farming peoples' migration routes over the mountain ranges of the island. These pathways, few in number, constitute not only the preferred vectors of population movement but also the channels of trade and of cultural and technological diffusion. While in an archipelago the seas between the islands are the "highways" of cultural diffusion (cf. Fox 1957:4), it is nonetheless appropriate not to underestimate the importance of the mountain trails in the case of an island as huge as Borneo.

It is evident, then, that the Punan, living as they do in enclaves surrounded by other peoples who, moreover, travel across their territory, are not cultural isolates cut off from the outside world. Although some bands have indeed remained extremely isolated, the Punan as a whole are integrated, directly or indirectly, into a network of political and economic relations on the scale of the entire island. In their contacts with some of their neighbors, the Punan groups engage in trade. This has undoubtedly been the case for a good many of these groups over the past two or three centuries. These Punan gather, besides what they need for their own survival, forest products specifically for trade (see the survey of these products in Chapter 2); but the exploitation of the forest by the nomads is in every instance oriented first and foremost toward subsistence, and only secondarily toward trade. It will be argued below that the theory presented by some writers, that trade in forest products is the sole reason for the nomadic hunter-gatherers' existence, has no basis in fact.

Both in aims and means, the exploitation of forest products has undergone many changes over the course of the centuries, due to improvements in technology, such as the introduction of metal, and also to a notable intensification and qualitative variation in the demand for forest products by downriver markets. These changes, in turn, have exerted a strong influence over the nomads and their environment.

Subsistence Economy

Sago

Punan subsistence is based on a small number of species of palms whose trunk contains a pith rich in starch, from which is extracted a flour high in energy value: sago (between 350 and 400 calories per 100 grams; see T.A.D. 1981). The most common of these palms, *Eugeissona utilis* Becc., is therefore of the greatest importance in the Punan diet. Groves of *Eugeissona* palm are irregularly scattered over the ridges and slopes below 1,000 meters' altitude. A half-dozen other species of sago palms, belonging to the genera *Caryota, Corypha, Arenga,* and *Metroxylon* (this last apparently limited to swampy plains), are noted in the literature (Johnson 1977:67; Seitz 1981:291; Anderson et al. 1982:118; Kedit 1982:257; etc.). It appears that the Punan use at least three or four of these species, according to the authors cited, and Sandin (1967–1968:228) mentions eight species used by the Beketan.

Sago flour is obtained by felling the palm tree, extracting its pith, pounding this pith, and then straining it. The fine flour thus obtained, sago in the narrow sense, forms the basis for a variety of food preparations. The palm is also frequently felled in certain regions for its edible heart, the palm-cabbage (Brosius 1986:177). One trunk of the *Eugeissona* palm provides about four kilos of sago flour, enough to feed one person for a week (Kedit 1982:257; see also Harrisson 1949:137 and Urquhart 1951:523). These small palm trees are therefore of a very low yield by comparison with the stout *Metroxylon,* which provides more than 150 kilos of sago per trunk (Jackson 1968:104–108).

A quick calculation indicates that a band of twenty-five people would need fifteen or twenty of these smaller palm trees a week, or between 800 and 1,000 palms per year. If a single palm grove, like the many I have seen, may contain from fifty to a hundred trees, of which perhaps only a half have grown to usable size, then the band would have to leave it for another grove after a week or two. This important factor regulates the movements of the band. A palm grove thus harvested may be revisited a year or two later; there will always be new palms reaching maturity. According to Brosius (1986:117), the grove is left to regenerate over several years. *Eugeissona* is said to take no more than five or six years to reach its full growth (Johnson 1977:67), though Kedit notes that the same palm when planted takes from ten to fifteen years to mature (1982:235). Whatever the case, the bands do revisit the same palm groves after a certain lapse of time (Anderson et al. 1982:118).

From these few figures, one can get an idea of the number of palm groves that a band of twenty-five people needs to have available within its nomadic range: at a very rough estimate, fifty or so. The highly variable regional density of the palm groves does not permit a further deduction of the estimated area of such a territory.

Men and women share the work. The sago palm is felled, chopped up, and split open by men; the pith is crushed by both men and women; and women strain and prepare the sago flour (see Urquhart 1951:523; Kedit 1982:257). Brosius (1986:177) describes a process of sago production taking place over two days: the first day is spent in felling the trees and carrying them to the stream, and the second in the actual preparation of the sago. In this way the band can produce 100 to 150 pounds (45 to nearly 70 kilos) of sago flour. Arnold (1967:98) notes that the different families of the band take turns working the palm grove, and that the sago is shared out equally among all (like the yield of the hunt and of gathering; see also Harrisson 1949:137; Needham 1954b:230).

There is no need to describe in detail here the vegetable diet of the Punan. Some fifty types of fruit are considered edible (Anderson et al. 1982:118), as well as leaves, ferns, bamboo shoots, and certain flowerbuds. Some tubers, the Dioscorea (*Dioscorea* spp.), grow wild in the forest (T.A.D. 1981:30). These are eaten by the nomads of peninsular Malaysia, and, in time of famine, by the farmers of Borneo (Budowski 1978, cited by T.A.D. 1981); but I have found no specific mention of their being eaten by Punan groups. Another point worth noting is the direct link between the interest shared by Punan and wild pigs in the forest fruits, whose time of ripening is irregular, and the interest of the Punan in the wild pigs themselves.

Hunting

Most older sources place sago-gathering and hunting on an equal footing, apparently believing that sago is of no greater importance to the Punan diet than is wild pig (*Sus barbatus barbatus;* for

more on this important animal, see Pfeffer and Caldecott 1986). However, more recent studies stress the preeminence of sago in the Punan
diet (see, for example, Needham 1954b:231). It would seem that even
if wild pig is highly desirable prey, it is far from being on the menu
every day. Hunting is nevertheless an important activity in the nomad
economy. As has been noted, Punan hunt with either blowpipes or
spears, and discussions of this weaponry relate directly to the question
of Punan origins.

Several writers (from Hose and McDougall 1912:II, 191, to Seitz
1981) have laid some stress on the fact that the blowpipe could not
possibly be an item of technology developed by an autonomous culture of hunter-gatherers, as iron is necessary to bore the hard wood of
which the blowpipe is made. Similarly, the hunting spear has a metal
blade. Since nomads have to obtain the metal they use from farmers,
Seitz concludes that the blowpipe must be associated with farming cultures (1981:287) and that Punan hunting methods are indistinguish-
able from those of the farmers. Over the last few decades, therefore,
some writers have been inclined, after Harrisson (1949), to see in
Punan culture an offshoot of the farmers' culture, specialized in the
economic exploitation of the primary forest. Some (like Hoffman,
1983 and 1984) have gone so far as to affirm that this specialization is
wholly founded upon the commercial exploitation of the forest, and
that but for these commercial considerations humans would be unable
to live in the forest environment.

It is true that the question of the blowpipe as an item of technology
is complex and further complicated by the recent differences in the
evolution of the various Punan groups. Writers who have studied the
relationships between the farming groups and their Punan neighbors
report conflicting data. Sometimes the Punan obtain their blowpipes
from the farmers and for the most part are unable to manufacture
them themselves (Harrisson 1949:141; Urquhart 1951:525–526;
Sloan 1975:148; Seitz 1981:287; and others); sometimes, conversely,
the Punan provide the farmers with blowpipes (van Walchren 1907:
842; Lumholtz 1920:218–219, 246; Whittier 1973:130; Kedit 1982:
237–238).

Although the use of iron undeniably spread first from farmers to
nomads, the direction in which the blowpipe as a finished product
may circulate is not really relevant. It is known that certain Punan
groups, having learned from the farmers how to make dugout canoes,
now in turn make these boats for them. To further complicate the

issue, some Punan have become excellent blacksmiths and now supply their sedentary former teachers with the bush knives used to fell forest trees (see Seitz 1981:303–304). Some Punan even have acquired enough technical skill to extract the metal from its ore (see Needham 1972:180). The Punan Murung, having learned techniques of metallurgy from the Long Gelat, have probably been providing their protectors with tools and weapons since the last quarter of the nineteenth century (Sellato 1986b:229).

Whether or not they have acquired the techniques of iron-smelting, whether or not they know how to forge the metal, and whatever may be their ability to produce the blowpipe as a final product, it is clear that all Punan groups have mastered the use of this weapon. Numerous authors have stressed that the Punan are highly skilled in handling the blowpipe, even more so than the farmers (for example, Elshout 1926:244).

A fact that many writers mention in passing, without attaching particular importance to it, is the profound knowledge the Punan have of plant poisons (see von Kessel 1857:409; Nieuwenhuis 1904–1907:I, 198; Elshout 1926:244; Mjöberg 1934; up to Hildebrand 1982:278). As well as the various poisons used for fishing, the Punan make for their blowpipe darts poisons that have a high reputation among the farming groups, who go to the Punan for their supplies. This specialization in poisons, and the fact that most of the plants which provide the raw materials for them grow in the primary forest, would seem to suggest that the technology of these poisons belongs to a culture of forest hunter-gatherers, and that it has been only partially transmitted to the farmers, in whose environment these plants are not always readily accessible.

What can the literature tell us of the weaponry and tools used by the Punan before the introduction of iron? Perhaps the oldest suggestion, that of von Kessel (1857:408), is that the original weapons of the nomads were clubs and wooden spears. There is a fairly widespread theory that the culture of the hunter-gatherers of the equatorial forest, before iron, was based upon wood. A good fire-hardened point is indeed almost as effective as a metal blade. For that matter, Schwaner (1853–1854) notes that the blade attached to the blowpipe may be of bamboo.

But this theory of a wood-based culture is rejected by certain writers, among them Testart (1981), who believes that the hunter-gatherers must necessarily have used stone before the introduction of metal. In support of this contrary view we may instance the evidence of J. Nicolaisen (1976a:229; 1976b:44): his Penan informants state that before they acquired iron from the farmers, they used tools of stone. My own Aoheng informants say that their ancestors had stone axes, and I have seen quadrangular stone blades in the upper Mahakam. While long-term farmers call them "fangs of thunder," and believe that they result from the petrification of wood struck by lightning, the Aoheng, partly of nomadic origin, are perfectly well able to identify these blades as axes (or adzes, depending on how they were hafted). We may note, with Harrisson (1984:317), that isolated Kelabit farmers in 1945 still made use of stone tools along with their metal ones.

According to certain specialists (see Avé and King 1986:15), the technology of ironworking may have reached Borneo between the fifth and the tenth century of our era. Subsequently, it would have slowly diffused from the coasts toward the interior. Taking into account the relatively shallow temporal depth of the nomads' collective memory (they recall hardly more than a century or two of their history), one may easily accept that such stone tools may still have been in common use at a fairly recent date among some extremely isolated groups.

Although these stone tools, hafted as clubs, may on occasion have served to supplement the wooden spear as a hunting weapon, it is more important to consider their use in the extraction of sago. Hacking through the tough trunk of the palm would certainly have been a longer job with a stone axe than with one of iron, but it could still be done. It would have been equally possible to split the trunk, with the aid of stone tools and wooden wedges (see Seitz 1981:292). As for the crushing of the pith, MacCarthy (1953, cited in Avé 1977:23) notes the use of stone mallets for this purpose in central Borneo.

The nomads' choice of prey may shed further light on their traditional stock of weapons. According to Seitz (1981:285), Punan hunting is specifically focused on the wild pig, and Brosius (1986:178) notes that the Penan Gang have no particular interest in small game. An estimate of five hundred wild pigs eaten each year by a nomadic band of thirty persons is presented by Pfeffer and Caldecott (1986: 96), and Brosius gives, for hunting expeditions after wild pigs with spears and dogs, an average success rate of 90 percent (1986:178). However, the situation is not likely to be the same in every area. Wild pigs appear irregularly, their presence depending (as already noted) upon the ripening of wild fruits, and the nomads cannot in general afford to neglect smaller prey. Much more commonly than pig, they hunt monkeys and mousedeer (*Tragulus* spp.), according to Kedit (1982:257), and even squirrels. Seitz himself mentions (1981:286) forty species of birds that the Punan list as game.

This evident importance of arboreal game, and the sophisticated technology of plant poisons, strongly suggest the extended traditional presence of a hunting weapon which, like the blowpipe, hurls poisoned projectiles toward a target otherwise out of reach. J. Nicolaisen notes that the Penan claim never to have used the bow and arrow but that their language possesses terms for these weapons, and that, moreover, they have miniature bows which are used as toys (1976a:230; 1976b:49). The Aoheng apparently know nothing of the bow, but, curiously enough, they use the word *pana* (in Indonesian *panah*, arrow) to designate a rifle or shotgun, as well as a kind of harpoon-gun that they make to use when diving after fish in deep river-pools. It is interesting to note, after Avé and King (1986:127), that the bow and arrow were used by certain groups to catch fish: weapons of this type were displayed at the exhibition of Borneo artifacts in Leiden in 1986.

Therefore, it cannot be excluded that the Punan did, up to a few centuries ago, use the bow and poisoned arrows, not only for fishing, but also for hunting (like certain groups in the Philippines). But it seems equally reasonable to suggest that there may have existed, before iron was available for the rods needed to bore a hardwood blowpipe, a blowpipe made of bamboo, like those used by the hunter-gatherers of peninsular Malaysia (see Schebesta 1973). The availability of iron would then have allowed the Punan to improve their stock of weaponry by making blowpipes that were sturdier and more lasting, perhaps also more accurate. As Nicolaisen points out (1976a: 213), hunters may well minimize their labor and maximize its yield by adopting new techniques from the farmers, as has happened in the case of the dugout canoe, the iron axe, and the dog. Here I note also the curious fact, whose meaning I cannot explain, that in different ethnic groups the blowpipe may be bored either from base to tip or (which seems less practicable) from tip to base.

In any case, it is probable that the two methods of hunting have long coexisted, each having its specific purpose: hunting with the metal-bladed or wooden spear, with or without dogs, for the pursuit of large terrestrial game animals; and hunting with the blowpipe or bow for birds, monkeys, and other small animals. However, one must note that big game still is sometimes hunted with the blowpipe, though this method may entail a long period of trailing the wounded prey, as the poison is slow to act on large animals. Tillema (1939: 142), describing the hunting of the rhinoceros, states that the wounded animal must sometimes be tracked for weeks. Finally, it is important to note that the spear and the blowpipe are mutually exclusive, in that the nomad sets out to hunt with one or the other, never with both, although a spearblade bound to the end of the blowpipe will serve to dispatch a large animal should the need arise.

Seitz (1981:288) suggests that the spear as a hunting weapon became important to the Punan only with the introduction of dogs. It does in fact appear that the early Punan had no dogs. Sloan (1975: 146), for example, states that the Punan Busang obtained their first dogs from the Kayan. Hose (quoted by J. Nicolaisen, 1976b:47) describes how the Punan, in a small group armed with spears, hunted wild pigs without using dogs. Nicolaisen himself reports (1976a:229) that the Penan remember a period before dogs when they chased wild pig with spears. This would necessarily have involved a beat hunt, in which beaters drive the animals toward those who do the killing. As a collective economic activity, this should be distinguished from hunting with the blowpipe, which is generally done by a solitary hunter. One may note that even long-term farmers like the Kelabit, living in a very remote area, also recall a time before dogs, when, according to Harrisson (1984:318), they sometimes hunted with the help of a tame yellow-throated marten. The existence of a beat hunt with spears (with wooden spears, before the introduction of metal) is entirely congruous with what is known of hunting practices among hunter-gatherers in other parts of the world. Although the adoption of the metal-bladed spear in place of the wooden spear probably led to little change in hunting techniques, the introduction of dogs made it possible to increase the success rate of hunts for terrestrial mammals while involving fewer participants.

The bush knife, a type of machete, does not seem to have been a tool or weapon of traditional Punan culture. Some writers mention that the nomads obtain theirs from the farmers (see Chapter 2; and Bock 1887:89). The bush knife in fact appears to be of no great use to hunter-gatherers. Even today, one may see members of former nomad groups (Hovongan, Kereho, Bukat) bending small branches out of their way by hand as they slip through the underbrush rather than taking their bush knife out of their pack to slash a path (not a habit that makes it easy for a taller foreigner to follow them).

One important point, of which I have seen no mention in the literature, is the practice of hunting by women. Seitz notes (1981:285) that the hunt is men's business. To my own knowledge, Bukat, Hovongan, and Kereho women commonly used to hunt, and some still do. Similarly, among those Aoheng who were nomads, women also hunted. Although this fact has not been remarked upon for the Penan of Sarawak, it has been reported for the Agta hunter-gatherers of Luzon (Griffin, in Dahlberg 1981). This does appear to be a cultural trait specific, in Borneo, to the Punan groups, and it seems to me to be a strong argument against the theory of devolution. Like sago and the products of gathering, the yield of the hunt is shared out equally among all the members of the band (Urquhart 1951:521; Arnold 1967:98).

In conclusion, we may note, with Seitz (1981:290), that the hunt is the occasion for no special ceremony, and that rituals and beliefs associated with hunting are extremely undramatic, if they exist at all. This is equally true for the collection of sago. A certain number of earlier authors have in fact stressed this near absence of rituals related to the quest for food.

Fishing

If hunting is not of major significance to Punan subsistence compared with the collection of sago, fishing is evidently of even lesser importance. This fact, already indicated in the discussion of the Bukat, is stressed in particular by recent writers (J. Nicolaisen 1976a: 210; Seitz 1981:304; Kedit 1982:257; Anderson et al. 1982:119). Present-day Punan commonly fish with hook and line (J. Nicolaisen 1976a:209); Kedit 1982:233). Some groups even use nets and fish traps. These nets (cast nets and stake nets) and the fish traps are of recent introduction (J. Nicolaisen 1976b:50), and it is probable that the fishhook has also been recently borrowed.

The traditional Punan fishing technique seems to have involved the use of plant poisons. This technique is often mentioned in the literature (Lumholtz 1920:II, 430); Needham 1972:178; J. Nicolaisen 1976b:50; Kedit 1982:257). A section of the river is barricaded, a large quantity of poisonous roots is gathered, pounded, and thrown in the water, and everybody present, child or adult, male or female, joins in scooping out the stunned fish by hand. According to Kedit, the poison used by the Punan is different from *tuba* (the poisonous root

Derris elliptica) in general use among the farmers. This special knowledge of fishing poisons is in keeping with Punan knowledge of the poisons used in hunting with the blowpipe.

Among the groups of the Müller mountains (Hovongan, Kereho) and the Bukat, women, who (as noted earlier) hunt just as men do, also fish, even to using the cast net. J. Nicolaisen (1976a:209) notes that fishing with hook and line, among the Penan of Sarawak, is generally done by women.

In former times, according to Seitz (1981:304), sago and wild game were so abundant that fishing was unnecessary. As was noted in the discussion of the Bukat, the Punan generally live away from major rivers, and in the regions where stands of wild sago grow the watercourses are commonly no more than small streams, from which there is little hope of a good catch of fish. Indeed, as many authors report, most Punan do not know how to swim, unlike the Dayak, who live on the banks of larger rivers and are all fine swimmers.

It is generally accepted that the Punan groups traditionally do not know how to make dugout canoes and do not possess them. It has been seen that this is true for the Kereho and the Bukat. The Punan Murung most probably borrowed the dugout from the Ot Danum at the turn of the century (Sellato 1986b:271). The Punan Bah of Sarawak had no boats while they were still nomads (I. Nicolaisen 1976:76). A Penan myth mentions the use of rafts in place of boats (Arnold 1958:72). The Uma' Long (very probably former nomads) had no boats and were afraid to travel on water (van Walchren 1907:804). The Penan of the Plieran now make boats, but are clumsy and fearful in using them (Arnold 1958:69). This fear of water no doubt derives from the nomads' inability to swim. Nevertheless, all the Punan groups I have been able to visit are currently able to make dugouts, though these are generally of very poor workmanship. There is only one mention in the literature, to my knowledge, of bark canoes made by Penan (Arnold 1958:69).

Although fish seem less important than game in the Punan diet, and the search for animal protein seems itself to be subordinate in the economic order of priorities to that for vegetable carbohydrates (sago), it is nevertheless true that these techniques of hunting and fishing, based on a unique familiarity with plant poisons, appear to be specific to a hunter-gatherer culture, owing nothing to the cultures of neighboring farming peoples. The absence of a sexual division of labor in the prac-

tice of these various hunting and fishing techniques, traditional or borrowed, seems to confirm the autonomy of Punan culture with regard
to the farmers' world.

Food Storage

The question of the storage and preservation of food supplies
should be briefly debated here. While J. Nicolaisen states that sago
flour can be stored, though not for long (1976a:231), Seitz declares
that the Punan do not store it (1981:291). Enthoven reports that the
nomads of the Kapuas were storing sago flour at one site, to be used
when they returned there (1903:87). Urquhart notes that only after
ten days does the liquid pulp produced by filtering become sago flour
(1951:523). A recent study (Strickland 1986) mentions that the wet
flour may be stored for long periods in tightly sealed jars. This implies
that the wet flour goes bad when exposed to air, and therefore that the
Punan probably cannot store it for long except in a relatively settled
situation, since they do not carry jars when they move.

A similar problem exists with regard to the storage of products of
animal origin. According to Seitz (1981:286), the Punan do not preserve meat. J. Nicolaisen (1976a:231) notes that meat may be kept for
some weeks above the fire, but that it deteriorates. My experience of
forest living indicates that meat or fish can be kept for a week at most,
and this only on condition that a very smoky fire be maintained to
keep the flies away. The nomads do not salt meat. The ethnic groups
of the Müller mountains preserve raw meat (pork, venison, or even
fatty fish), cut into cubes and mixed with finely chopped leaves from
the bush *peang* (*payang* in Kayan; probably *Pangium edule* Reinw.;
see Chai 1978:251). Such a mixture, if well made, remains edible for a
month, though it acquires a strongly gamy flavor.

Two food substances keep well, honey and animal fat. All the
Punan groups keep pig fat (or the oil of fish, or indeed of snakes) in
bamboo containers, using it for various food preparations or, if necessary, as a source of illumination. It should be noted that, in any case,
the crucial concern here is not the extent to which food products can
be stored, so much as the regulation of access to and control of stored
resources (see the discussion of ownership in Chapter 5).

Subsistence and Trade

The borrowing of elements of technology from the farmers,
as noted above (after J. Nicolaisen 1976a:213), allows the Punan to

minimize their labor and increase the yield of their subsistence activities. Thus the iron axe greatly facilitates the felling of sago palms. Experiment has shown that the energy output needed to fell one trunk is five times greater with the use of a stone axe than with one of metal (see Rousseau 1977:132). Besides this, the iron rod permits the drilling of a durable and accurate blowpipe, and the use of dogs reduces the number of people required in the hunt for terrestrial game.

Two direct consequences become apparent. First, the Punan become dependent upon their farming neighbors for their iron. Second, the Punan, who may have been engaged in a full-time search for food before they possessed these new items of technology, now have more free time. It is evident that these two consequences are linked, in that to obtain their iron the Punan have to give something in exchange, and that, having iron, they also have more time to devote to the hunt for commercial forest products.

I argue here that the establishment, or at least the intensification, of trade relations between farmers and nomads is intrinsically linked to the introduction of the above-mentioned items of technology; that the farmers, in their eagerness to obtain from the Punan commercial products in demand by coastal markets, played an initiatory role in Punan society; and that the Punan could not have become regular suppliers of these products without the savings in labor and time that resulted from the introduction of these items of technology.

This discussion of the Punan subsistence economy must conclude with a few words about salt. As stated, salt is an important article of trade. Nevertheless, it is apparently not always indispensable, according to two of the writers most familiar with the Punan: the Punan Magoh said they could live quite satisfactorily without salt (Harrisson 1949:140), and the Penan Lusong and Penan Gang seem to have been able to do without it for periods of several years (Urquhart 1951:513). They knew of saline springs but did not use them, unlike the farmers who, in times of scarcity, boiled these waters to extract their salt. It is probable that the nomadic Punan find all the salt they need in their food. They eat every part of their prey, including the blood and the intestines. Harrisson mentions the existence of a salt substitute obtained from a palm (1949:139–140), but as far as I know he is alone in reporting an indigenous product of this sort.

At the end of these few pages on the nomads' subsistence economy, I am led to the conclusion, which was also Harrisson's, that of the three main articles of trade obtained by the Punan, metal, salt and tobacco, none is in fact absolutely indispensable to their subsistence (1949:139). A hunting-gathering economy may very well have been able to function in the forests of Borneo before the introduction of these articles.

Mobility, Territory, Aggression

It has been seen that the territory of a nomad group is defined, at any particular moment, by its interfaces with neighboring groups. Each one of these contact zones is unstable over time, varying according to political and economic relations between the group and its neighbors. It is important, in discussing territoriality, to distinguish between the band, as a residential and economic unit, and the ethnic group, which is made up of a certain number of bands more or less closely akin.

Mobility and Subsistence

The band as an economic unit moves from place to place in order to secure its subsistence. In an ecological environment whose resources are abundant and constant (that is to say, nonseasonal), the Punan could choose to exploit these resources either by short but frequent expeditions from a permanent base camp, or by periodic relocations of the entire camp. Many studies have shown just how advantageous nomadism may be to hunter-gatherers (Testart 1981).

We have only a very limited understanding of the patterns of Punan movements. As Urquhart notes, the Punan are unable to explain the rules that dictate their relocations (1951:509). The essential for them is that they should always be within a reasonable distance of a grove of sago palms that they can exploit. Harrisson reports for one group a nomadic round lasting four months and covering a distance of fifty kilometers, using fifteen successive camping sites (1949:135). Enthoven notes that they rarely stay more than three months in the same place (1903:87). Kedit speaks of more or less circular movements around a point central to the territory (1982:256). Brosius notes that a camp may be used for a time varying from a few days to six months (1986:176), according to the availability of sago palms. My own data suggest an average period of residence in any given camp of two to four weeks (see also Harrisson 1949:136).

As stated above, the usable palms in a grove of average size will probably be depleted after a week or two. This does not necessarily mean that the camp must then move. Indeed, a single camp may be used as a base for the exploitation of several groves located around it, within a radius of two to three hours' walk (see Kedit 1982:257).

The paths along which the Punan travel link the palm groves (or, more precisely, the location of the palm groves determines the configuration of the network of paths: see Anderson et al. 1982:118). These paths also connect the camp sites, always the same sites, strategically selected with regard to the locations of the groves (see Huehne 1959–1960:201).

Thus the band is mobile, and what remains to be determined is whether or not the range of these movements is territorially limited. It may be useful to introduce at this stage a distinction between "internal" migrations (short-range movements for reasons of subsistence) and "long-range" migrations (literally, emigrations over long distances and for reasons of security, often with no return). We shall concern ourselves for the moment only with the first case.

Concepts of Territory

One basic point is subject to some ambiguity. Writers dealing with territoriality often do not specify whether they mean the territory of a band or the territory of an ethnic group. Thus in the literature one finds opposing views: the Punan do indeed have bounded territories and possess a concept of what they consider to be their territory (see, for example, Bouman 1924; Stöhr 1959:163; Huehne 1959–1960: 201; Schwaner 1968: CXCVI; Kedit 1982:256; Brosius 1986); or, the Punan have no particular territory, their migrations are unrestricted, and they have no concept of territoriality (Needham 1972:178; J. Nicolaisen 1976a:208; Seitz 1981:289).

The case of the Bukat, examined above, offers an approach to this question. The territory of the Bukat as an ethnic group, considered at any given moment of their history, has boundaries set by features that are either natural (for example, the river Kapuas, south of which the Bukat apparently never lived) or human (interfaces with other ethnic groups). It is evident that the boundaries of Bukat territory have changed over time (gradual withdrawal from the Baleh, advance toward the Mahakam). I shall return to this point below.

The territory of any given Bukat band, within (by definition) Bukat territory, is another matter. Maps 8.2 and 8.3 give the impression of a kind of Brownian movement, a random dance of molecules. It has been noted that each band is autonomous with regard to its movements. In Seitz' view, it is because of the small size and low density of Punan population that no fixed boundaries are established around the areas in which sago palms grow, and no territorial claims are made. Similarly, Needham notes that when local groups meet, a highly infrequent event, the contacts are marked by a sense of mutual concern (1971:204).

It is probable that this has not always been the case. If the realm of the nomads (as defined above) has been reduced in extent by swidden farmers' penetration into the interior (due in particular to their use of metal) and by the conversion of nomads to farming, it is nonetheless almost certain that the nomad population was in the past far larger than it is today. It seems reasonable not to exclude a priori the possibility of specific instances of competition between two bands over resources, which could have occurred whatever the concept these nomads may have had of their territories. Schwaner, writing of the Punan of the basin of the river Barito in the middle of the last century, notes that skirmishes between bands over territorial incursions could at times take place (1968: CXCVI). This holds true also for other groups (such as the Bukat). It is especially likely that trouble would arise between two bands of a single Punan group which had allied themselves with two different farming groups that themselves were in a state of conflict, as happened in the case of the Punan Murung (Sellato 1986b:264).

However, I believe that such conflicts among bands of a single ethnic group would remain relatively rare, and that, as Seitz says (1981), there has generally been a superabundance of resources relative to the number of persons to be supported, so that bands can move around within the territory of the ethnic group without having to establish borders between themselves. But a state of affairs valid in times of peace, when there is no threat to the security of the territory as a whole, will undoubtedly change in times of war, when territories may become smaller and resources scarce (as, for example, when the Bukat withdrew en masse to the lower Mendalam, to escape Bukitan and Iban headhunters). At such times frictions that can be avoided in peacetime may lead to armed conflicts over the palm groves.

Although the concept of territory at the level of the band seems not to be particularly well defined, other than that the first to arrive in an area acquires rights over it that may be invoked in time of crisis, these bands do seem for the most part to have a certain concept of the territory of the ethnic group to which they belong. In any case, people have some idea of a home territory in which their group had its origin (the cases of Bukat and Kereho are fairly striking) or in which they say they have always lived (see, for example, Kedit 1982:256).

One finds in certain instances the idea of an ethnic territory having a "center" around which the bands circle, or from which they see themselves as having spread. Thus, as early as 1849, Becker mentions a central gathering place of the Njawong (the Kereho) near the headwaters of the Melawi (1849b:326), which is confirmed by present-day Kereho informants: indeed, it is from the upper Kereho that all the Kereho say they originate, and from which some of them left for the Busang. Similarly, the Bukat say that they all originate in the Mendalam, which they call Buköt. All the Punan Murung say that their own center of dispersal was the site of Tarun Tapan, on the upper Murung (Sellato 1986b:225). Kedit mentions such a central point for the Penan of Mount Mulu (1982:256). It is not impossible that a similar "center" may have existed for the Punan Aput on the upper Balui (see Tuton Kaboy 1974). Such a "homeland" constitutes a grid for historical and genealogical information (see Brosius 1986:175) and thereby provides a firm foundation for ethnic identity, indeed for modern territorial claims. As is evident from what was said above, and from many other cases, the toponym of this "center" is often the source of the general ethnonym of a given ethnic group.

Considerable attention was accorded above to the question of Bukat and Kereho ethnonyms. The autonyms of Punan groups correspond to toponyms of their region of origin. But innumerable exonyms have been applied to them, of two sorts: first, regional names referring to nomads without distinguishing among them (Ot, Ukit, Bukitan, Punan, Penan, Basap, etc.); and second, local toponyms, designating the place where a given group lives. The autonym used by the people of the group itself is either a toponym from the territory where they believe they have always lived (Bukat, Hovongan), or a toponym from the oldest territory they remember (the Lisum, for example), chosen without much concern for the exonyms locally applied to them. One exception is that of the Punan living on the Murung, here called Punan Murung but who in fact claim the name of Punan with no qualifying term (Sellato 1986b:223). On the whole, the nomads pay little attention to these exonyms, readily accepting them, but only in the context of their interactions with the settled farmers. What matters to them is their autonym, which is used within the group.

It appears that the concept of ethnic territory, the knowledge (or the memory) of this territory, and the ethnonym that relates to it are the bases for the sense of ethnic identity of a Punan group. These concepts, which emerge in the oral literature, are perhaps, along with language, the only currently surviving social expressions of this sense of identity. This may no longer be true in the case of bands with an extensive history of long-distance migrations: the Lisum of the upper Belayan seem to have forgotten their original homeland on the Rejang, as well as the ethnonym that relates to it.

Defense of the Territory

While the various bands of a single ethnic group seem generally able to avoid conflict among themselves, relations between different nomad groups are often hostile. There were bloody clashes between Acue and Halunge in the headwaters of the Mahakam (Sellato 1986b:311), between Bukat and Hovongan-Kereho, between Bukat and Bukitan, between Kereho and Punan Murung (1986b:236), and between Punan Murung and Punan Merah (1986b:247). Long-lasting feuds are mentioned as having existed between the Lisum and the Punan Kelai (Hoffman 1983:111) and between the Penan and the Punan Busang (Urquhart 1951:530). The "sense of mutual concern" noted by Needham (1971:204) may be no more than a recent phenomenon, developed in the peaceful context of modern Sarawak.

It must be stressed that these hostilities involve bands confronting each other at the fringes of ethnic territories rather than entire ethnic groups. Thus, a band of Bukat might clash with a band of Beketan at the zone of contact between the two groups, but there has never in the history of the Bukat been a coalition of bands against a common enemy (except perhaps at the instigation of their sedentary patrons, as, for example, in the case of Bukat attacks against the Hovongan). It would appear that in a similar situation, whereas two bands of the same ethnic group are likely to settle matters amicably, two bands from different ethnic groups may well fight each other, if, according to Bukat informants, they are not careful to keep away from the common border of their ethnic territories. As the nomads increasingly turn to headhunting and slave-raiding for the benefit of their farming neighbors, clashes thus provoked among nomad groups markedly intensify.

As a result, the borders of the territories of different nomad groups are in effect no-man's-lands, ventured into only by the ill-intentioned (headhunters) or by bands that have been driven out of their own territory by other enemies and therefore appear to local bands as competitors for food resources. In both cases, these are intruders; in both, there is a conflict of interest.

Relations between nomads and farmers take place in a different mode. The political and economic relations between these two cultures will be examined below; here we are concerned only with the effect that the proximity of the farmers may have on the nomads' territory. As has been described, this consists of a vast stretch of primary forest, most often mountainous, extending over the upper basins of several river systems. It forms an enclave open toward several downstream areas, culturally and ethnically different from each other, offering interfaces or zones of interaction with several different farming groups. Roughly speaking, these farming groups may be distinguished as "allies" or "enemies" of the nomads. It should be noted that this distinction may hold for one band but not necessarily for another, nor for the nomad group as a whole: the "allies" of one band may well be the "enemies" of the neighboring band (see the case of the Punan Murung, in Sellato 1986b:263).

Toward enemy or neutral groups, the nomads' usual attitude, as seen in past chapters, is one of withdrawal. The borderlands of their territories are most often undefended, a habit apparently common among hunting groups (see Service 1966:30). The Punan avoid hostile interaction with these neighbors, keeping away from the zone of contact between their lands. As Urquhart notes, they prefer to retreat from their enemies rather than kill them, even when they might be able to commit such killings with complete impunity (1951:501). However, this remark of Urquhart's should be qualified on two points.

The first concerns the nomads' real vulnerability. It is true that the nomad warriors are virtually untouchable when they are away from their own home base, raiding the farming peoples; we have seen how the Kereho harassed the Ot Danum, and the Acue harried the Kayan in the same way (Sellato 1986b:316). But the bands are very vulnerable when attacked on their home ground by groups of warriors, whether nomads or farmers, as reported by Elshout (1926:243). And there is no lack of references in the literature to massacres of Punan by headhunters, all across Borneo (see Deshon 1901a, 1901b; Dalton, in Hildebrand 1982:223; Rutten 1916:245; etc.). The impunity, and immunity, of Punan in their forests is therefore mythical, and their suspicion and withdrawal are entirely justified.

The second point concerns the ability of the nomads to fight for their territory. If any given interface with an enemy farming group is "static," that is, if there is hostility on the part of the farmers but no desire to take over nomad territory, the nomads keep their distance from the limit of their territory and from possible headhunting raids. On the other hand, if the farming group tries to take over for their own farming needs some of the territory where the nomads are living, the nomads apparently try to defend it. Thus, as has been seen, the Bukat of the Baleh (the Ukit) resisted the invasion of Iban pioneering new farmlands, over every foot of ground and for a period of several decades, until, decimated, they finally gave up the struggle. The Lisum, Beketan, Punan Aput, and other groups of Sarawak apparently also took up arms against the Iban, waging a guerrilla war of rearguard actions, retaliating against Iban incursions even while they slowly retreated.

Once again, one notes that this resistance is the work of isolated local bands directly affected by outside aggression rather than a coalition of all the bands within the nomad group joining to force the enemy back out of the ethnic territory. It is a limited and local response to an immediate and concrete threat, and bands not directly concerned do not mobilize against what is for them only a potential danger.

The abandonment of a particular watershed under military pressure from an enemy group means, for the nomads, a migration to another watershed in their territory, or a long-distance emigration. Bukat refugees from the river Baleh split up between the headwaters of the Mahakam and those of the Kapuas. The Punan Murung moved back and forth over the divide between the headwaters of the Murung and the Mahakam, that is, between the two groups of swidden farmers who were contesting the right to claim them as clients (Sellato 1986b: 264). The Punan Aput also traveled back and forth between the upper Balui and the Apo Kayan (see Tuton Kaboy 1974). Thus the Punan groups, responding to the circumstances of local politics, occupy or abandon parts of their territories or leave them permanently to seek a safer neighborhood.

It is appropriate to mention here the possibility of an expansion of nomad territory through the conquest of farmers' lands. The case of the Kereho of the Busang is, to my knowledge, the only instance of the expansion by warfare of a Punan group. It may, however, be noted that the joint military actions of the different nomad groups of the Müller mountains against the Ot Danum of the Busang could probably only have been mounted in the field with the direct or indirect intervention of the Aoheng and Seputan, who were already sedentary and were the sponsors and masterminds of this conquest.

It must therefore be admitted that the Punan, though more often hunted than hunters, and careful to avoid as far as possible any clash with their nomad or farmer neighbors (some, indeed, like the Punan Murung, readily describe themselves as nonviolent and claim that they have never attacked anyone; Sellato 1986b:264), have nevertheless been capable of taking up arms to defend their nomadic territory if it is threatened and, on occasion, under certain specific conditions, have even been able to conquer new territories.

Zones of Contact with Settled Patrons

The relations of the nomads with the farming groups that are their "allies" often remain fairly cool. As has been said, such alliances, linking a particular village of swidden farmers with a particular band, do not (as in the case of the Bukat) create ties between entire ethnic groups. A village, or more often its chief, may patronize and protect an allied nomad band for a number of political and economic reasons, to be explored in detail below. Thus the Bukat of the Mendalam were under the protection of the Kayan; the Aoheng Huvung chiefs defended the territory of "their" Bukat against the Iban; and the Lisum, many of whom had been the victims of Iban massacres, placed themselves under the protection of the Kenyah Lepo' Tau (Elshout 1926:243), as the Punan of the Ratah did with the Bahau of the middle Mahakam (Sellato 1986b:247).

The zone of contact between nomads and allied farmers is an "active" interface, unlike the border between Punan and enemy groups. It is at this active interface that interactions of all types occur. It is here, too, that the borders of the territories are most precisely determined, both geographically and legally, by virtue of the alliance. Thus the boundary between Bukat and Kayan on the Mendalam was set at the junction of the Hovat, confirming de jure the previously existing de facto situation. Nomads in flight, establishing themselves close to new protectors and partners, are formally allotted their own specific territory. Such was the case with the Lisum, to whom the Kenyah gave lands on the Boh; nomadic Semukung, coming from

Sarawak via the headwaters of the Kapuas, bought a small territory from the Aoheng of the upper Mahakam for the price of a slave and a gong (Sellato 1986b:325); and some of the Beketan bought land on the river Kakus (Sandin 1967–1968:231). In place of a vague, de facto boundary with an enemy group, there is a precise, legally established boundary with an ally.

It may be supposed that it is at these active interfaces, owing to the geographic proximity of their neighbors and to the more or less intense relations with them, that the concept of territory is most marked among the Punan. Here there is no no-man's-land, no attitude of withdrawal. It is at these interfaces that the cultural shift from nomadism to agriculture may eventually occur, as well as shifts in ethnic identity (Bukat becoming Kayan, "Ot" becoming Murung, Beketan becoming Iban, and so on). We shall return to this phenomenon in Chapter 5.

Nevertheless, even with their allies the Punan remain reserved and aloof. At this stage they have already become relatively dependent upon the farmers, and in fact find themselves in the position of subjects to overlords who can be demanding. The farmers make use of the nomads in many different circumstances; particularly, and of special interest here, they compel them to move outside their territories. Thus some of the Punan Murung were moved to the river Kacu by the Long Gelat, and when the Long Gelat split up, the group's two chiefs probably divided up their Punan as well (Sellato 1986b:263). Similarly, the Sebop brought their Punan clients along with them in their flight from the Plieran to the Tinjar (Arnold 1967:172). When the Kayan Malaran (Uma' Laran) moved, "their" Punan Bahau came with them (Hoffman 1983:108). The Lisum were resettled on the upper Belayan by the Kenyah when the latter moved there; and the Long Gelat moved the Punan Merah of the middle Mahakam around as they chose.

Moreover, it can happen that the farmers, having an urgent need for a head or a human sacrifice for one of their rituals, help themselves directly to one of their nomad protégés: the Modang of the Wahau did this (von Dewall 1849:124), and the Long Gelat of the Mahakam (another Modang group) may also have done so (Sellato 1986b:263). The Punan therefore have a tendency to be suspicious of the farmers' stratagems and try not to let themselves be manipulated. According to Testart (1981), the extreme mobility and fluidity of enclave hunter-gatherers is a reflection of their desire to escape the dominance of the farmers around them. This is also the view of Seitz (1981:293), who notes that if the Punan keep their distance, it is in order to escape social submission to the farmers.

The influence of the major agricultural groups upon the nomads with regard to processes of fission, long-distance emigration, and the present-day distribution of nomad groups has probably been underestimated in the past. This stage of the farmers' influence upon the nomads precedes in time the stage in which they constrain them to settle down.

Aggression

In the Dutch literature of the nineteenth and the early twentieth centuries (but to a lesser degree in the literature of Sarawak, which tends rather to portray them as victims), the Punan generally have the reputation of being savage killers and fanatical headhunters, even the Punan Murung, who now describe themselves as having always been peaceable. In reality, as has been said, they are much more often hunted than hunters, and headhunting is not part of their culture.

It has been indicated, with the help of bibliographic references from the nineteenth century, that the Bukat became headhunters and slave-raiders in response to a commercial demand on the part of the farmers. This is equally true of the Bukitan, the Kereho, and the Punan of the Apo Kayan (see von Kessel 1857:403; Elshout 1926:244), who killed, took heads, and abducted children for their overlords. These are special expeditions, with or without the participation of their sponsors, beyond the borders of the territory of the nomads concerned, often to a great distance; and the fruits of the expeditions, for which the nomads have no use, are turned over to the chief of the farming group who backed them. Whether heads and captives are part of a trade deal, or whether they represent a "service" obligingly offered to the settled group, the hunt for human game is an activity instigated among the nomads by the farming peoples.

However, some Punan groups, having acquired the habit of headhunting through contact with their neighbors, integrate this trait into their own culture as they settle and subsequently hunt heads for themselves. Thus the Aoheng, a group formed originally from a mingling of nomads and the relatively unwarlike Pin, became headhunters as zealous as their Kayan or Long Gelat neighbors (see Sellato 1986b).

The nomads find further occasion to play the warrior in another type of situation with regard to outsiders who are professional collectors of forest products. It appears that this too, like headhunting, is a secondary phenomenon, instigated from outside. Indeed, a band of Punan exploiting the forest only for their own subsistence would hardly be bothered by the presence of professionals interested in collecting commercial products (rotan, resins, etc.) rather than food: Punan and collectors, whether they avoid each other or enter into contact, would not be competitors.

On the other hand, for Punan who are beginning to become heavily dependent economically upon the gathering of commercial products, these professional collectors would be economic competitors. If the Punan do not realize this themselves, their settled patrons and customers, concerned to preserve the revenues of what they consider their territory (the territory of "their" Punan) and the monopoly over its yield, make it their business to increase Punan awareness of what is happening and charge them to prevent intruders' access to their collecting grounds. Thus the Bukat (with the Aoheng) killed Iban collectors who ventured into the headwaters of the Mahakam; chief Bang Juk of the Long Gelat sent his Punan to hunt down the Iban (Elshout 1926:244); the Punan Murung attacked Bekumpai intruders not authorized by their patrons (Sellato 1986b:266); and the Hovongan killed anyone who came to collect forest products on the Bungan, to the point that the colonial government had to declare this region off-limits to professional collectors (Enthoven 1903:85). It is probably in the context of this type of defense of the group's collecting ground that one should interpret references like that of von Dewall to supposedly "gratuitous" attacks by Punan of the Tidung region, who kill "out of habit, taking no heads" (1855:444). This, then, is likely to be an attitude arising out of the economic changes undergone by the Punan groups who, from hunters and gatherers of their own food, have made themselves into commercial collectors (further discussed in Chapter 5).

Among nomads whose economy is based almost exclusively upon the exploitation of the forest for food, a strategy of territorial defense is activated only when the food resources of the territory are threatened (by the intrusion of other competing nomads or by an attempt at conquest on the part of neighboring farmers). The same happens among Punan whose economy has become dependent on commercial gathering when it is the commercial resources of the territory that are threatened. This suggests that the concept of territory, for the Punan, pertains not so much to the realm of ideology as it does to a simple, pragmatic appreciation of economic realities.

Social Organization

The following sections will examine certain important aspects of the organization of traditional nomad societies before they become subject to major modifications under the impact of the economic changes that they undergo or initiate.

The Band

The band is the migratory unit, as shown in the reconstructions of the histories of groups like the Bukat or the Kereho. The expression "migratory unit" is to be taken here in the broadest sense: its primary meaning, of course, is the unit of residence and of movement but, more than this, also the economic unit (of production and consumption) and the political unit. This is true for any given band at any given moment, even if the composition and membership of the band fluctuate over time.

It seems that no Punan language contains a term specifically designating the band. The term *puhu'* (in Bukat, Kereho, and other languages) generally designates the extended family, or a group of extended families having a common ancestor, and thus denotes the recognition of a genealogical (therefore diachronic) link, rather than the synchronic link of common residence. Thus, and this is often the case, two separate bands may recognize that they belong to a single *puhu'*. The *puhu'* may be envisioned either as an ascending group (Ego-focused), or as a descending group (ancestor-focused). It is possible that the Punan Murung term *vevuhan* (designating the band or the extended family; Sellato 1986b:273) is a cognate of *puhu'*.

The band is therefore composed, in practice, of a core group comprising a section of a *puhu'* (a branch of the family or a line of descent), supplemented by affinal relatives and even by "outsiders" (related by neither blood nor marriage). It will be seen that this core group of the *puhu'*, as the founding component of the band, plays a certain political role.

The band is relatively small. Some authors provide figures. The five Penan bands of the Plieran comprise an average of about fifty people each (Arnold 1967:95). Needham gives an average figure of thirty-two persons (1971:204). Urquhart indicates a range of from twenty-five to forty persons (1959:78). It should be noted that in the case of bands that are already partially settled population figures must be treated with suspicion, as official figures may be higher than the actual population. An average figure of from twenty-five to fifty persons per band seems valid for all the nomad groups of Borneo. This figure probably represents a compromise between an economic determinant (the need to find food for the whole band without having to move too often) and a social determinant (the need to maintain, without risk, the practice of band endogamy).

There appears never to be any form of political organization above the level of the band, which is completely autonomous in its decisions. It has already been noted that Bukat bands never formed alliances against an enemy. Harrisson reports that Punan may be "loosely federated in an area group of several bands" (1949:139), but what he means by "federated" is not very clear; it may simply be that these bands recognize that they belong to the same ethnic group. Needham remarks that there is little recognition of common interest between bands except when they are relatively close geographically and genealogically, and no occasions for cooperation (1971:204). The nomadic local group (the band) can be seen, according to Needham, as a segmentary society in an extreme form (1971:204).

For nomadic Punan bands, indeed, there are none of those seasonal activities or migrations that may bring other hunter-gatherer groups together each year in particular locations, providing a break in the bands' isolation. In this equatorial environment, where the seasons are hardly perceptible, most resources are available all year round, and those which are not (fruits, wild pig) are unpredictable. There is no recurring annual event, no cycle, to give a rhythm to the passage of time for the Punan. Chance meetings in the course of migrations, trade encounters, or official summonses (see Harrisson 1949:143) are all that may bring bands into contact.

Nor are there, above the level of the band, economic or ritual activities that bring together several bands. Each band is autonomous in this regard (Needham 1971:204). No form of organization, whether political, economic, or ritual, exists therefore at the level of the ethnic group, or even of a possible local federation of bands. This does not mean that there is no economic and social interaction among bands. Trade goods undoubtedly circulate between "peripheral" bands living close to the farming groups and bands living in the center of the ethnic territory. Besides this, a certain percentage of marriages between members of different bands bears witness to the existence of interaction.

Members of a band, individuals or nuclear families, show a degree of mutual solidarity, especially in subsistence activities. People take turns working in the palm groves, and sago and the products of hunting and gathering are shared equally among all. According to Needham (1971:204), concerted commitment to moral values connected with their joint survival maintains unity among the members of the band, who support each other. In other words, the band represents something important for its members (see Needham 1954b:232). It is indeed likely, though this is a topic about which it is hard to be precise, that within the band there exists a particular feeling of community, reinforced by coresidence and common activities as much as by the bonds of kinship, which are multiple given the practice of band endogamy. With regard to its relations with farmers and the nomad bands of other ethnic groups, the band apparently acts as a political unit.

The Nuclear Family

The nuclear family is called by the term *kevian* among all the groups of the Müller mountains (Aoheng, Seputan, Kereho, and Hovongan), *kajan* among the Bukat, and *vevuhan* among the Punan Murung. Interestingly, once the nomads have become sedentary, the same term designates the extended or stem family inhabiting the same hut or the same longhouse apartment. Thus these terms should perhaps be considered as referring originally to the minimal residential unit, the nomads' temporary shelter or lean-to, and to its inhabitants, more than to a unit of kinship, the nuclear family.

In any case, among the nomads the minimal residential unit and the nuclear family are generally identical. According to the literature, a shelter is shared only by a couple and their unmarried children. It is rare to have a third generation represented (see Harrisson 1949:139) or to find a sibling of one spouse. A shelter might be inhabited by only one person, for example, an aged widower. Kedit gives, for the Penan of the Mulu region, an average of 6.6 persons per shelter (1982:228). This number is certainly lower for many other groups less demographically dynamic (see, for example, Huehne 1959–1960:199).

Each one of these minimal units has a certain autonomy within the band concerning its own decisions. Although each unit is expected to participate in activities related to the band's subsistence economy, it may leave the band at any time if there is a conflict between its own interests or choices and those of the band. The unit has responsibilities and rights deriving from its presence in the band, but this very presence, its affiliation to the band, may be called into question at any moment. Although considerations relating to security or the presence of food resources, or a sense of band loyalty, may act to promote cohesion, there is nothing in the social organization of the band that might prevent a nuclear family from leaving it.

However, it appears that once having left its band, a nuclear family has no choice but to join another. The Punan probably consider that it is undesirable for a migratory unit to have too few members—hence the lower figure of the range given earlier, of twenty to twenty-five persons. Band security may be one reason for this, and perhaps also efficiency in the search for and production of food.

In fact, what is most often observed is band fission, in which one band becomes two new bands, not necessarily equal in size. The cause of this fission is a disagreement between heads of families about the movements or future of the band. This process has been shown in action among the Bukat. The history of the Punan Murung also shows many such fissions (Sellato 1986b). Ellis reports that the Punan Busang, after discussing the increasing scarcity of sago palms in their region, could come to no consensus as to a solution and separated into two bands (1972:237). Tuton Kaboy reports an identical process among the Punan Aput (1974:287). It is probable that an increase in population within a band, making the search for food more difficult, often plays a role in band fission.

These new bands maintain relations, on the basis of their kinship ties (they belong to the same *puhu'*), and may on occasion subsequently reunite. This process of successive fission and fusion is particularly striking in the history of the Punan Murung (Sellato 1986b: 283). As Seitz notes, band membership is rarely stable over a long period of time, as the band divides and reforms (1981:295; see also Urquhart 1959:78). Thus nuclear families move from band to band in accordance with instances of fission and fusion, which accounts for the common presence in each band of a certain percentage of "outsiders." If the history of a nomad group is made up of the juxtaposed histories of the bands that comprise it, it may also be said that the particular history of each nuclear family cuts across the history of the bands (see the history of Sekudan's movements in Chapter 2). The band, even though it represents something to its members and on occasion acts as a political unit, seems to be a highly unstable structure. In fact, one may wonder whether the concept of a band, other than as a functional economic unit, makes sense at all.

Production and Consumption

As mentioned above, in the period before the introduction of dogs and iron, among the nomad groups certain economic activities existed that entailed the collective participation of members of the band. Among these was the beat hunt for terrestrial game, especially wild pig. This type of hunt would have required the participation of all able-bodied individuals, a fairly common custom among hunter-gatherers of the world. The introduction of dogs, at dates no doubt varying for different groups, led to the disappearance of this type of cooperative hunt among the Punan. But this certainly did not mean that hunting with dogs became a solitary activity, and the Punan still prefer to go out with their dogs in groups of several people, for the sake, no doubt, of a greater yield of game. Hunting with the blowpipe is often, though not always, the job of a solitary hunter. As for the traditional Punan method of fishing, with poison, this is indisputably a collective activity.

Work in the sago palm groves, as already stated, is carried out by mixed groups of men and women. This is a complex activity, a many-staged and relatively long process. Although certain writers, like Arnold (1967), claim that the different families of the band work alternately to produce sago, my observations suggest that most often several families will do the work together, completing the various phases of the work in an unbroken sequence (see also Harrisson 1949: 137). As for gathering, it is definitely an activity carried out cooperatively by women, old people, and children, who scatter in small groups in every direction, the better to comb through a sector of the forest.

The type of sexual division of labor found among the Punan seems to be specific to them and apparently independent of that practiced by the farmers. As described above, the different tasks in the production of sago are shared: men are responsible for felling the palm trunks and extracting the pith, either men and women may pound it, and women are responsible for straining it. While gathering seems to be primarily a job for women, hunting, at least among certain groups, is done by both men and women, and so is fishing.

Other tasks that regularly fall to women are the hauling of water and the collection of firewood (see Urquhart 1959:82), the final preparation of sago and cooking in general, and the construction of the shelters (among Bukat and Kereho). Two types of hard labor requiring strength and endurance are also considered women's work, the carrying of goods and children when the band moves (among many groups), and the collection of rotan for household use (at least among the Kereho). Sometimes, as among the Kereho, women are expected to find and bring home the game killed by the men (see Lumholtz 1920:174). Men hunt and have exclusive responsibility for the collection of honey and beeswax, an extremely dangerous job. As well as this, they guard the band as it moves.

An explanation for the comparatively heavy burden of work placed on women may lie in the preeminent place sago occupies in Punan subsistence, and in the difficulty of felling the palm trees before iron was introduced: men must have had to spend most of their time at this work (five times as much as today). The sexual division of labor observed today would then be a survival from this previous state of affairs. In sum, it is feasible to conclude that the allocation of work is made pragmatically, on the basis of aptitude, rather than ideologically, on the basis of gender: young women in good physical condition go hunting, while old men, no longer able to hunt, turn to gathering.

It appears that from the time when trade with the farming groups began to be of notable importance in the Punan economy, one may observe a distinct reorientation of male activity toward the collecting of commercial products, while women come to be concerned exclusively with gathering for purposes of subsistence. This new form of sexual specialization becomes even more striking as the Punan begin to turn to farming.

In any case, sago and the yield of hunting and gathering are evenly divided among all the members of the band (see Harrisson 1949:137; Needham 1971:204). According to Needham, this sharing is not just common practice but a formal and scrupulous obligation among the Western Penan (1954b:230). The leader of the band has no special privileges in this regard.

The almost total lack of any possibility of long-term preservation of food means that every edible produced must quickly be consumed. Many writers have described how the Punan gorge themselves with food when it is abundant and go empty thereafter if food is scarce. A similar attitude toward food has been noted for many groups of hunter-gatherers the world round. This impossibility of accumulating foodstuffs reflects both the nomadic way of life and the de facto egalitarianism of Punan bands (see Testart 1981). But though the edibles produced by collective or individual economic activity may be pooled, this does not mean that they are consumed in common. The unit of consumption seems to be the residential unit, the shelter group, or the nuclear family (probably with some exceptions). Each family eats the same things, in equal amounts, but apparently each does its own cooking.

Residential Patterns

There are many descriptions of Punan residential patterns in the literature. While camps for the night, in the course of a migration, can be set up almost anywhere along the forest footpath, camps meant to be lived in for several weeks are established on special sites already occupied in the past. These sites are within easy reach of several sago palm groves and very close to a small stream. Each camp is made up of a certain number of independent structures, whose size varies according to the number of people they are intended to shelter. The simplest are platforms of branches barely raised above the ground (sometimes, indeed, no more than a litter of leaves on the ground itself), with a single slanting windbreak or lean-to roof thatched with leaves. A camp of such structures can be constructed in less than an hour (Harrisson 1949:138). More elaborate housing consists of a hut with a double-sloped roof of leaves covering a branch-floored sleeping space raised on posts, and a hearth. Such a shelter or hut, the minimal residential unit, houses from one to a dozen persons, according to the size of the nuclear family.

One point that should be discussed here is the use of caves as habitations by the Punan. That Punan sometimes do live in caves is reported by Hose (1894–1895:158, 173), Hose and McDougall (1912:I, 232, II, 182), J. Nicolaisen (1976a:229, 1976b:44), and Seitz (1981:298). Caves must be taken here as including rock shelters at the foot of an overhanging cliff or under boulders, as well as true fossil karst networks in limestone massifs. I visited many such shelters and caves in the Müller mountains and elsewhere, and all or almost all showed traces of human occupation. Of course, the presence of caves is dependent upon the geologic context. In regions where karst networks are well developed within limestone formations, there is no doubt that the dry caves have been regularly used as shelters. Such caves were mentioned in the discussion of the Bukat. All the sites of former camps of the Punan Murung are close to caves (Sellato 1986b: 280–281). Similarly, more than half of the old campsites of the Seputan on the Kacu and the Penane are in caves. On the upper Kacu there is even a site consisting of once inhabited caves lying one above the other. Archaeological excavations in such sites would be of enormous interest. Kedit (1982:256) mentions caves in the center of the territory of the Penan of Mount Mulu, but up to now there seems to be no evidence of their having been inhabited.

Without going so far as to claim that the Punan were committed cave dwellers—an impossible argument, if only because not all of the regions where Punan live have appropriate caves—it does seem logical that caves would be preferred sites of shelter for the Punan, given the undeniable advantages they offer: protection against rain and the cold, a saving in the labor of shelter construction, and a place to hide in case of danger.

The Aoheng used the caves in their territory as refuges during the Iban war. These caves are still regularly used by groups of hunters when they go on expeditions of several days, and I myself have often spent nights in them. It may be noted that while the farming peoples (Kayan and Long Gelat) commonly used such caves as places to deposit the coffins of their dead, the Punan in general did not, as will be seen below.

Leadership

Are the nomadic Punan hunter-gatherers an egalitarian society? The descriptions in the literature of their social organization, and in particular of their system of leadership, present a somewhat ambiguous picture. Written sources generally provide no term that serves to designate the leader, or leaders, among still nomadic Punan. At best they may offer the term *tuai rumah* (for example, Jayl Langub 1972), but this is a regional expression in the Malay lingua franca or in Iban, in use among sedentary groups, which has become an administrative title given to community leaders.

In preceding chapters, mention was made of certain terms and expressions that designate leaders. Though the term *sipoi* used by the Bukat is a loan word, corresponding to nothing in their social organization, the Kereho term *dino tohokan* and the Punan Murung *roko* (Sellato 1986b:273) both refer to the "old person," the elder, leader of the band. The term *ketuke* used by the Punan Aput (Tuton Kaboy 1974:290) seems to have the same meaning. It should be noted that these words are often used in the plural, and are applied not so much to the elderly as to persons who are mature and experienced. In all cases, the category referred to is one of age rather than hierarchy.

The expression *lino tangön* used by the Bukat (cognate with the Aoheng term *tongon,* referring to the sow that leads a herd of wild pigs), relates to the concept of authority. This choice of the name of a female animal, leader of the group (adult boars are usually solitary), is noteworthy in relation to the fact, to which few references exist in the literature, that women may be band leaders: Penganun, leader of the Halunge (Sellato 1986b:311), was a woman; Bulan, leader of the Punan Murung, was famous in that entire region as "queen of the Punan" (Sellato 1986b:236); and I know of other cases among the Lisum and the Beketan. References here to leaders as male should therefore be understood to include this possibility.

The choice of a band leader is made, according to the literature, in a variety of ways. According to Arnold (1958:58), the role of leader passes from father to son in all the groups (see also 1967:98), and in particular among the Penan Menawan (1958:55). Among the Penan Lusong, the role is called "semi-hereditary" (Urquhart 1951:500). According to Needham, it is not hereditary, but nevertheless often passes from father to son (1972:179). Jayl Langub notes that there are three possible modes of selection: one of the elders may be accepted as leader, the leader may be elected, or the role may be inherited (1972: 219). It should be noted, however, that most of these studies do not distinguish, in their remarks on the choice of a leader, between what happens in nomadic bands and in settled or semisettled groups, nor between the spontaneous choice or election of a leader and a decision required of the group by the authorities for administrative purposes.

Whatever may be the process by which the leader is chosen, his status, at least in groups not converted to agriculture, is not very different from that of the other members of the band. There is nothing sacred about his role, and it entails no particular privileges (J. Nicolaisen 1976a:214), except that leaders may sometimes have several wives (Urquhart 1959:80). The leader has little formal authority, his power being based only on his personal qualities (see Jayl Langub 1972:219; Needham 1954b:231; J. Nicolaisen 1976a:214). According to Needham, no difference in status is marked or ascribed (1971:204).

What, then, is the use of a leader, under these conditions? Since he has no formal power, his influence depends on his experience, his wisdom, his ability to make good decisions—though, for that matter, it appears that decisions may be made only after a general discussion in which everyone has a voice (see Jayl Langub 1972:220).

Thus the prestige of a band leader derives, not from his status or from his skill as a hunter or his ability as a provider (see Needham

1954b:231), but from his leadership qualities. The leader must be hardworking, an eloquent speaker, experienced, and fully familiar with the group's history and traditions (Jayl Langub 1972:219; this last quality will be further discussed below).

Another important factor is the leader's suitability as a representative of the band in its interactions with the outside world, and in particular with the farming groups and the government (see Harrisson 1949:143; Seitz 1981:297). In these circumstances, mastery of the neighbors' language, or of the national or regional language, is a highly desirable leadership skill. The Punan, anxious to meet the farmers on an equal footing, want a leader of whom they can be proud. The prestige of the leader reflects upon the group. Conversely, these external connections, integral to the leader's role as representative, can only increase his prestige within the band. This is probably the process that gave rise, among certain groups such as the Aoheng (Sellato 1986b:384, 403), to temptations toward social inequality. I shall return to this point below.

Each individual or nuclear family possesses in principle a certain autonomy in relation to the band, and conflicts among them may lead to its fission. These are not conflicts of power, but rather conflicts of choice concerning migrations, trading partners, or, more recently, way of life (nomadic or sedentary). Conflicts may also result from a clear failure of the acting leader, when his decisions have proved disastrous for the band. In this case, under the leadership of another elder, a group of families who no longer accept the leader's options will choose to secede, and the two bands go their separate ways.

Conversely, the prestige of a leader known for his wisdom may attract individuals or families from other bands to join his own. Thus it happens, as has been said above, that a band is generally made up of a founding descent group *(puhu')* plus a certain number of affines or "outsiders" who have become members.

We return now to the question of the transmission of the role of leader. Whatever the process of selection, it is highly likely that the new leader will be closely related to the old, since the majority of the members of the band belong to its founding *puhu'*. It should also be noted that, since investigations are often carried out in Indonesian or in the Malay lingua franca, nephews or cousins, even distant cousins, are often included in the classificatory category of sons, and thus the succession may appear to be more strictly hereditary than it actually is. In practice, the new leader may be a younger brother or a cousin, a son, a nephew, or a cousin of the younger generation, or a son-in-law or other affine of the former leader. It is probable that the whole of the band, or perhaps the leader himself (see Rousseau 1985:41), selects the future leader, choosing the best possible candidate among the experienced adults of the band. Although there is doubtless no ideal of strict hereditary transmission of the role, there may be a tendency to choose a future leader from among the band's founding *puhu'* rather than from among "outsiders."

There is also an observable tendency toward a retroactive establishment of fictive kinship ties between successive leaders. Thus the Lisum (or Punan Lisum) stress the fact that such and such a leader was the "brother," "son," or "grandson" of the one preceding, whereas a study of genealogies shows that he was in fact only his cousin (even a cousin by marriage), or his son-in-law, the nephew or son of a cousin, or a grandnephew. This appears to confirm the existence of an ideal of close relationship (real or fictive) between a leader and his predecessor, a fact to be linked to the practice of band endogamy in the context of a composite band such as has been described above.

Thus, although the absence of a specific term to designate the leader, and the absence of any real formal authority granted him, imply an absence of social differentiation within the nomad band and an ideal of egalitarianism put into practice, nevertheless the band as an endogamous family unit seeks to maintain itself as such by keeping leadership within the *puhu'*, or by establishing a posteriori fictive consanguine links between successive leaders. In the case of this latter process, the egalitarian ideal manages to resolve in practice the latent opposition between the two social categories of founders and newcomers, and to integrate this second group into the band. It is, however, possible that this opposition, like the ideal of keeping leadership within the *puhu'* (the source of this opposition), is itself due to the influence of the stratified farming peoples. As the nomads convert to agriculture, this ideal may be put into actual practice (as happened among the Aoheng: see Sellato 1986b:403; also J. Nicolaisen 1976a:214).

Kinship

The system of kinship terminology of the Punan groups is of the Eskimo type, with assimilation of cousins to siblings (see J. Nicolaisen 1976a:215). It will not be described in detail here. A comparative study of Punan kinship systems is in preparation. Some points may, however, be noted. These systems often do not distinguish birth order, and the contrast between elder and younger sibling therefore appears to be irrelevant; for consanguines, sex is distinguished only for parents and, though not in all cases, for parents' siblings; there may be no specific term designating the spouse, and when there is one it is reciprocal—that is, without mark of gender; nephews are sometimes, in a wrench of the generational principle, assimilated to grandsons; and there are generally no specific terms for great-grandparent and great-grandchild, five generations only being recognized. In affinal terminology, terms of reference for the parent of a spouse and the spouse of a child seem usually to be borrowings, while the equivalent terms of address refer to blood relationships; and finally, for affines of Ego's generation, systems of two or three separate terms take into account both the sex of the speaker and the sex of the person addressed or referred to (see Sellato 1983b).

We should also note the existence of a remarkable system of necronyms, including from ten to several dozen terms. In striking contrast to kinship terms, these necronyms strongly stress the birth order and the sex both of the person named and of the deceased. Certain systems of necronyms, in use among the Penan of Sarawak, have been studied in detail (see, for example, Needham 1954c, J. Nicolaisen 1978, and Brosius 1992).

Rituals and Religion

This section will focus upon the sphere of the sacred and its manifestations, as well as upon certain features of Punan àdat (customary law) which are associated with this sphere, and which I have therefore chosen to treat here. The subsections describing marriage and funeral customs, most fully treated in the literature, are particularly comprehensive, while the last subsection, on the nomads' religious beliefs and practices, is by comparison fairly brief.

Marriage and Postmarital Residence

The existence of band endogamy has already been mentioned. Whether or not this is explicitly stated to be the ideal, it is preferred (see Needham 1971:204) and constitutes a social feature common to a great number of Punan groups. It is expressed in practice by marriages between people closely related by blood, and in *adat* by a certain vagueness in the proscriptive rules of marriage.

Marriage between first cousins is practiced among the Bukat and the Kereho, as it is among the Punan Murung (Sellato 1986b:274), the Hovongan, the Lisum, and the Beketan of the Tabang region, and the Seputan. The same practice is confirmed for other groups in Sarawak by J. Nicolaisen (1976a:216) and Needham (1966:6), but it appears not to be universal, as certain groups, perhaps under the influence of sedentary neighbors, prohibit this type of marriage (see Seitz 1981: 297). There have been reports of other cases of marriage between close blood relatives, in particular with an uncle or an aunt (see Urquhart 1959:80; J. Nicolaisen 1976a:216), but this probably only happens if the couple are relatively close in age. Indeed, the Punan apparently disapprove of marriages in which there is a considerable difference in age between husband and wife (see Seitz 1981:297). One might conclude that the Punan attach greater importance to the more immediate category of age group than to the principle of generational differences.

Generally speaking, proscriptive rules of marriage are few, being reduced to the minimum in order to facilitate marriage within the community (Seitz 1981:294), and the concept of incest is fairly vague (Urquhart 1959:80). For that matter, no specific term for incest exists in the Punan languages. It should, however, be noted that no case of marriage between siblings has ever been reported, to my knowledge (though this does occur in certain origin myths).

Jayl Langub (1972:220) states that only 10 percent of marriages take place between members of different bands (and this among groups already settled; see also Seitz 1981:294). If these marriages are rare, marriages between ethnic groups are probably even more so, at least as long as the Punan are still nomadic and have only limited interactions with their sedentary neighbors. Van Naerssen (in Hildebrand 1982:85) reports extreme endogamy among the four villages of the Hovongan.

Several particular types of marriage may be mentioned in passing. The sororate (in which a man marries his deceased wife's sister) is present among the Aoheng (Sellato 1986b:406), and would appear to exist as well among the Punan Kelai (Anonymous 1968:123). Among the Seputan there was a custom in which two brothers would marry two sisters, and another in which two brothers would marry a mother and her daughter (Sellato 1986b:406); a band of Punan Benalui, as described by Pfeffer (1963:125), is made up of three families whose heads are three brothers who married six sisters. These traditional customs, whose effect is to multiply the bonds of alliance between two families, may well be specific to the nomad groups.

Polygyny was practiced by a certain number of groups. As well as in those cases already mentioned, it has been reported, most often for leaders, by Urquhart (1959:80) and Harrisson (1949:142). Polygyny has also been noted among the Punan Murung (Sellato 1986b:274), and I know of several present-day cases among the Hovongan. Moreover, Seitz reports a single reference to a case of polyandry (1981: 296). But certain groups would appear to be strictly monogamous (Lumholtz 1920:216–217; Urquhart 1951:519).

It is probable that monogamy is normal practice among the Punan in general, but that there is no strict rule or explicit ideal on the subject. Cases of polygyny, fairly rare on the whole, may be the result of several situations: a demographic imbalance between the sexes (following an enemy attack, for example) and an attempt at recovery by the band involving the mobilization of all the members of an age to bear children; the desire of a leader for increased prestige among his sedentary neighbors (whose chiefs often have several wives or take concubines); or the first wife's barrenness (the case in one of the Hovongan polygynous marriages). As I see it, the compelling principle is the optimal utilization of the band's reproductive potential; the absence of strict marriage rules permits the flexibility necessary to attain this goal, which is congruent with the vagueness of the concept of incest in the context of the endogamous band.

Marriage rites are minimal, indeed sometimes nonexistent. As described in the preceding chapter and as the literature confirms, in many groups marriage is entirely informal (see Urquhart 1951:519; Jayl Langub 1972:220). The Seputan say they had no ritual of marriage, except for leaders, who were the descendants of Long Gelat swidden farmers.

The informal aspect of marriage is confirmed by the extremely limited practice of the marriage gift or payment. Certain groups have no system of marriage payments, among them the Punan Batu, the Punan Binai, the Punan Berun, the Punan Benyawung, and the Punan Kelai (Hoffman 1983:84); it may have been the same with the Bukat. Gifts are given by the man to his prospective bride among several groups: for example, a Punan Musang should present her with glass beads and a bush knife (Tillema 1934–1935:22). But often this gift is optional: a Punan Aput gives his future bride a valuable old bead, but only if he happens to have one (Tuton Kaboy 1974:291). Similarly, among the Punan Murung (Sellato 1986b:274), the marriage payment is transferred by installments, a little at a time, and often left unchecked (see also J. Nicolaisen 1976a:215).

It is quite possible that traditional practice among the nomads was for the woman to make a gift to her future husband, as certain reports indicate. Schwaner (in Roth 1968: CXCVII) states that among the Ot of the Barito it is the woman who chooses the man and offers him weapons. Such a custom may have been prevalent among the Bukat. According to Sitsen, it is the young woman, among the Punan Musang, who offers a blowpipe to her intended. The same occurs among the nomads of the Tidung area (Tillema 1934–1935:22).

Among the Kereho, as we saw, the traditional custom of the gift of a weapon coexisted with the custom borrowed from the Seputan of a marriage payment in the form of gongs (see Stolk 1907:25), the second practice being restricted to "tribal chiefs," the descendants of neighboring Seputan farmers. It is interesting in this regard to see how this cultural trait passed from the Long Gelat swidden farmers to the leaders of the Seputan when they settled, and from them to the leaders of the Kereho, to become the norm, along with the rule of uxorilocality, among the Kereho of today.

The gift of a weapon to the young man by his father-in-law enables him to provide for his future family and symbolizes the responsibility toward them that he is assuming. But one may well imagine that when two young people set up housekeeping, this new relationship, informally recognized by the band with no associated ritual, may be substantiated (see Seitz 1981:294) by some material help not strictly defined by custom, given by the parents of the bride or groom (or more probably by both), in the form of weapons, tools, or the utensils necessary to the economic functioning of this new family unit within the band.

The rules of postmarital residence, according to the literature, seem somewhat unclear; all the more since writers very often do not distinguish between what happens in still nomadic bands and customs among settled groups.

The Penan Lusong practice uxorilocality, while their neighbors the Penan Gang show a tendency toward ambilocality (living alternately with the wife's family and the husband's), or more rarely, neolocality (Urquhart 1951:519). Among other Penan, the young couple join the

parents of either partner (utrolocality), but may also establish a neolocal residence (Jayl Langub 1972:220). According to J. Nicolaisen, in
the case of a marriage between members of two different bands, the
couple moves back and forth between their original local groups
(1976a:215; 1976b:40). In a marriage between band members, the
new couple remains in the band and no doubt quickly sets up a neolocal establishment; that is, the two build their own shelter, even if they
may previously (before the birth of the first child, for instance: see
Seitz 1981:294) have lived for some time in the shelter of the parents
of either spouse (utrolocality within the band, or shelter utrolocality).
In a marriage in which husband and wife belong to two separate
bands, the couple will join either one band or the other (band utrolocality), whether or not they set up a neolocal shelter; or they may practice band ambilocality, that is, live alternately with both bands.

As Seitz notes (1981:294), there is no rigid rule of residence. Residence seems to be a matter of the personal choice of the couple, or of
an arrangement between the families to optimize the economic functioning of the nuclear families or bands concerned. If certain Punan
groups state that they have a rule of uxorilocality, this is almost certainly a borrowing from agricultural groups, as among the Kereho
Busang. In the case of those Punan groups which are already settled,
living in huts in small villages, it is probable that neolocality, dominant in the nomadic bands where the residential unit is the nuclear
family, gives way to utrolocality, since the huts, being larger and more
permanent, can accommodate stem families or extended families.

Disposal of the Dead

Like marriages, deaths in traditional nomad society are not
occasions for elaborate ritual. The literature is curiously rich in
descriptions of types of funerals among the Punan groups. In their
details these practices vary, the common characteristic being that they
are of a relatively rudimentary character compared to those of farming
societies. The body may simply be abandoned, just as it is, on a flat
stone (in the case of the Kereho), on a platform of branches hastily set
up in the forest, or in the shelter where the death occurred (Jayl
Langub 1974:296). In certain cases the body is wrapped in a sheet of
bark or a mat before being left on a platform (Harrisson 1949:142) or
buried (Sulaiman 1968:25–26). Among certain groups the body is
buried without a coffin (Jayl Langub 1974:296; Harrisson 1949:142)
under the hearth of the shelter (J. Nicolaisen 1978:33), or at a dis-

tance from the camp (Urquhart 1951:511), downstream from the camp (Sulaiman 1968:25–26) or, conversely, upstream (Arnold 1958: 59–60; 1967:97), or just anywhere (Sandin 1957:135). Among other groups the body, in a coffin, is buried under the hut (Urquhart 1951: 512), or elsewhere (Sandin 1965:187), or left under a lean-to (Tuton Kaboy 1974:292; see also Urquhart 1951:511) or on a platform in the forest (as among the Kereho).

Interment inside the trunk of a live tree is found in widely separated regions of Borneo, but only, it would appear, among the nomads, including the Penan of Niah (Sandin 1957:135) and the Punan La'ong (Sandin 1965:187), and the Ot of the headwaters of the Barito (Schwaner, in Roth 1968: CXCVII). This type of tomb was also in use among the Aoheng; in the case of a birth of twins, the babies, who were believed to bring bad luck, were immured alive inside a cavity hollowed out of a tree and closed up with its own bark.

In rare cases, mention is made of a secondary treatment of the bones of the dead, among the Bukitan (Sandin 1956:66) and the Punan Benalui (Pfeffer 1963). There is an equally exceptional mention made by Perelaer of the practice of cremation by a nomad group, the Kereho (in Meyners d'Estrey 1891:320); here cremation appears to be associated, indeed, with interment inside a tree.

Most commonly, no form of ceremony accompanies the disposal of the body. Most authors make no mention of funeral rituals, and others explicitly state that these are nearly or wholly nonexistent (Stöhr 1959:164; Arnold 1967:97; Lumholtz 1920). Besides a shroud of plant materials (either bark or a woven mat), a coffin, a platform, or a lean-to windbreak, there are only rare mentions of any objects being left with the body (Arnold 1967:97) and of sacrifice of an animal or a human being made (Stolk 1907:25). Generally speaking, there are neither grave gifts nor sacrifices.

A common custom among all known Punan groups is the immediate abandonment of the body, of the place where the death occurred, of the camp, and sometimes of that entire sector of the territory (see, above, the discussion of the Bukat, and Mjöberg 1934; Harrisson 1949:142; Urquhart 1951:512; Arnold 1958:59–60; Stöhr 1959: 164; Huehne 1959:201; Ellis 1972:240; Jayl Langub 1974:296; Tuton Kaboy 1974:292; J. Nicolaisen 1978:33). Among several groups, the camp, or at least the hut of the deceased, is wrecked or burned before being abandoned (Urquhart 1951:512, 532; J. Nicolaisen 1978:33).

The band may move only a short way from the abandoned camp, or a very long way. A particular manner of withdrawing is described for two widely separated groups, the Punan Kelai (Sulaiman 1968:25–26; Anonymous 1968:127) and the Penan Gang (Urquhart 1951: 510). The band moves a short distance and makes a new camp in which it stays for three days, after which it repeats this process two more times; only then is it once more free to go where it likes. Although, according to Needham (1954b:232), the Punan never abandon old people and the sick, it nevertheless appears that among certain groups, such as the Bukat, the dying were indeed abandoned (see Bouman 1924:175–176).

Common to the Punan groups, therefore, is this standard practice of immediate flight from death. In general, they maintain no contacts with their dead (see Tillema 1939:208–209). This trait is specific to them and is not to be found, except in extreme cases (for example, in a time of epidemic), among the sedentary peoples who, having their graveyards near their villages, must live in relatively close proximity to their dead. Rituals by which the soul is escorted to its last abode, similar to those the farmers perform to make sure that the ghost of the dead person is dispatched once and for all, were mentioned in the discussion of the Bukat, but there they appear to have been borrowed from the Aoheng; such rituals are apparently not reported among other nomad groups.

The simplicity of death rites, the near total absence of grave gifts, sacrifices, or a ritual escorting of the soul, all of which hold true for the entire island, indicate a sharp distinction between hunter-gatherer culture and the cultures of the farming groups. Curiously, the culture of the forest nomads of Africa (Woodburn 1982) includes traits very like those of the Punan: destruction of the dead person's hut, occasional desertion of the dying, the immediate abandonment of the camp, a scarcity of rituals or prohibitions relative to death, and the absence of belief in an afterworld.

Punan Religion

The simplicity, both material and ritual, of Punan death practices may no doubt be linked to the concept the Punan have of what happens after death, a very vague concept, often borrowed, according to certain writers. Generally speaking, the Punan, like the farmers, seem to acknowledge the existence of a soul (or more than one) which, at the death of the individual, becomes a spirit that is potentially dangerous. But, unlike the farmers, who defuse this risk by ritually escorting the soul to an afterworld, the Punan, apparently having no belief in the existence of a final home for the souls of the dead, see every death as a serious spiritual danger, as the spirit of the deceased remains to wander the earth. Hence the necessity of flight from the place of death, to give the site time to "cool down." It is interesting to note that, even after a period of intensive contact with farming peoples and the adoption of belief in a final home for the dead and of certain funerary rituals, the practice of abandoning the site of a death still persists.

We may note, without going too deeply into the matter, that other expressions of Punan ritual life are in general just as minimal as those relating to marriage and death. The Punan have few or no prohibitions, omens or auguries, curing or purification ceremonies for the sick, or rituals related to the extraction of sago, hunting, or gathering (see Harrisson 1949:142; Urquhart 1951:512, 521–522; Kedit 1982: 243). When they do have them, they seem to be traits that have been borrowed and considerably simplified. This does not prevent certain Punan groups, or at least certain individuals, from enjoying reputations as shamanistic curers among their sedentary neighbors (see Hose and McDougall 1912:II, 190). Considered by these neighbors as beings intermediate between human and animal, between culture alienated from the realm of spirits and raw nature in constant contact with them, the Punan are by their very essence the best of mediators. It is not uncommon to find, in the myths of the farming groups, Punan playing the role of messengers of the spirits (see Revel-Macdonald 1978, Sellato 1983a). Looked down upon for their way of life, Punan regain a little respect due, paradoxically, to the animal qualities ascribed to them by their farmer neighbors.

The Bukat and Punan groups of the Müller mountains recognize a couple or pair of creator deities (whose relationship and gender vary), Kito and Minang. They are viewed as having withdrawn from the affairs of the world and are rarely or never called upon. Kito, also called Ake' Kito (Grandfather Kito), preserved in the Aoheng pantheon, appears as the deity Aki Kato of the Punan Busang (Needham 1954a:522), as well as among the Lisum and the Beketan of the region of Tabang, which is not unexpected given that all these groups— Bukat, Beketan, Lisum, Lugat, Punan Busang, Punan Aput, and Punan Merah—are related. Kito is also present among the Kenyah, who are believed (for other reasons) to be former Punan. It would be interesting to make an inventory of the traditional deities of other Punan groups. Whatever the case may be, there is to my knowledge no creator deity named Kito among the major groups of long-established farmers.

The remarkable absence of rites of passage (J. Nicolaisen 1976a: 215), indeed, of any sort of rite, and the presence of a half-forgotten but specific pantheon, suggest that the religion of Punan societies represents a system of belief and practice distinct from that of the farming groups. Contrary to Seitz (1981:290), who concludes that no autonomous religion common to all the Punan groups exists, I tend to concur in the conclusion of J. Nicolaisen (1976a:231) that all the Punan groups very probably have in common a core of religious beliefs unique to them. Nevertheless, I would tend to view the Punan band as a "secular" society, pragmatic and little given to religious belief or behavior, like the Basseri nomads of South Persia (see Barth 1964; Douglas 1982). This idea, in its relationship with what has been described of the Punan way of life and social organization, will be further explored in the following chapter.

Summary

The Punan groups traditionally inhabit a specific ecological niche, the vast primary forest, which is also an economic niche from which they derive their daily subsistence. The forest environment allows for them total self-sufficiency in matters of diet. I believe it has been demonstrated that the Punan subsistence economy is capable of functioning in complete independence. The techniques they use in the extraction of sago and in hunting, fishing, and gathering would have been entirely effective before the introduction of new items of technology, such as metal. Indeed, traditional Punan society and culture could well have existed in the absence of any commercial contact whatsoever with the farming peoples. Findings concerning the Punan concept of territory, the way in which their "segmentary" society functions, their system of leadership, their collective activities, their ideal of endogamy, and their "secular" attitude toward marriage, death, and rituals, all lead to the conclusion that their culture and type of society are autonomous with respect to the cultures and societies of the farmers who live around them.

CHAPTER 5
PROCESSES OF CHANGE

I ARGUED in the last chapter that the cultures of the nomadic hunter-gatherers of Borneo may be subsumed into a single culture which I call Punan culture, and that this culture is independent of the cultures of the farming groups surrounding the nomads' enclaves. In the following pages I will first discuss the conversion of the Punan from a food-oriented, hunting-gathering economy to one heavily dependent upon commercial collecting; then the process of change to various forms of agriculture; and finally, the transformations affecting Punan society during these periods of transition. This sequence may seem arbitrary, and a certain amount of repetition and cross-referencing cannot be avoided. It is one among a number of possible ways of making sense of a vast array of facts from different spheres—political, social, economic, commercial, and religious—and of their causal relationships and development over time.

I will try to show that the economy of the nomadic Punan, capable of complete self-sufficiency, changes in response to strategies that the farming groups initiate under pressure from coastal markets in order to obtain forest products—strategies with which the Punan readily concur. The conversion of the Punan to rice cultivation, an unintended and paradoxical side-effect of these strategies, causes a reduction in the supply of forest products. But the Punan, choosing to avoid too great a dietary dependence upon rice, develop economic systems of mixed subsistence, which, being both stable and flexible, permit them to remain the professional collectors that they have opted to become. It is important to stress that these processes historically gave rise to situations that could be both consecutive in time in a given region and contiguous in space at a given time.

The Shift to Commercial Collecting

It has been shown that in the past the Punan bands could function with potentially complete self-sufficiency, without contacts of any sort with farming groups. They could get along without metal and were, as they still are, able to live without salt. I emphasize "potentially," because at present it seems impossible to prove that they in fact had no contact with the farmers.

It is true that markets for forest products had already existed more than a thousand years ago. But it is essential to take a diachronic perspective: forests and forest nomads of that time covered a far larger area than they do today (see, on this subject, Hildebrand 1982:34), and the "peripheral" nomad bands, ranging along the coasts and main rivers and therefore close to centers of trade, had already been integrated into trade networks as commercial collectors, whereas the bands of the interior, which had no direct contact with markets, remained autonomous. The peripheral bands, as they were gradually absorbed into farming groups, passed on the job of commercial collecting to bands living farther upriver, in this way promoting the assimilation of these nomads, in turn, into farming groups as well as the further extension into the headwaters of trade networks, and therefore of commercial collecting. This is the process by which downriver Bukat were absorbed into Kayan communities, becoming farmers and middlemen in the trade with the upriver Bukat, who in turn became the commercial collectors the first group had ceased to be.

Stone tools, as we saw earlier, were still in use until fairly recently in certain isolated areas, even among farming peoples. It is therefore reasonable to believe that even though the nomads of Borneo as a whole have a thousand-year history of trading contacts with the coasts, the last totally autonomous bands of the deep hinterland may have been integrated into trading networks only recently, most probably within the past two centuries.

Development of Economic Dependence

The members of an autonomous nomadic band, limited to stone tools and hunting without the help of dogs, would no doubt have been engaged in a full-time quest for food. Even if they wanted to take up commercial collecting, they would hardly have had the time for it. All that changes with the introduction of metal and the dog, at the time of the nomads' first trade contacts with farming groups. The felling of sago palms is now made far easier by iron axes, which, as noted above, reduce by four-fifths the energy output and therefore also the time required for the work. Accurate and durable blowpipes can now be made of hardwood, and with these and the use of dogs the hunt becomes much more productive. A proportion of the nomads' work time is therefore saved. As they have no reason to produce more food, nor any means of preserving it, this time saved is free time.

But metal and dogs are not to be had for the asking, and the process through which the Punan are to become economically dependent is set in motion. Like all hunter-gatherers, the Punan have nothing to give in exchange but the yield of their hunting and gathering (see Testart 1981) and perhaps certain manufactured objects (mats and baskets have been mentioned, and plant poisons). The commercial demand for forest products, relayed from the coasts up to the most distant farmers of the headwaters, and probably more and more strongly from the colonial period onward to modern times, places pressure on the nomads. The farmers, who make an attractive profit on the trade in these products (as reported by many writers, beginning with Anonymous 1859:481), compete to form patron-client relationships with the nomad groups.

It is important to understand that forest products play a far from negligible part in the total economic system of the farming groups of the headwaters. Those groups which have no nomads at their command find themselves, if not economically handicapped, at any rate markedly less rich and powerful. Kwing Irang, a Kayan chief of the Mahakam, who had no nearby nomads with whom to trade for forest products, called in professional collectors from the Barito to exploit the forest resources of his territory (Nieuwenhuis 1904–1907:I, 276). The farmers resort to a variety of strategies to attach their Punan clients to themselves—that is, to initiate relations of trade with the nomads, draw more bands into a trade relationship, and maintain their monopoly. Although the farmers are undoubtedly the first to solicit trade goods, the Punan, as will be seen, soon find themselves trapped by the needs that the farmers induce, and themselves begin to ask for things that in the past they could well have done without: metal, salt, tobacco, cloth, glass beads, and more.

The strategies the farmers adopt to establish and maintain trade connections exhibit both economic and political components. Among the first, as just mentioned, is the need created among the Punan for items recently introduced. It seems self-evident that once they have tried felling sago palms with an iron axe, the Punan do not want to keep on using axes of stone. Tobacco also seems to be a great commercial success. Later, when the Punan, a bit more experienced and less gullible, no longer simply accept without bargaining what is offered in exchange for their goods but are able to compare the quality and amount of what they can get from different potential trading partners, they set up situations in which the farming groups have to compete with each other to offer a better deal in order to keep their Punan clients. Finally, the time-honored system of revolving credit, still practiced on a wide scale today, allows the farmers to keep the Punan in the position of permanent debtors, which not only binds them as clients but tends to increase their productivity.

Political strategies include the two systems of alliance, by exchange of blood and by marriage, between nomads and farmers. Through these alliances, the Punan are placed under a moral obligation to trade with specific partners, who thereby obtain a monopoly. Once the leader of a band has become the blood brother of a farmer chief, it is unthinkable that he should trade with anyone else. Besides this, the farmers' chiefs are entitled to prohibit, not only their own followers (see van Walchren 1907:797), but also members of subject groups (Sellato 1986b:266), from trading with the nomads. The existence of this monopoly then allows the farmer chief to increase his profit. Generally speaking, it appears that these political strategies are developed, in the case of any given Punan band, subsequent to the economic strategies mentioned above. Later still, sociocultural strategies would come to be applied.

Well and truly hooked, the Punan are now caught between their newly felt needs for imported articles, their position as debtors, and their moral obligations toward their allies. The farmers keep pressuring them to bring in more and more forest products and to this end are ready to create among them new needs for cloth, beads, and gimcrack ornaments. At a later stage of interaction, the need arises for value objects such as gongs and jars. In the 1980s the same system centered around such things as wristwatches, transistor radios, and tape cassette players.

From their position of creditors, the farmers have every opportunity to impose their demands upon the Punan, reflecting the fluctuating demands of the downriver markets. They direct Punan efforts toward the most lucrative products, and it may be, as Testart notes (1981), that this reorientation toward gathering takes place at the expense of the hunt. Although some of the products in greatest demand are obtained by hunting (rhinoceros horn, bezoar stones, hornbill casques and feathers), the bulk of the transactions probably involve articles such as resins or rotan.

Intensification of Relations

In every case, the Punan find themselves obliged to provide, in the context of strictly commercial exchanges, an ever-increasing supply of forest products. But in these transactions everybody gains. The farmers grow richer, certainly; but the Punan too benefit economically, given the time they save through the use of their new acquisitions (again, primarily, metal and dogs). In the time they save, they gather what their farmer patrons ask for, but without any great concern for productivity. How long the farmer may have to wait for his products is not a matter of much importance to the Punan. Iron axes are slow to wear out, and dogs quick to reproduce.

The Punan, from being gatherers only for their own subsistence, have become part-time professional collectors. There is a kind of point of no return intrinsic to the first trade contacts, which, once passed, means that the Punan can never again do without commercial collecting as part of their economy, which becomes more and more dependent upon outside contacts. Parallel to the intensification of economic ties with the farmers runs a more subtle intensification of their political and cultural influence on Punan society.

At the stage envisioned here, the Punan bands are still entirely nomadic, living their traditional lives, except that they have occasional trade contacts with the farmers. Ironically, these contacts often seem to be of the type called "silent trade" or trade without contact, in which goods are exchanged in absentia, no meeting taking place between the trading partners. Only a few of the farmers, specialists in trade with the Punan, know where and when to find them. Subsequently, as they gain confidence, the Punan accept face-to-face meetings with their partners, in places and at times agreed upon in advance (days being reckoned by the knots in a strip of cane). Nevertheless, they stay deep within their remote forests, and only the above-mentioned specialists, whose help the colonial authorities would also call upon, know how to contact them (see Urquhart 1951:501).

At a third stage of interaction, as shown above, contacts intensify. A trading center may be established where the territories of the two groups meet, or, a little later, the Punan may risk descending from their hills to the first farming village. This kind of trading center corresponds to what I have called elsewhere a pivotal point (1986b:255). It is a place where cultures meet and mingle, an interface between two ethnic, economic, and cultural systems. Here a flow of population moving downward from the headwaters meets and crosses a "flow of culture" moving in the opposite direction; here the Punan bands of the interior contact peripheral bands for trade; and here alliances are formed. And it is around these trading centers that the Punan are later to plant their first crops. On balance, at this early stage of contact, the results for the Punan are beneficial. In proof one may cite the slow drift of numerous Bukat bands from the headwaters down to the trading center of Nanga Hovat, and the flow of Kereho from West Kalimantan to the trading center of Tamalue-Telusan. According to all the evidence, the Punan want to trade.

Thus, if the Punan are in effect trapped economically (and morally) in their trade relationship with the farmers, I argue that for the most part they made a deliberate decision to play the game of commercial collecting because they found it advantageous. On the whole they live better, because it is easier for them to feed themselves. A similar situation, that of some Native Americans at the beginning of the fur trade, seems to have given rise to a considerable increase in population (Kay 1984). The Penan of the upper Balui, better integrated into commercial trading networks, would seem to be more prolific than the Punan Busang, who are demographically on the road to disappearing altogether (see Huehne 1959–1960:199).

Other alternative choices would be offered to the Punan in later years (to remain nomads or start to farm; to rely on rice or to keep on collecting for the market). We shall see, first, that nuclear families and bands make their own autonomous decisions on each occasion, and second, that these decisions most often lead to maintaining or increasing the place of commercial collecting in their total economy. The economic dependence of the Punan upon the farmers brings with it, a little later and with the intensification of interaction, political dependence as well.

Development of Political Dependence

At this stage of the transition, when trading centers have been established, it may be stated, with the support of data from the literature, that the relationship between nomadic Punan and farming groups changes. From partners whose favor must be wooed, the Punan become followers, political subordinates. Indeed, we may say that at this stage the political component of this relationship becomes, not more important than the economic component, but more visible, more blatant.

It is true that this relationship is readily described as "symbiotic," a word that may describe a situation but hardly explains it. In reality, one may well call this a relationship between subjects and overlords. The abundant mentions in the older literature of Punan groups that are "under the orders" of the farmers, or over whom the farmer chiefs exercise "great power" (for example, Weddick 1849:97; Nieuwenhuis 1904–1907:II, 389), seem to me entirely valid. The same is true for notes on the types of "services" the Punan render to the farmers: they are, in turn, border guards, guides or porters for expeditions, hired henchmen for raids, and hunters of heads or slaves (see von Kessel 1857:403; Knappert 1905:604; Elshout 1926:244; Pauwels 1935: 350; and many others). These services have been mentioned above several times, and for examples we need only refer to the history of relations between the Bukat and the Kayan.

In short, as Knappert put it, the Punan are extremely useful to the farmers (1905:613). So useful, indeed, that when the farmers migrate, they are eager to bring "their" Punan along. These relationships, which some writers consider symbiotic, are described by others (for example, Rousseau, personal communication) as distinctly exploitative. In exchange, the Punan receive from the farmers what may be considered a minimal and undefined degree of protection. In some cases this protection may be military (though this apparently was very rare); more often it is political or diplomatic. It also seems that the farmers may, in cases of extreme need at a time of crisis, give the Punan some material aid (in particular, food).

How do the Punan come to be transformed from trading partners into subjects or followers? This may perhaps be best explained in economic terms. In this context, it is appropriate to see the services the Punan render to the farmers as actual presentations of service, and thus as trade goods just like forest products. If one doubts this, one has only to consider heads and slaves, very definitely marketable trade goods, which the Punan obtain in the course of raids and turn over to their backers.

Debtors in trade, the Punan agree to render these services, which, for them, have no meaning and are of no economic value. After all, if the farmers want to be paid in this way, why not? But this alone is surely not enough to explain the subordinate status of the Punan. Other factors need to be taken into consideration. An alliance with a farmer chief is morally binding on the leader of a Punan band, and if the chief asks for a free service, the Punan considers himself obliged to provide it, especially if he is the farmer's son-in-law. Besides this, it can be observed that the Punan have a certain feeling of cultural inferiority with respect to farmers (stratified farmers, in particular), reinforced by the contempt that farmers generally feel for nomads. The prestige of a farmer chief is probably enough, in certain cases, to give him all the authority he needs to obtain free gifts from the Punan (who often blame themselves afterward for not having dared to refuse). Finally, later, after a certain degree of cultural integration of the nomads (or ex-nomads) into the farmer community, the chiefs of the farmers find it easy enough to mobilize the Punan in the name of a professed common interest or common culture.

But the farmer chiefs may go too far with their manipulations and demands, and the Punan, after having grumblingly borne a great deal, may finally feel they have had enough. Thus the Punan Kohi of the Langasa, when the Uma' Suling of the Meraseh (a Kayan group) imposed upon them an excessive burden of corvée labor, left the region overnight. Other nomads elsewhere deserted their hamlets under the pressure of obligations placed on them by the colonial government, in particular the duty of sending their children to school (in the case of the Bukat) or of paying door tax (see Tillema 1934–1935:11).

It appears, then, that the political domination of the Punan by the farmers is established in part on the basis (or the pretext) of a commercial exchange, services for goods, and in part on the exploitation by the farmers of relationships of alliance and a situation of psychological ascendency. For another thing, it is probable that the colonial authorities often held farmer chiefs responsible for "their" nomads, which further legitimized their political dominance.

This political dominance by the farmers, unlike its economic equivalent, seems to be rather poorly tolerated by the Punan. To be asked to furnish services in exchange for trade goods seems to them entirely appropriate, but to have the same tasks imposed upon them without tangible reward, in the name of abstract principles, is less acceptable. It is probable that as long as they remain nomadic, the Punan will do what they can to escape the farmers' domination and to evade their demands; but they have little recourse other than their mobility. Nevertheless, they suppress their reluctance with regard to this problem of political dependence in order to give priority to their new economic activity, commercial collecting; and to do this they choose, paradoxically, to settle.

Sedentarization of the Nomads

We return now to the stage at which a trading center is established. It is a point of articulation at once territorial (a territorial interface), economic (a site of the exchange of goods), and political (a focus of alliances). Here, too, sociocultural interactions take place, and sociocultural strategies are mobilized (by the farmers) that lead to a shift, first, in the way of life of the Punan, from nomadism to agriculture and, later, in their very ethnic identity.

It would appear that more or less all over Borneo farming peoples exerted pressure on the Punan bands to make them settle around a trading center. This is what happened in the case of the Kereho and the Bukat. The Acue nomads, precursors of the Aoheng, were compelled to settle by the Long Gelat chiefs of the upper Mahakam, first by force, then through negotiation (Sellato 1986b:319). For many of the Penan groups of Sarawak, sedentarization took place through the intervention first of the farmers then of the government. This process is simplified and summed up in an example given by Seitz (1981:302): a Dusun chief of Brunei encountered a group of Penan in the 1930s, traded with them, met them regularly, obtained their allegiance, and finally, in the 1960s, got them to settle. In certain cases, the farmers went so far as to build a little village for their Punan (who still had to pay for it with forest products; Tillema 1934–1935:7). This eagerness of the farming groups to sedentarize their hunter-gatherer neighbors appears to be a common trait in the Philippines as well (see Estioko and Griffin 1975; Headland 1975; Maceda 1975; and Eder 1977, cited by Bulbeck, personal communication). We shall see below that in the minds of the farming peoples of Borneo, settling the nomads does not mean turning them into swidden farmers—far from it. It is important to keep this distinction in mind.

In the first phase of this process, the farmers, represented by a few of their men who live at the trading center with Punan wives, introduce the cultivation of bananas and cassava (or probably of other tubers in the years before cassava appeared from the Americas). Such a state of affairs is widely reported in the literature, and we shall return to it below. This is a simple type of farming, based on hardy cultigens that require little care and can be harvested all year round. At the same time a more permanent camp of huts is constructed, for use as needed. Only a few families in the band invest some of their time in this farming activity, while the others continue to live as nomads; and even those families who have taken up this type of horti- culture readily abandon their fields for months on end to go and live in the forest. These bands with a versatile economy are what the litera- ture refers to as seminomadic Punan.

In a second phase, the Punan, or at least certain families in the band, try their hand at rice cultivation. Their swiddens are small and poorly kept, and their harvests meager. But in consequence these fami- lies come to spend a greater percentage of their time in the village, though this does not keep them from going to live on sago in the forest whenever they feel the need (see Jayl Langub 1974:297; J. Nicolaisen 1976b:43; Kedit 1982:251). It is often in this phase of the beginnings of rice cultivation that the Punan build their first longhouse, modeled on those of the farmers (as the Kereho and Bukat did). It should be noted that certain groups may stop short of this second phase.

In some cases, the sedentarization of the nomads and the introduc- tion of cassava and rice are due to the intervention of the authorities, who for a variety of reasons (taking a census, raising taxes) want to gain the power to control the nomads. Adopting, curiously enough, regional standards of value, the government seeks to make the Punan conform to the norms of the farming peoples. Progress and develop- ment mean standardization on the dominant model of the farmers: rice farming to the point of self-sufficiency in food where possible, longhouse living, and all the rest. Thus numerous Punan groups were set to work in the fields under pressure from the authorities; the Hovongan were compelled to live in longhouses (van Naerssen 1951– 1952:139; at least, up to the time the Indonesian government decided to have the longhouses destroyed); and the authorities in Sarawak went so far as to build longhouses for the Penan (Kedit 1982:251). But this type of dwelling is not one that the Punan find congenial: the Punan Gang of Long Jek in Sarawak, after living in three longhouses successively, left the last in 1985 to return to separate huts (Brosius 1986:183).

The farming groups often undertook to settle the Punan on their own initiative. If the aims of the authorities were based on motives that were in large part administrative and humanitarian, what may have been the motives of the farmers? Administration was hardly their business, and they were not philanthropists. A fact of the greatest importance is noted by Bouman (1924:175): at this particular stage of a "seminomadic" mixed economy based, in proportions varying with different families, on sago, cassava, and rice, the Bukat developed a new system of sexual division of labor, in which women engaged in farm work, men in commercial collecting. This is equally true for the present-day Kajang, who have a similarly mixed economy in which 70 percent of agricultural work is done by women (I. Nicolaisen 1984: 18–19, 36, 55). This may be linked to the fact, reported by Nieuwenhuis, that at the turn of the century Punan and Bukat men married to Kayan women spent most of their time in the forest rather than in the swidden farms of their in-laws and supported their families by hunting (and, one may suppose, by commercial collecting; 1904–1907:I, 197).

I argue here that the sedentarization of the nomads represents the outcome of a commercial strategy brought to bear by the farmers in order, on the one hand, to guarantee the continuity of their supply of forest products and, on the other, to increase the productivity of the collectors. Indeed, once women, children, and the elderly settle down and begin to grow crops in the neighborhood of a trading center, the farmers can be certain that what the men collect will not be marketed elsewhere. Moreover, a mixed subsistence economy permits the men to spend a markedly higher percentage of their time in commercial collecting. While women take care of the crops, these men become true professional collectors.

It should be said that though this new situation may first arise as the result of a tactical move on the farmers' part, it is very readily accepted by the Punan, who see it as highly advantageous to themselves. Thus, as with the earliest trade contacts, one may recognize an original initiative taken by the farmers, followed by a markedly favorable response from the Punan. Their new subsistence economy, more diversified and flexible, is also more secure, and commercial collecting pays for what they need in the way of imported objects. While the Punan as subsistence hunter-gatherers prefer the advantages of nomadic living (Chapter 4), the Punan as commercial collectors favor this mixed economy incorporating a certain degree of sedentarization. For the farmers, this is the ideal state of affairs: their trade relations are dependable and permanent, bringing in a maximum return, and profits are excellent. They have the Punan close at hand if they need their services; and these Punan attract to the neighborhood other still nomadic bands, which means even more trade.

It is conceivable that the colonial government may also have tried to set up similar situations in order to penetrate a trade network and divert the trade for their own benefit (see Chapter 2 for the case of the Bukat). Later, especially in Sarawak, the authorities, on the contrary, intervened to monitor prices and protect the Punan, who were often cheated in the course of trade transactions with the farmers.

In different political circumstances, however, the Punan may abandon such a mixed economy completely to return to their former nomadic way of life. The Punan Lusong, who had begun to grow rice in 1941, went back to the forest when the Japanese arrived; not until 1961 did they settle again (Jayl Langub 1974:296–298). Similar cases occurred, as described above, among the Bukat of the Mahakam. Certain bands of Punan Murung, after their first contacts with agriculture, went off again to live in the forest, not to settle for good until over a half-century later (Sellato 1986b:286).

But there comes a time, as sociocultural interaction and mixed marriages increase, when an irreversible shift takes place from one economic system to the other. The family investment of labor in rice farming increases, as does the proportion of rice in their diet; later generations of Punan, mingling more and more with the farmers, increasingly identify with them, and fewer and fewer men devote their time to commercial collecting. This process of economic, cultural, and ultimately ethnic assimilation of nomads to farmers has been encountered on several previous occasions, among the downriver Bukat who became Kayan, the Beketan who became Iban, and most lately the Bukat of the Mahakam, who are becoming Aoheng. The nomads of the upper Barito also went through such a shift from one ethnocultural category to another, from "Ot" to "Dayak" (Sellato 1986b:255).

From being professional collectors, these Punan become farmers. If there are no other bands farther upriver to collect forest products, the supply dries up. This of course runs counter to the wishes of the original farmer groups, which see their profits melting away. The forest is then open to professional collectors brought in from the coasts or from downriver. Thus it is absolutely legitimate for Seitz to state that the farmers disapprove of Punan taking to agriculture (1981:302). Tillema reports that the chiefs of the farmers saw to it that "their" Punans remained hunter-gatherers, some, like the Segai, going so far as to spread dark tales of taboos forbidding nomads to practice agriculture (1939:138–139). The government, trying to convert the nomads to rice farming, met with opposition from the farmer chiefs (Pauwels 1935:352–353). A qualification is called for: what the farmers disapprove of is not the practice of agriculture in itself, but the possibility that the Punan might come to depend too heavily on rice. As the farmers would say, everybody knows that Punan are supposed to be collectors, and people ought to do what they are supposed to do. Besides the loss of the profits they make on forest products, the farmers are concerned about territorial claims made by Punan farmers, who tend to come settle in the lowlands; and they also fear the loss of their political control over the Punan. Thus, the ultimate consequences of the sedentarization of the nomads are the opposite of the effects of its early stages. At the start, horticulture, and even rice cultivation, combine in mixed economies in which commercial collecting achieves its greatest productivity; but once a certain degree of dietary dependence on rice is reached, rice cultivation places limits on the time available for collecting, and the flow of forest products dries up.

I believe that the farmers' strategy is to settle the Punan, for reasons amply detailed above, but not to convert them to agriculture, which runs counter to their interests. However, once the Punan reach the stage of sedentarization and early horticulture, the farmers no longer have any control over the process. And they are fated, in some cases, to see "their" Punan escape from their economic domination.

Control now, to a certain extent, belongs to the Punan themselves. They are the ones to decide whether they want to become full-time farmers or remain professional collectors in a mixed subsistence economy. Although certain groups, like the downriver Bukat, the Beketan of Sarawak, the Penan of Niah, the Seputan, and probably groups such as the Kenyah and Sebop, actually did become full-time farmers —and some of them very good ones—other groups chose to preserve mixed economic systems (see below), which guaranteed them an abundant and varied diet and allowed them to devote an optimum amount of time to commercial collecting. Among these groups are the Hovongan, the Kereho, the Punan Murung (Sellato 1986b), and certain Penan groups of Sarawak (see, in particular, Ellis 1972:240; J. Nicolaisen 1976a:213; Kedit 1982). It is noteworthy that the Hovongan, for example, have maintained this type of mixed economy from the end of the last century up to the present day and have refused to commit themselves more fully to dependence upon rice, in order to be able to keep on exploiting the commercial potential of their forests.

Conversion to Agriculture

In what has just been said, I have drawn upon the concept of an active interface between farmers and nomads, a zone of contact in which interchanges of all types take place, and also upon the concept of a pivotal point at which one type of economy, culture, and sometimes even ethnic identity shifts into another. These processes are accompanied by movements of population from the headwaters downstream, or from the forest to the lowlands, toward the pivotal point. The data presented in Chapters 2 and 3 bring, to my way of thinking, diachronic confirmation (over approximately two centuries) of the processes of the nomads' sedentarization and conversion to agriculture, processes that have been recognized and studied in Sarawak since the Second World War. We are undoubtedly dealing here with an evolutionary tendency, in operation over more than two centuries in the center of Borneo (since this tendency may most appropriately be described within specific spatial and temporal limits), which transforms fully nomadic hunter-gatherers into relatively sedentary groups dependent upon farming for an appreciable proportion of their food. There is absolutely no suggestion here of a general, planetwide evolutionary process conducing hunter-gatherers to take up agriculture; I am speaking here only of an evolutionary tendency at a regional level. It should also be recalled that these processes of conversion have been linked to the appearance of commercial collecting in the nomad economy.

Here I wish to reiterate my categorical dismissal of the notion of a formal and absolute opposition, in Borneo, between nomads and rice farmers. The cultivation of rice in swidden clearings or irrigated fields is in no sense the most sophisticated or the most reliable, efficient, or intrinsically superior form of agriculture in Borneo, and it should not be taken to be the ultimate goal of every conversion to agriculture. There has been some discussion in the literature of the cultivation of tubers and fruit trees as a possible "intermediate stage" in this conversion. Although it has happened that certain groups have lived for some time in a subsistence economy based on tubers, that does not mean that this is a necessary stage in the process of shifting from hunting and gathering to rice farming.

I intend to show, in the case of the Punan and other formerly nomadic groups, that there exists a continuum of economic systems displaying a variety of combinations of rice farming, horticulture, gathering, and hunting. These systems are not adulterated or transitional forms lined up between two polar opposites, nomadic hunting-gathering and rice monoculture, but are stable and functional in themselves. Certain groups have chosen and persisted in one or another of these flexible and reliable systems in order to keep on collecting for the market. I also intend to argue, to further support my refutation of an opposition between nomads and rice farmers, that in the past there were societies of sedentary horticulturalists, sophisticated in culture and technology, who occupied significant territories in the center of Borneo.

Before turning to this subject, I shall touch upon the modes of adoption of horticulture and rice farming in Punan societies undergoing the conversion to agriculture. But it should first be stressed that, according to some sources, certain nomad groups who have long been in contact with stratified farmers nevertheless, up to a short time ago, practiced no form of agriculture (the Punan Kelai, see Simandjuntak 1967: 40; the Punan Malinau, see Marcus 1970:70; and some bands in Sarawak).

Horticulture

One of the first points to be taken into account in a discussion of horticulture concerns the sago palm. It is known that, in general, the nomads "manage" the wild sago groves so that they can use them again within the shortest possible period of time (see Sellato 1986b: 261). This type of stewardship already stands at the boundary between gathering and horticulture: it has been called "protected gathering" (see Haudricout and Hédin 1987). Besides this, it is known that there are some interior groups, former nomads or long-term farmers, who cultivate sago palms, among them the Kenyah (T.A.D. 1981:20), the Modang (Guerreiro 1984:246), the Berawan (Metcalf 1982), and the Kajang (I. Nicolaisen 1984), not to mention those who intensively farm the lowland palm *Metroxylon* (Kajang and Melanau, and some groups of the lower Barito). Indeed, it has been reported that some Penan groups have begun to plant sago palms, in particular *Eugeissona* (Kedit 1982:235), which is apparently not hard to do. It should be noted, and this is an important point, that sago was found to have a ratio of energy return to labor (in kcal/hour) around two to four times as high as hill rice (see Strickland 1986:131–132).

Nevertheless, the yield of mountain sago palms is low and their cycle of growth relatively long, and if the band no longer travels through the forest in search of food, it will soon have to acquire other cultigens with a higher yield and a shorter cycle of growth (see Sellato 1986b:261).

Among the yams and their relatives, certain tubers, the Dioscorea (*Dioscorea* spp.) are known to grow wild in the forests of Borneo. Although no study specifically mentions their being eaten by the Punan, some early writers report that the Punan eat "roots" (for example, Molengraaff 1900:196; 1902:187). It would be highly surprising if an edible were to exist in the forest that the Punan do not know about and do not eat. Three species of Dioscorea are gathered by the Moken sea nomads of south Thailand (Ivanoff 1985). Besides this, it is possible that at a time already far in the past the Punan may have recognized and learned to make use of the ability of tubers to grow from fragments. According to Bellwood (1983:74), tubers are commonly replanted among many groups of hunter-gatherers. It should, however, be noted that these tubers have a far lower caloric value than sago (a hundred or so calories per hundred grams, compared to 350 or 400 for sago; see T.A.D. 1981). Unearthing these deeply buried tubers may call for as much labor as the extraction of sago, and this for a food lower in caloric value; the nomads' motivation for undertaking the cultivation of these tubers is therefore not likely to be very high.

But the introduction of cassava (manioc, *Manihot utilissima,* native to South and Central America) into central Borneo, at an unspecified date, was to offer the ideal cultigen to nomads in the process of settling. And in the early stages of Punan sedentarization, it is most often upon cassava that they base their agriculture and the portion of their diet that comes from farming (Nieuwenhuis 1907:123; Sulaiman 1968:29; Jayl Langub 1972:220, 1974:298; J. Nicolaisen 1976a: 208). The Penan Gang of Long Jek, who settled in 1969, began by planting cassava irregularly over three or four years (Brosius 1986). This is probably what happened among the Punan Murung (Sellato 1986b:260). Associated with cassava, in these first stages, is the banana, another high-yield and short-cycle cultigen (see, for example, Tillema 1939:139, for the Punan of the Tubu and of Sambaliung).

Cassava and the different species and varieties of bananas are extremely easy to plant, require little care, can be harvested all year round, and do not exhaust soil fertility (see Seitz 1981:301). For a minimal investment of labor (a little clearing of the ground to begin with, a little weeding from time to time), people get a stable supply of food. There is no need to schedule farm work in advance, no need to save seed. Moreover, cassava flour (tapioca) can be cooked as a paste not unlike sago, and cassava leaves are also eaten as a vegetable.

Among other cultigens in these early stages of sedentarization, one may note a domesticated species of Dioscorea *(Dioscorea alata)*, taro *(Colocasia esculenta)*, other plants of American origin such as the sweet potato *(Ipomoea batatas)*, corn or maize *(Zea mais)* and sugar cane, and vegetables such as gourds or squash and leaf greens similar to spinach. Job's tears *(Coix lacryma Jobi* L.), an ancient cultigen, may perhaps also be added to the list, though little is known about its presence in Borneo.

Along with tubers and vegetables, the Punan plant fruit trees. Among these in particular may be mentioned the jackfruit *(Artocarpus heterophyllus)*, whose large fruit has a high caloric value, and the durian, the rambutan, the mango, and others, of which wild varieties exist. Fruit trees no doubt require even less work than tubers. Indeed, it is possible that the Punan planted fruit seeds and thus developed wild orchards in the hills even before they settled. Urquhart mentions Bukitan, Ukit, and Sian orchards in the mountains (1951:496). Orchards were planted by the Bukat, as mentioned above, and also by the Punan Murung (Sellato 1986b:227).

Thus a first type of mixed economy is established, based in part on horticulture and in part on wild sago, which provides increased food reliability for a lesser output of time and energy than does an economy based exclusively upon the exploitation of wild sago. As J. Nicolaisen notes (1976a:213), some Punan seem to think that a combination of hunting and gathering with the cultivation of cassava and bananas around a fixed settlement is an easier way of life than hunting and gathering alone. Once they find themselves in this economic situation, itself attractive and functional in that it permits them to spend significant amounts of time in commercial collecting, the Punan have available the option of starting to cultivate rice.

Rice growing has undeniable drawbacks for the Punan: it is a major investment of labor for long-term results, entailing advance scheduling of activities and the storage of seed grains, the need for their full-time presence on the site at certain times of year, the use of a technology less rudimentary than that required for tubers; also, Punan dislike of the taste of rice. More crucially, rice cultivation cuts into the time they can spend in commercial collecting. There is no doubt that this last

factor has contributed to the refusal of numerous families—if not of
entire groups—to turn to rice farming, and to the persistence of what
we shall call the cassava-sago economy.

Rice Cultivation

Alongside the cassava-sago economy, other types of mixed
economies may be found that combine one or the other of these two
staples, or both of them, with rice in varying proportions. Among the
factors that make Punan reluctant to cultivate rice, we have mentioned
the need for advance planning, which the rice cycle requires: scheduling work and setting aside and storing seed grain are difficult tasks for
the Punan, whose hunting-gathering economy is oriented toward
immediate consumption rather than careful, long-term investment. It
is quite credible that the Punan would find themselves at a disadvan-
tage in this regard. The amount of work they have to do and the new
technology they have to learn are minor problems; the Punan are neither indolent nor incompetent and seem able to adapt easily enough to
these practical requirements. But advance planning represents a radi-
cal change in their way of thinking about their economy and their life
in general.

A factor worthy of note is the lack of interest, even aversion, that
Punan have for rice as a food. It has been said that the Bukat, even
today, do not much care for rice. Harrisson reports that the Punan eat
rice only reluctantly (1949:143; see also Urquhart 1951:532–533).
The Penan of Niah refused to eat it before they settled (Sandin 1957:
135). The Kejaman and the Punan Bah made only small swidden
farms, but cultivated palm trees and showed a distinct preference for
sago (Low 1882). It appears that the taste for sago, perhaps because of
this aversion to rice, was sometimes transposed into a taste for cassava, as happened with some groups of the upper Rejang (see Seitz
1981:301). Indeed, cassava in some of its culinary aspects is very similar to sago. This aversion to rice serves to underline once again, if it
were necessary, the improbability of a "devolutionary" origin for the
Punan. However, it did not prevent them from eating the farmers' rice
in the absence of anything better, when they came to trade in the farmers' villages (as the Bukat did).

In any case, certain Punan groups did begin to cultivate rice. An
important factor in this choice is undoubtedly the presence of men
from the farming groups married to Punan women and living in the
trading centers. These men, often the sons-in-law of band leaders,

sometimes become leaders in these hamlets and farm rice for themselves and their families, or indeed impose the practice upon the entire community.

It was noted above (in the discussion of the Bukat) that nuclear families involved in agriculture and others which are still nomadic may coexist within the same band, and that even within the nuclear family a wife may mind small swidden fields while her husband ranges the forest seeking products for the market (see Bouman 1924:175). Thus within a single band may exist every possible combination of two or three of the economic staples, rice, cassava, and sago. This, indeed, is what studies of the Punan show. The percentage of dietary dependence upon rice is extremely variable. The Penan Gang of Long Jek remain dependent upon sago for nine months out of the year (Brosius 1986:174, 179). And J. Nicolaisen reports that most of the Penan families who cultivate rice obtain barely enough to feed themselves for two to five months after the harvest (1976a:208; see also Kedit 1982: 252). Bouman makes a similar remark with regard to the Bukat of the Mendalam (1924), and the same point has been noted above for the Kereho. Enthoven, for the Bukitan (1903:66), and Schneeberger, for the Punan of the Merah and Belayan (1933:11), find that although the nomads learn to farm, a high proportion of them continue to eat sago and hunt.

Indeed, Punan swidden fields are often very small and poorly cared for, left to themselves after sowing; Punan who come back for the harvest find only what pests have left them. This lack of interest and investment in labor and care derives from the fact that farming is in direct competition with commercial collecting. Punan families for whom commercial collecting has become an economic priority have adapted their dietary economy to facilitate it, and efforts to maximize the productivity of their rice fields would be a serious hindrance to collecting.

Punan who cultivate rice therefore content themselves with small clearings and small harvests, which most often offer them less than half a year of self-sufficiency in rice. I argue here that this is evidence not of incompetence in rice farming but, on the contrary, of an economic strategy. We may examine the case of the Hovongan. At the turn of the century, the Hovongan lived in an economic system based on sago, cassava, and rice; they farmed small swiddens, which they abandoned between sowing and harvest, and wild sago remained their staple food (Nieuwenhuis 1900b:189, 1904–1907; Enthoven 1903:

85). For this reason Nieuwenhuis considers them, as a group, transitional between nomadic Bukat and farmers. In 1980 this system still functions, even if the relative proportions of the three staples have changed a little in favor of rice. The Hovongan have at their disposal an immense hunting-gathering territory, and still live in the forest several months a year.

We may note the possible existence of a sago-rice system, with no significant presence of cassava in the diet. The Kereho of the Busang may indeed have turned from sago to rice, with the help of their Seputan neighbors, and no mention is made of cassava in their history. Currently, however, their economic system is based on all three staples. It appears that certain Penan groups of the Mulu region also live in a sago-rice system (see Kedit 1982). The Punan Murung probably had a cassava-sago system, later abandoning sago and developing the cassava-rice system by which they live today (Sellato 1986b: 240, 260).

Some writers appear concerned to establish the average time required for a conversion from sago to rice. Thus J. Nicolaisen calculates that a "complete change from one type of economy to the other" would take at least thirty years (1976a:228), and Seitz thinks that at a more recent date this economic changeover would take less than a decade (1981:302). Such an effort is irrelevant. First, one may suppose that so complete a shift in the economy would mean achieving total self-sufficiency in rice. Among the groups I have studied, the Bukat, more than fifty years after the introduction of rice farming, are only about 50 percent self-sufficient in rice; the Punan Murung let a hundred and fifty years pass between their first direct contact with agriculture and their abandonment of sago as a food source, and, after a half-century of rice farming, are still for the most part far from self-sufficient; and the Kereho, after eighty years, still depend in large part on wild sago.

Some nomad groups, like the Penan of Niah (Sandin 1957), undeniably have become rice farmers. However, it is appropriate to regard with caution the case of other Penan groups in Sarawak, of whom it is too readily said that they have "converted completely to rice farming." Nothing could be more doubtful, since, engaged as they are in commercial collecting, and therefore to some degree in nomadic living, they must by necessity turn to sago for some of their subsistence. In any case, the heavy pressures exerted on them by the authorities should be taken into account. All this leads me to argue that if these

Punan groups have not yet achieved self-sufficiency in rice, despite a half-century or a century of experience in rice farming and the pressures upon them, it is simply because they have not wanted to. Those who have wanted to, like the Lugat assimilated into the Aoheng, have reached this state of self-sufficiency within two generations (Sellato 1986b:394).

I conclude, therefore, that of these groups who have begun to cultivate rice, a high proportion have chosen not to commit themselves to an intensive involvement in this activity. These Punan have integrated rice into a mixed subsistence system, in which it coexists with cassava and/or sago. Such a system, at once flexible and dependable, permits them to continue with commercial collecting. In the case of the Kereho, we have analyzed the factors instrumental in the development of this type of mixed system, in particular, the incompatibility between the political pressures that favor sedentarization and rice farming, and the economic pressures of the commercial demand for forest products. The Kereho have indeed settled, more or less, and taken to cultivating a little rice, but they have maintained their mobility and the flexibility of their subsistence economy as a whole.

An important factor in the economic choices made by the Punan is their own awareness, on a local scale, of their exclusive monopoly of commercial collecting. We may now note a difference related to the type of social structure characteristic of the farming groups that are the neighbors of the nomads under consideration. Where the farmers' society is egalitarian, members of the group will themselves engage in commercial collecting, thereby entering into direct economic competition with the nomads. Finding themselves deprived of their exclusive right to collect forest products, the nomads then have a choice between leaving the region or joining these collectors in the exploitation of the territory. If they choose to join them, they will soon come to be integrated into this farming group—all the more rapidly since the group's social organization easily accepts outsiders—and will become farmers and move altogether into another ethnocultural category (cases in point are the Sru and the Beketan of the Rejang, assimilated to the Iban; the Punan Murung; and perhaps the Bukit of the Meratus).

On the other hand, nomads who have a trading relationship with a group of farmers with a stratified social structure can be secure in their exclusive control of commercial collecting, simply because these farm-

ers generally do not collect forest products; their chiefs have claimed
for themselves the monopoly of trade and are intent on preserving
their source of revenue. Besides this, stratified societies do not permit
the easy integration of a group of outsiders. Thus the nomads will
maintain their economic preserve and also their way of life. If they settle, it will be in a separate village; and they will maintain a distinct
identity. (This is the case with most of the Punan groups associated
with the stratified Kayan, Kenyah, and Modang groups of the center
of the island.) The social and ideological aspects of this factor of geographical proximity will be examined more fully below. We should
note that this phenomenon of persisting separate identities appears not
only where nomads are in contact with stratified societies of the Kayan
type, but also in relations between the stratified Maloh and the Beketan, and even between the Punan Batu and the sultanate of Berau. It is
linked, therefore, with a social context of which inequality and exploitation are salient characteristics (monopolization of trade, or at least
of the profits of trade, by the dominant social category).

A discussion of agriculture would be incomplete without a word
about domestic animals. It is frequently reported that the Punan lack
interest in domestic animals or any taste for their meat (Harrisson
1949:143; Huehne 1959–1960:202; Seitz 1981:303). With regard to
their need for proteins of animal origin, the Punan have no use for
these animals, as they get all they require by hunting. Besides this, the
constraints of stock-rearing would limit their mobility: it is not possible to herd animals through the forest. Some groups of settled Punan
raise chickens, and some (the Bukat) even rear a few head of cattle,
but these animals are generally raised to be sold or, more rarely, sacrificed, rather than specifically to be eaten.

Stable Mixed Economic Systems

The Punan have chosen to give priority in their economy to
commercial collecting. They have become professional collectors.
This priority is expressed in a specific adaptation of their subsistence
system, which permits flexibility and mobility while at the same time
guaranteeing them their daily food, and consequently in a refusal to
invest more time in an activity, such as rice farming, that would
restrict their mobility. J. Nicolaisen's remark is appropriate here:
"There is good reason to believe that the more Penan turn to rice farming the less time they will have for hunting, for collecting rotan . . ."
(1976b:54). Nevertheless, it does appear that, up to a certain percent-

age of dependence on rice (25 percent, or 50?), the relationship of the investment of time (and labor) to the amount of food produced is about the same in rice farming as it is in the cultivation of tubers, and rice may without risk be integrated into a subsistence system based on three staples, as the cases of the present-day Hovongan and Kereho show.

J. Nicolaisen suggested that the Sarawak government permit the semisettled Penan to continue basing their subsistence on cassava, bananas, and fruit trees, instead of urging them to farm rice (1976b: 54). This suggestion should be qualified: of the three basic staples, rice, cassava, and sago, any sufficiently flexible combination is viable. Moreover, according to Seitz himself, even among the Punan he characterizes as "definitively sedentary," families periodically leave to spend some time in the forest, living on sago and wild pig, and this economic combination gives most sedentary families a certain security (1981:304). This suggests that these Punan are not self-sufficient in rice, and that they, too, live in a mixed economy (see my remarks above on those Penan groups of Sarawak supposed to have "completely converted" to rice farming).

A more extreme case is that of the Kenyah and the Sebop, among whom families may go off to range the forest for periods of two or three years, living only on sago and game (Urquhart 1957:114; 1959: 73). This strange phenomenon can be explained, no doubt, by the fact that these ethnic groups were once nomadic, and it shows that, even after two centuries of intensive rice farming, hunting and gathering remains an acceptable economic alternative, not only a recourse in times of famine. Moreover, it is these same Kenyah who cultivate the *Eugeissona* palm and maintain wild palm groves (T.A.D. 1981:20).

As an example, I would like to give here a brief summary of a remarkable study by I. Nicolaisen (1984) of the Kajang of Sarawak. The Kajang, a composite ethnic group probably made up at least in part of former nomads (see I. Nicolaisen 1976:76), have lived for at least the past century in a mixed economic system, combining rice farming, hunting and fishing, gathering for food, and commercial collecting. Sago, extracted from palms both cultivated (*Metroxylon,* imported from downriver) and wild, accounts for 35 percent of their diet and has as much social prestige as rice. The rice fields are rather small, but the palm groves are managed in such a way that they provide a large and constant supply of sago. This economy, tending to center on immediate consumption, is flexible and permits an extensive use of the territory, offering optimal conditions for agriculture, gathering, hunting, and fishing. The flexibility of this mode of subsistence permits the Kajang to devote a good part of their time to commercial collecting and other remunerative occupations. This is not a case of an incomplete conversion to agriculture, but of a particular form of ecological adaptation and specific economic priorities.

This summary brings out many of the ideas expressed above in relation to the Punan. The Kajang economy is indeed a specific form of mixed subsistence economy whose flexibility accommodates a significant proportion of commercial collecting. It is stable but not rigid, capable of change, and it allows the Kajang to keep their options open with regard to possible modern opportunities, such as wage labor.

The types of mixed economy found among the Kajang, the Hovongan, and the Kereho represent, in my opinion, highly refined systems developed and perfected over long periods of time. A mixed economy offers undeniable advantages over a rice monoculture: its diversification provides greater reliability of diet, whereas the rice harvest may fail and so endanger the subsistence of the rice-farming family; commercial collecting offers an integration on more advantageous terms into local networks of trade; and the flexibility of the system, finally, allows for a more efficient response to opportunities presented by the modern world (short-term wage labor, for instance), while rice farmers are chained to their work in the fields.

It is clear, to reiterate, that the development of such systems originated in the commercial demand for forest products and in the conscious choice made by these ethnic groups to respond to this demand by changing the orientation of their economy to give priority to commercial collecting.

To conclude this discussion of the conversion to agriculture as it relates to commercial collecting, a summary of the process may be proposed. Nomadic Punan, before the introduction of iron, gathered only for their own subsistence, having no time to collect for others and possibly no contact with farmers for whom to collect. Once they have iron tools, these nomadic Punan find themselves with free time, which they choose to devote to commercial collecting in response to the demands of downriver markets. To be able to give more time to this new activity, they opt for partial sedentarization and the development of mixed subsistence economies, stable and flexible, integrating certain forms of agriculture (horticulture and/or rice farming). Finally, those Punan who (often for "external" political reasons) become most dependent upon rice have to make a drastic reduction in their commercial collecting activities. The Punan, like their farmer neighbors and patrons, apparently have every interest, given the intense demand for forest products, in perfecting and preserving their strategies of mixed subsistence, which allow them to make their commercial collecting as productive as possible.

Horticultural Societies

It must first be specified that at the present state of our knowledge, all that follows in this section belongs to the realm of speculative history. A set of convergent indications, which are not proofs, guide the outlines of these speculations, and it would be a mistake to see in them anything more than working hypotheses and suggestions for future research.

I have written elsewhere of the Pin, that major ethnic group lost in the mists of the past, related to the Ot Danum of the Barito and occupying the upper Mahakam before the invasion of the Kayan groups in the second half of the eighteenth century; there I developed the hypothesis of a culture based on the cultivation of tubers, a "tuber culture" (Sellato 1986b:395–396). Certain historical indications do lead one to believe that these Pin, and perhaps also the former Siang and the Ot Danum of the Barito (1986b:256), were not familiar with rice farming. Other indications suggest that the Pin societies were fairly loosely organized, unstratified, and unwarlike, but that they possessed a sophisticated technology (smelting of iron ore, stone sculpture, pottery, weaving, fish-farming) and highly elaborate rituals, in particular funeral ceremonies, including secondary treatment of the bones and the great festival *pengosang* (1986b:408, 410–411). Some of these cultural traits suggest a possible relationship of the Pin with the Ngaju culture area, and more markedly with the culture of present-day Ot Danum. It therefore appears that these ethnic groups, which have been called Barito groups and whose culture extends over a large part of the southern half of Borneo and well into the Kapuas River basin and the middle Mahakam, once also occupied the upper Mahakam. I have chosen to call this ancient set of cultures the "Barito Complex."

On the arbitrary criterion of a combination of two cultural traits that seem to me to be diagnostic, first an economy based in large part on horticulture (that is, an economy of sedentary farmers, but lacking rice), and, second, complex funerary rituals (including cremation, or secondary treatment of the bones, or at least the defleshing of the body), I propose to take a look at some ethnic groups of the northern half of Borneo that have been the subject of published studies, and that seem to me to be of much interest. These two cultural traits are, in themselves, distinctive enough to bring out a contrast between the ethnic groups of the Barito Complex (including those briefly described below) and groups related to the Kayan, masters of rice farming. A third trait, relating to social organization, may also be examined. As I have tried to show in another publication (1987), the social organization of the Barito groups is more or less hierarchized, but not stratified, which it is both in ideology and in practice among the Kayan and related groups. I believe that the joint study of these three cultural traits in historical perspective will show considerable consistency, and thus help to support my hypothesis. Besides this, one should not exclude the possibility that the megalithic tradition known in certain regions of the island is associated with the same cultural context.

The Berawan of the Baram, in Sarawak, base their present-day economy on swidden rice, but are apparently far from being self-sufficient in rice; they rely to a great extent upon sago, which they take from palms cultivated close to the villages, and upon cassava. They seem to have become rice farmers more recently than their neighbors, and possess few rituals associated with rice. Hunting, fishing, and gathering in the forest play an important role. The funeral rituals of the Berawan seem to be extremely complex, at least for certain individuals. The body, in a coffin or a jar, is placed first in a grave hut; then, one or several years later, a second festival takes place in the course of which the bones may be cleaned and finally deposited in a larger edifice, a mausoleum (these data are taken from Metcalf 1982).

The Melanau are largely Islamicized societies of Sarawak's coastal regions. Although they grow rice, their economy relies to an almost equal extent upon cultivated sago palms *(Metroxylon)*, and on hunting, fishing, and the collection of marketable forest products (rattan, gutta-percha, resins, wax, and camphor). They are fully integrated into regional commercial networks, exporting not only these products but also their sago. These societies are stratified, in the manner of the Kayan, and the bones of a deceased aristocrat were subjected to secondary interment, being deposited in a great jar on a pillar of ironwood (this from Morris 1978 and 1983).

The Kajang were discussed above, and their economy described, on the basis of data from I. Nicolaisen (1984). They practice secondary treatment of the bones of the dead in a manner similar to the Melanau, making use of enormous carved pillars. These ancient funeral rituals, as among the Berawan, are considered part of these groups' particular cultural heritage and serve as symbols of their ethnic identity.

The historical connections between Kajang and Melanau are amply proven (see Morris 1978:37, de Martinoir 1974), and correlations between Kajang and Berawan have been proposed (Metcalf 1975; it is in part to this stimulating little article that I owe the origin of these remarks). Metcalf lists ethnic groups that practice secondary treatment of the bones of the dead (1975:57). Besides the groups already cited, he includes the Kelabit, the Lun Bawang and the Lun Dayeh, the Tring, and the Punan Bah (a subgroup of the Kajang). He suggests the existence of a "*nulang* arc" (so called from the name of this ceremony among the Berawan) extending across Sarawak, and considers that the ethnic groups in question represent an ancient cultural substratum in the north of Borneo. He draws a parallel with Ngaju culture, but does not appear to connect his *nulang* arc with the south of Borneo. This correlation is, however, suggested by de Martinoir (1974:268), who classes all these Sarawak groups with the Ngaju, an idea first proposed by Leach (1948).

Other, more widely scattered cultural traits seem to reconfirm the bonds between the *nulang* arc of northern Borneo and our Barito Complex. These Sarawak groups have almost certainly borrowed their system of social stratification from the Kayan groups, but the Kajang seem to have preserved through this borrowing something of an ideal of egalitarianism, since the common people may depose their aristocratic leader for incompetence, return power to the hands of a council of commoner elders, and even leave the village to express their disagreement (I. Nicolaisen 1984:16, 50), all of which would be highly exceptional in Kayan societies. This process of the control of leadership by the people strongly recalls the political system of the Aoheng (described in Sellato 1986b:403 and 1992b), who subverted, under the influence of their Pin elements, the stratified system borrowed from their Kayan protectors. The Berawan say that headhunting was not part of their culture (Metcalf 1982:27). Similarly, the Pin are described by the Aoheng of today as peaceable people whose customs went so far as to forbid the killing of human beings. Finally, the paraphernalia of secondary treatment of the dead, and even its terminology, are curiously similar in the northern *nulang* arc and the southern Barito Complex. I will not go into detail here, but this point deserves intensive investigation, as do the linguistic connections between these Kajang, Melanau, Berawan, and other northern languages and the languages of the Barito groups.

I suggest therefore, in conclusion to these remarks, that all the above-mentioned societies belonged to a major set of cultures of unstratified horticulturalists, possessing an elaborate technology and system of religion. This culture complex extended over a very great portion of Borneo, predating both the cultures of the stratified rice farmers (the Kayan type) and perhaps also the Malayo-Ibanic set of cultures of the west.

What is the place of the Punan in this picture? They were very early associates of the horticulturalists. A certain number of groups, Acue, Punan Murung, Seputan, Kereho, and Hovongan, were in contact with the various Pin and Ot Danum groups of the Mahakam and Barito (Sellato 1986b). The Beketan, Bukat, and other Lisum, for their part, were in contact with the horticulturalists of the Rejang River (some of whom would contribute to the formation of the Kajang).

Certain nomad groups joined with some of the horticulturalists to become composite ethnic groups, among which some developed mixed economies (the Kajang-Melanau and the Hovongan, for example), while others (the Aoheng and the Seputan; Sellato 1986b) came to depend upon rice under the influence of their rice-farming neighbors. Other nomads remained nomadic but maintained close connections with the former horticulturalists. It is, no doubt, for this reason that some of the Bukitan, neighbors of the Kajang, and the Punan Benalui, neighbors of the Lun Dayeh, practiced secondary treatment of the dead. Finally, some nomad bands, who have remained in extreme isolation much longer than others—like the Bukat, the Kereho, and certain Penan groups of Sarawak—today offer us a perspective on the traditional culture of the hunter-gatherers. I therefore suggest that in the history of Borneo there existed at least three independent traditional cultures: nomads, horticulturalists, and stratified rice farmers. A culture of unstratified rice farmers (of the Iban type) developed in the western part of the island, possibly out of the culture of the horticulturalists.

For the moment, I shall go into no further detail about these speculations. I believe, nevertheless, that they form a reasonably credible hypothesis, offering a new interpretation of the history of economic and social systems in Borneo; but it is clear that an immense amount of work remains to be done before this can be anything more than a hypothesis. Our knowledge of Borneo societies is in dire need of basic ethnographic studies.

Social Changes

As long as the Punan bands remain nomadic, their social interactions with the farmers are limited to contacts in the course of trade. With the establishment of trading centers, these interactions markedly intensify, including an increasing number of intermarriages. At this point, social conditions are established that give the farmers the power to place the Punan in a position of political dependence. These same conditions are the starting point for the process of assimilation of the nomads to their neighbors.

From the time of the first intermarriages, there is a perceptible imbalance in social relations between nomads and farmers. The farmers display a certain contempt for the savages they consider the nomads to be, and there is no reported instance of a woman from a farming group going to live with her nomadic Punan husband (see J. Nicolaisen 1976b:41). This point has been discussed in relation to the Bukat. A certain number of cases are reported in which Punan gave their daughters to farmers in marital alliances, but apparently more frequent were those in which farmer men would go to live with their Punan wives. Unwilling or unable to lead the nomadic life, they settle with their families at the trading center. There they create the nucleus of a village, and there they farm (as noted for the Kereho).

Thus these men from the farming groups, often the sons-in-law of band leaders, play an initiatory role in Punan society (see Seitz 1981: 297). Sometimes they themselves, or their children, become headmen of the hamlet that is forming. Several examples of this process have been noted above.

This core hamlet, center of trade and agricultural activities, quickly becomes a magnet for the nomadic families of the band and for other neighboring bands. The headman of the hamlet thus often acquires a status superior to that of the leaders of bands. He mediates the relations between nomads and farmers and plays an important role in the farmers' political domination and in the acculturation of the nomads. He also mediates commercial exchanges, appropriating to himself the role of middleman, a role he can exploit to his own profit. Moreover, in certain cases, he becomes the representative before the government authorities of his semisettled band and other still nomadic bands of the region. At this pivotal point that is the trading center, a variety of social changes begin to appear, gradually diffusing among those still nomadic bands farther upstream who are beginning to feel the pull of this magnetic site.

Residence Patterns, Ownership, Territoriality

From making forest camps, temporary shelter for a night or a month, the Punan turn to building huts that form a little hamlet. These are more solid, permanent structures, but they are inhabited no more than a few weeks or a few months per year, depending on whether the families or the band come only to trade or also to farm a little. Although the hut remains the property of the family who built it or, more generally, of the band to which this family belongs, it still stands empty and abandoned for a good part of the year, and no ritual seems to be associated with its construction or its occupation. Such a hut shelters an extended family when its members come to stay in the village, and no longer only a nuclear family.

By the time that all the families of the local group (no longer to be called a band) have come to depend in part on agriculture, its residence pattern may include, as for the Kereho, three types of habitation: a core village of huts built to last (of impervious ironwood), isolated farm huts, and temporary forest camps. In certain cases, and often under outside influence, some groups (the Bukat, for example) build a longhouse. These dwellings (huts or apartments) are the absolute and inheritable property of the extended families, who leave their belongings there (including the value objects, gongs and jars, which make up their estate), and they are the setting for family rituals (borrowed from the farmers). Each household is in principle represented in the political and ritual life of the hamlet, but it is not rare for the hamlet to be all but deserted, families being off in the forest or on long journeys, and this representation is then purely nominal.

With the acquisition of social stratification and the achievement of self-sufficiency in rice, the longhouse becomes the legal and ritual center of the community and the permanent home of all its families. The affiliation of individuals to the household, by birth, marriage, or adoption, is subject to strict and definite rules, and so is the affiliation of the household to the longhouse. The permanence and continuity of the household as a corporate body, and of its social, political, and ritual status, must be secured, and the transmission of goods and status is similarly regulated by *adat,* or customary law.

To what degree residence is permanent is a function of the group's way of life and economic system. As the density of residence increases, and to a still greater extent as social stratification is adopted, the residential unit becomes the extended family rather than the nuclear family as in the past, and the affiliation of this unit to the wider community is strengthened ("closure of the group," in Rousseau's phrase, 1985:41), as is its political and ritual presence and role within the community.

So far as subsistence is concerned, it has been shown that wild groves of sago palms and other food resources of the forest are not the focus of any concept of private property (except in "modern" contexts; see, for example, Brosius 1986:175–176). As soon as farming appears, this type of collective property ceases to exist, and swidden fields, cultivated sago palms, and fruit trees become the private property of the family that cleared or planted them. Each family works to fulfill its own needs, and interfamilial cooperation diminishes (see Seitz 1981:302), to the point that it may become, as among the Aoheng, an exchange of labor with accounts strictly kept.

Similarly, the profits of commercial collecting are apparently the property of the collector and will be divided among the men who go out as a group to collect together. In no way do these profits become the collective property of the band, at least among semisettled groups. However, certain forms of redistribution persist among relatives or neighbors, with regard to the products of hunting or fishing.

It seems reasonable to conclude that the practice of collective ownership exists only within the limited context of the exploitation of wild resources for food, and disappears as soon as exploitation involves marketable goods or cultivated food resources. It seems also to disappear at a certain stage of sedentarization, at which even game and fish cease to be shared out equally in a process of generalized exchange. When, with rice farming, the economy is reoriented toward the storage of foodstuffs, it is probable that the concept of private property becomes still more marked.

With the intensification of contact with the farmers, as described earlier, the concept of territory becomes more precise and better defined, geographically and legally. As commercial collecting develops, the Punan, under the influence of their farmer patrons, become conscious of the need to take up arms to defend the marketable resources of their territory against rival collectors. Nevertheless, this defense strategy consists only of brief responses by separate bands to specific threats, leading to no concerted resistance to their enemies. Apparently it is only after these societies have attained a certain degree of cohesion, involving a regrouping in villages, the acquisition of agriculture, and perhaps social stratification, that one may observe organized, armed defensive responses.

The territory of Punan groups who have become sedentary farmers is composed of their ancestral territories, redefined or formally confirmed de jure, and/or territories acquired or bought from neighboring farmers. In every case, and particularly among those groups with mixed economic systems, this territory is physically occupied, frequently traversed, and extensively exploited, and is based upon a concept of collective property whose guardians are the leaders (or the aristocrats). This concept of territory is reinforced in modern times by administrative apportionments.

Social Organization

In the course of the process of sedentarization, the hamlet that is the trading center and pivotal point gathers to it a population generally greater than that of the average band. Indeed, the hamlet drains families from other bands still living as nomads upriver. Sometimes several bands settle in the village at the same time (see Seitz 1981: 299). Moreover, farmers live there for short periods or settle there as the result of intermarriages. This dual aspect of the new community, its increase in size and heterogeneity, is the source of a number of agents of social transformation: the reduction of band endogamy, the decline in collective activities and traditions of sharing resources, and the emergence of a new form of leadership.

A greater blending of population, and the concomitant presence of different bands, extends the range of potential marriage partners, in other bands or among farmer neighbors. Band endogamy loses ground not only in practice but also as an ideal. First, the hamlet, this new community, gradually replaces the band as a residential and political unit, and hamlet endogamy replaces band endogamy in the group's ideology. Besides this, the extended family has replaced the nuclear family as a minimal residential unit, and the hut of the settled Punan now shelters an average of ten people: an older couple, several children and their husbands or wives, and grandchildren (see Jayl Langub 1972:220). At the same time, in connection with this new residential pattern and under the influence of neighboring farmers, the concept of incest is broadened and made more precise. It becomes linked to residence: two first cousins, who might have been able to marry in the nomad band, are no longer able to do so in the setting of the village, because they have lived in the same hut as children and are therefore looked upon, from the farmer point of view, as siblings. In the same way, a marriage with an uncle or aunt becomes undesirable. This extension of the definition of incest, limiting the number of potential partners, favors ethnic and cultural intermingling.

The newly married couple, who in the nomadic band would soon have set up their nuclear family in a neolocal residence, now more often live utrolocally, moving into the hut of either spouse's parents. Residence with parents seems to develop in particular in the context of longhouse living, which slows down the establishment of neolocal cells. Among some groups, under the influence of farmer neighbors, the new couple ideally, if not always in practice, lives with the parents of the bride. This tendency to uxorilocality, at least in principle, is particularly marked among Punan settled near uxorilocal groups. Similarly under the influence of neighbors, there may also appear some cases of polygyny, practiced most notably by leaders.

Changes in the kinship system are not easy to ascertain; however, the borrowing of terms designating parents-in-law and son- or daughter-in-law suggests that contact with the farmers produces a reinforcement of the formal aspects of affinal relations. This question is the topic of studies now under way, and no definitive conclusions have yet emerged. It seems, nevertheless, to be quite common for enclave hunter-gatherers to have a tendency to model their kinship system on that of their neighbors (see Testart 1981 and 1987). In any case, permanent dwellings and intermarriages with the farmers bring about modifications in the structure of the Punan family unit.

Mention was made above of the appearance (or at least the development) of the concept of private property with the introduction of commercial collecting and agriculture. It seems fairly clear that the settled Punan no longer, or more rarely, cooperate in economic activities. Even the coordination of such activities is limited (see I. Nicolaisen 1986:107). The economic unit from this time onward is the extended family, the residential unit. Curiously, this new unit is intermediate between the band, the former economic unit, and the nuclear family, the former residential unit. It was noted above that the term *kevian* in the languages of the groups of the Müller mountains, originally designating the nuclear family, carries the implication of coresidence; and this term designates among fixed groups the household, therefore the extended (or stem) family. The fair distribution of food, which among nomadic Punan is inseparable from its collective production, disappears among farming Punan. Among the Kajang, an institution-alized exchange of game and fish among all the families of the local group once existed but has now disappeared (I. Nicolaisen 1984:42). Among the Aoheng, the exchange of game and fish is restricted to a narrow circle of relatives and close neighbors. It appears, therefore, that sedentarization, generally associated with a distinct increase in population density, leads (as Smith has reported for the Ojibwa 1974: 757) to some reduction of traditional behaviors related to sharing and generosity, and of perceived obligations toward the kin group. More generally, the sense of solidarity, very marked in the nomad band, is to a considerable degree dissipated as the Punan settle and integrate themselves into a larger community (see Needham 1971:204–205).

Another new element appears with intensive commercial collecting and agriculture, a form of sexual division of labor linked to the new economic system: women's work is redirected toward the subsistence economy and agriculture in particular, while men devote themselves to commercial collecting. But when the group becomes more heav-ily dependent upon farming and rice, men neglect commercial col-lecting in order to devote most of their time to working in the fields, and this type of sexual division of labor is transformed again, as men and women come to specialize in the different phases of farm work.

With the intensification of relations with the farmers and, even more, with more permanent forms of dwelling, changes take place in the customs associated with marriage payments and postmarital resi-dence. In a nomadic band the neolocal establishment of a newlywed couple may be the occasion for the parents to provide material help, not strictly regulated by custom. However, it is certain that as Punan in the process of sedentarization come to marry into the farming groups, they must submit to the demands of farmer *adat* law. Thus the marriage payment, normally made by the man's family to the wom-an's, is brought into conformity with the prevailing practice among the farmers. In the first stages of settling, this affects only those Punan leaders who establish marital alliances with the farmers. Thus, as shown above, there coexisted among the Kereho at the beginning of this century two types of custom regarding marriage payments: the traditional type and another, borrowed type, applicable to leaders. Among the Seputan, marriage rites were absent except in the case of leaders. This confirms that it is indeed via the leaders of the groups that borrowed rituals make their way into Punan society. It should also be noted, in this regard, that among stratified farmers the marriage payment is of far greater value for aristocratic marriages than it is for commoners. Punan leaders who marry into noble farmer families have to pay a high price and, in order to do so, have to exploit their status for their own economic benefit.

As time passes and the Punan become more sedentary, the custom of the marriage payment spreads throughout the local group: all the peoples I have studied, whether influenced by the stratified groups of the Mahakam and the Kapuas or by the unstratified groups of the Barito, now practice it among themselves. Probably these versions of the custom are simpler and less lavish than their models. However, the groups that have been sedentary for the longest time are not necessarily those whose marriage payments are largest. It should also be remembered that the payment agreed upon is often not delivered in full—or indeed at all—and that the Punan, though they may have adopted the custom in principle, may not attach so much importance to it in practice. Besides this, it seems that among a number of very recently settled groups in Sarawak marriage gifts are still made only when the Punan marry into farmer families.

It may be noted that the system of marriage payments, such as it is, introduces a new sociological element into Punan society: it confers upon women a new value, which they seem not to have had in the band, above and beyond their potential as workers and mothers. From this time on, this potential must be paid for in every marriage, and most especially when the man desires to act counter to a rule of uxorilocality. Although this system changes the status of women, who are strictly equal to men in the nomadic band, it is hard to measure its effects in settled Punan society.

In postmarital residence as in the marriage payment, the Punan in general take a fairly detached view of the rules they borrow. While the Kereho of Tamalue do indeed practice uxorilocality, the Punan Murung, the Aoheng, and many others practice utrolocality despite a professed ideal of uxorilocality. Surprisingly, the Kereho, unlike the other groups above, have not found the constraints of uxorilocality to be an economic handicap.

This combination of geographic, ecological, economic, and cultural factors provides the conditions for the emergence, common but not inevitable, of a new type of leadership among the settled Punan. A good band leader is not necessarily a good village headman: the qualities required are not the same. In this critical period of transition, the Punan look to a younger individual, more adaptable, more open to the outside world, capable of introducing a new way of life. Moreover, several bands may live together in a single hamlet, and the traditional authority of a band's leader does not extend to other bands. Conflicts of power follow, which may not have existed in the nomadic band, because in these sedentary circumstances the challengers no longer have the option of simply leaving. Tensions also exist within the bands, between those who favor tradition, wanting to remain nomads, and those who favor change, wanting to settle. This is as much as to say that what happens depends in large part on the leader who is chosen, or imposes himself, in this settled hamlet.

In this open, unorganized context, a notable individual may come to the fore. This may be simply the leader of a band, well known for his leadership skills, his convictions, and his capacity for furthering change, who gains power through his influence over others and who is accepted as leader by other bands. Charismatic personalities such as these, uniters of their people with a vision of the future, are long remembered: Sekudan, leader of the Bukat of the Kapuas; Bulan Jihat, "queen" of the Punan Murung (Sellato 1986b:248); Tingang Senean, the first historic chief of the Aoheng (Sellato 1986b:310). Sandin reports that a local Beketan leader, Nyalang, became chief of all the Beketan of the region after having brought them all together (1967–1968:230).

The emergence of these personalities is facilitated by regional political circumstances, notably the support of an important chief among neighboring farmers or that of the administrative authorities. Sekudan, as he undertook to unite his group, had the confidence of the Dutch government. A certain Entinggi became influential among other Beketan leaders because he had married his son to the daughter of an Iban chief (Sandin 1967–1968:229).

A farmer who becomes the son-in-law of a band leader is well placed to take advantage of this alliance and of his prestige as a farmer in a context of conversion to agriculture, to take the lead in the local group and succeed his father-in-law. An Iban, Kuling, thus became the leader of the Kereho of Tamalue. Another Iban, settled among the

Beketan of the Balui, became their leader (Sandin 1967–1968:233). Other cases have been reported among the Lisum. These "outsiders" acted as innovators and catalysts among the Punan, introducing new technologies, new cultural features.

Thus it is not surprising that ancient "sons-in-law" took on, with time, the stature of culture heroes in the history and myths of certain ethnic groups. The figure of the Tiger among the Aoheng, Seputan, and Hovongan, who initiated rice farming and certain prohibitions and rituals among them, represents Liju Aya', the great Long Gelat chief, but also all the minor Long Gelat "sons-in-law" who came to live with them (Sellato 1986b:329). The children of these men benefit from the prestige of their grandfather, leader of the band, and of their father the initiator; they benefit also from the support of the group's farmer protectors, and often, in consequence, from recognition by the administrative authorities in the form of a title, *temenggung, penghulu,* or *tuai tumah.* The authority of such a leader over the settled Punan is incomparably greater than that which a nomad leader might have over his band.

With the increase in population density, the restriction on mobility linked to the development of agriculture, and the more rigidly structured affiliation of families to the community, a greater need arises for political coordination, in particular with regard to neighboring groups and the government. To an ever greater extent, the leader is the representative of his community to the outside world. Now the temptation to social inequality begins to be felt. The leader, as he comes to deal on an equal footing with farmer chiefs, becomes conscious of his status and seeks to obtain the standing necessary to give outsiders a good impression of himself and his group. In this he often has the support and aid of members of his community, who, suffering from a sense of inferiority to the farmers, feel the need for a leader with prestige. Thus the leader will induce his people to contribute (in labor and in kind) to help him build a larger and finer house, acquire valuable objects (gongs and jars), and, as described earlier, get together the marriage payment that will bring into the family, as his wife or his son's wife, the daughter of a farmer chief. Friedman (1975) has demonstrated in the case of the Kachin to what point the mere existence of the marriage payment contains the seeds of social differentiation, thus of inequality. The temptation to social inequality will be sharper in contacts with stratified farmers than with unstratified farmers, among whom payments are generally less unequal and more affordable.

The temptation to social inequality, as I refer to it here, seems to be made up of three component temptations: the economic exploitation of power, the hereditary transmission of power, and social stratification, as a corollary to the first two (in the case of those groups with stratified farmer neighbors). These components, which seem to be closely interdependent, are linked to the new and specific politicoeconomic situation in which the headman of the Punan hamlet finds himself.

The history of the groups studied above seems to indicate that whether a group yields to these temptations and puts social inequality into practice depends in part on the personality of the leader, in part on the community's reactions. Economic exploitation of the status of leader is relatively easy. The leader has a certain latitude in levying community contributions, in the form of goods (taxes in kind) or services (corvée labor), in more or less the same way as the farmer chiefs obtain services from the nomads. He can call upon the need to maintain his own prestige before outsiders, the moral obligations of his people, his ties of blood or marriage with them, his personal influence, and his charisma. Besides all this, his role as political and economic mediator may allow him to make a substantial profit from every transaction with traders and neighboring farmers. This does not necessarily mean that the leader actually will exploit his position. As Rousseau notes (1985:42), economic exploitation is not an inevitable corollary of power: unlike Kwakiutl chiefs, Tikopia chiefs make no great profit from their status. It seems that on the whole the Punan leaders did not abuse their positions.

The second component of social inequality, the hereditary transmission of power, meets with somewhat more success (though often temporarily) among the Punan. The strategy described just above, of a pursuit of reputation and prestige based on the accumulation of goods and aristocratic alliances, leads to the establishment of a line, or "house," of leaders in the community. This is one of the opportunities that are by-products of commercial collecting: the profits so gained make it easier to acquire gongs, with which a Punan may obtain in marriage the daughter of a farmer chief. Enormous prestige accrues to the descendants of a Punan leader through such a marriage, especially when the group lives in close association with stratified farmers. A certain tendency to rank endogamy makes itself felt, which serves to draw yet tighter the ties between the Punan leader's descendants and noble farmer families. This process is conspicuous in the history of the

Aoheng and the Seputan, whose prominent families constantly sought to create ties with the aristocracy of the major stratified groups around them. Thus, in order to gain dominance among their own villagers, respectable Aoheng families laid great stress on their alliances with Kayan and Long Gelat aristocrats, and on the fact that these nobles recognized them as their counterparts (Sellato 1986b). The Punan Bah, in similar fashion, created an aristocracy closely linked to noble families among their Kayan neighbors.

In the case of nomad groups settling near an unstratified group, as the Kereho and the Punan Murung did in the recent phase of their history, the gaining and keeping of power may in part depend upon prestige activities, such as funeral festivals, which reinforce the dominant status of certain individuals or families as "rich" people opposed to "poor" (see the next section).

This nascent social inequality, the natural outgrowth of kinship ties and marital alliances, soon gives rise, in the appropriate regional social circumstances, to stratification. All that is necessary is for one of these Punan leaders to buy or capture slaves for himself, in imitation of the farmers and to enhance his prestige: the society then finds itself (in practice if not in the ideal) divided into three categories—slaves, those who own them, and everybody else. All the elements of classic social stratification are present: aristocrats, freemen (or commoners), and slaves. It is in this way, or so one may suppose, that the Aoheng, the Seputan, the Kajang, and others became stratified societies. The new aristocrats tend to behave like their farmer counterparts. They try to introduce from the stratified farming societies those customs which are advantageous to them, such as obligatory contributions of corvée labor, prestige feasts, and rituals, all of which place an economic burden upon the people.

In certain cases, they do manage to establish a stratified society more or less conformable to its model. This is probably what happened with the Kenyah. But most often the common people oppose, more or less vigorously, explicitly or through inertia, the establishment of stratification or even, still earlier, the attempt to impose a hereditary transmission of leadership. Aoheng and Kajang communities, which accepted stratification, took exception to the dictatorial nature of leadership that it implies and maintained a certain degree of power to control or even depose their aristocrats, which preserved the relatively democratic character of their societies. Commoners of a certain category among the Aoheng, the *kovi maum,* have maintained a political and ritual role that leaves them the final word in all decision-making (Sellato 1986b); Kajang commoners may even impeach their ruler and temporarily replace him by a council of elders (I. Nicolaisen 1984).

Other groups, after flirting with stratification, finally reject it as undesirable. This is the case with the upriver Punan Murung, some of whose leaders tried, in vain, to establish a noble line of descent (Sellato 1986b:273). The Punan Biau (a Kajang group), unlike their cousins the Punan Bah, have neither aristocrats nor slaves (I. Nicolaisen 1976:72). The Kereho and the Hovongan, though they had close relationships with stratified ethnic groups, did not permit stratification to penetrate their society. This was not an explicit rejection of stratification, but the consequence of their choice of an economic system excluding any strongly centralized form of power. The extreme family autonomy, mobility, lack of cohesion, and widely scattered dwellings associated with their mixed rice-cassava-sago economy placed constraints on what they could borrow: in the course of their partial sedentarization, they took from their settled neighbors only those sociocultural traits which did not conflict with the priorities of this economic system or call into question the balance between their life in the forest and their life as farmers. Even those sociocultural traits which they did borrow were flexibly adapted to their economic options.

The Bukat, for their part, explicitly and firmly rejected every attempt by their leaders to establish hereditary chieftainships, as their recent history adequately shows. In spite of their close acquaintance with the strictly stratified society of the Kayan, they remained in a permanent state of "*gumlao* revolt" (see Leach 1954) against attempts to import their neighbors' social system into their own. They have preserved and put into practice their ideas of equality and individual autonomy up to the present day.

As may be seen, unmixed Punan societies have, in general, resisted the temptation to inequality. Those societies that have given way to this temptation, Kajang, Aoheng, and Seputan among them, were composite ethnic groups, made up of nomads mixed with horticulturalists, and it appears that the egalitarian horticultural societies, perhaps because they were already sedentary, were more inclined to let stratification develop than were the nomadic Punan bands.

These unmixed Punan therefore may have had a true ideal of egalitarianism. They also had economic options to which they were

strongly attached, flexible and adaptable options based in all proba-
bility on a particular ideal of individualism. The kind of stratified society proposed to them was incompatible with these options, and they
rejected it. This resistance to social innovations likely to undermine
the foundations of a traditional society is apparently not uncommon
(see, for example, Asch 1979:92). Besides this, it was noted above
that the stratified societies' economic structures themselves acted to
preserve the exclusive monopoly the Punan had on commercial collecting and, at the same time, allowed them to maintain their relative
isolation and their identity. In general, it appears that very few Punan
groups adopted social stratification, and those who lived close to
stratified groups remained distinct from them.

Conversely, it appears that numerous nomad groups, Beketan,
Lugat, Tanyung, and Sru, assimilated relatively easily to the unstratified Iban. These more open Iban societies, whose families enjoyed a
certain autonomy with regard to their movements and economic
choices, must have seemed to the Punan more compatible with their
own priorities. Moreover, the economic system of these societies was
not of a type that would permit the nomads to retain their monopoly
on commercial collecting. Furthermore, according to some authors,
certain ritual and cosmological aspects of Iban society enhanced its
power of sociocultural assimilation of groups at its fringes (McKinley
1978). A similar phenomenon of assimilation has been described elsewhere with regard to the Ot and the ethnic groups of the Barito (Sellato 1986b:254–257).

I suggest here that, for the Punan, the idea of a political organization above the level of the family has no appeal. Fundamentally individualistic and pragmatic, they prefer to content themselves with their
"nomad-style" political system, concerning themselves primarily with
their respective economic options at the expense of a political vision at
the level of the group.

Studies of the retention and acquisition of sociocultural elements,
and of innovation, provide an idea of which elements are fundamental
and which are (or have become) secondary in the course of the process
of conversion from a hunting-gathering economy to one in which agriculture plays a part. It appears obvious that the Punan value highly
such elements of their culture as their ideals of equality and individualism and their preference for mobility and variety in their activities.
Besides this, commercial collecting, from its beginnings and increasingly thereafter, has shown itself to be an essential element in the new

Punan culture. A little later, a mixed subsistence system becomes, in turn, an essential element.

In this perspective on the new Punan culture, it appears that these ideological and economic elements are very closely linked. Ideology seems to find its most important application in the economic sphere; it is here, indeed, that ideology acts most positively, most constructively, leading to the invention of new economic systems. In the political sphere, ideology is expressed by inertia, in the rejection of social transformations and the preservation of a "nomad-style" political system. Whatever the case may be, these elements, whether of the ancient ideology or the newly developed economy, were held to be so important by the Punan groups that they sought to preserve if not indeed to enhance them over long periods of time after the abandonment of a strictly nomadic way of life.

Rituals, Religion, Ideology

This section will be limited to a rapid survey of transformations in some of the areas of *adat* that seem particularly important or easy to observe, a selection dictated by the data available in the literature.

It has been said that rites of passage in traditional Punan culture are virtually absent, and in fact almost no references are found to rituals concerning, for instance, pregnancy or birth. A discussion of life-cycle rituals must therefore center on marriage and death. In the course of sedentarization other rituals may appear, principally those associated with the house and with agriculture.

It is important to note that some Punan groups may have been subject to multiple or multiphased religious influences, according to the contacts they had with different major ethnic groups. Thus the Kereho of the Busang absorbed the *adat* of the stratified groups of the Mahakam, by way of the Seputan, before becoming subject to the influence of the Ot Danum of the Barito. Similarly, the Punan Murung of the headwaters and those of the Ratah were doubly influenced by the Bahau and the Long Gelat of the Mahakam, and by the Barito groups (Sellato 1986b:273–274).

With regard to borrowed marriage rituals, data are scarce. Certain rites pertaining to the fertility of the couple and the solidity of matrimonial ties have probably been integrated into the *adat* of some Punan groups, but marriage does not seem to have acquired among the Punan the importance it has in the ritual life of the farmers. However, to the extent that marriages with the farmers made it necessary, the Punan more readily accepted customs associated with marriage as an economic transaction, in particular the marriage payment and post-marital residence (which has some impact on the economy as a whole, as noted above).

Death rites, like marriage rites, may be described as impoverished versions of an imported ritual system. The Seputan and the Bukat adopted the Kayan and Long Gelat type of interment (a coffin placed in a cave or, more recently, in a graveyard); the Kereho adopted secondary rituals from the Ot Danum. The practice of offerings and sacrifices, and rituals for the escorting of the soul, traditionally absent or extremely minimal among the Punan, were adopted in connection with certain borrowed ideas of the hereafter.

Indeed, with sedentarization, it is no longer possible to flee from a death (though this still tends to happen if there is a death among commercial collectors living in temporary forest camps). The living must continue to dwell near the final resting places of their dead, as the farmers do, and therefore must learn to dispatch the spirits of the dead. In the same way, the Punan adopt customs such as formally lamenting the dead, observing a mourning period, and certain prohibitions.

A further word on funeral rites of the Ot Danum type. The Kereho, like the Punan Murung (Sellato 1986b:276), have integrated these rituals into their culture in a simplified form; but to hold them still constitutes a quest for prestige, extremely expensive for the family of the deceased, as is the case among the Ot Danum but not in stratified societies, in which the entire village contributes to the cost. In those Punan groups which resisted stratification, funeral feasts are opportunities for individuals to claim or reinforce their social standing in a context in which the only relevant opposition is that of rich to poor, a characteristic of societies I have called "hierarchized" (see above; and Sellato 1987).

Rituals of healing and purification of the sick, apparently absent or nearly so in traditional Punan society, have been borrowed and adapted in various ways, and, it would seem, not very earnestly. The nomads seem as lacking in ritual recourse when faced with sickness as they are when faced with death. However, it has been noted that, paradoxically, some farmers value them as effective shamanistic healers and ideal mediators between humans and deities or souls, for all that the rituals the nomads hold are pale imitations of their own.

Certain rituals associated with sedentary dwellings, from small family offerings to household spirits up to the general purification of the village, have long existed among settled ethnic groups like the Aoheng and Seputan, having apparently been in part inherited from the Pin and in part borrowed from the Kayan and Long Gelat. The Kereho of the Busang have household and village rituals that they acquired from the Seputan and Ot Danum. The Bukat of the Mendalam may have borrowed from the Kayan, together with the longhouse, certain rituals associated with it, which, like the longhouse itself, have subsequently disappeared. The hut or house of recently sedentarized Punan seems, however, to be no more an object of rituals than is the nomad shelter. It is simply a material structure, a roof.

The case of rice farming displays this same reluctance of the Punan to borrow rituals along with the cultural elements they relate to. While the Aoheng, and to a lesser extent the Seputan, have adopted the rice cult as their neighbors practice it, the Punan in general took up rice farming divested of its rituals (see Seitz 1981:290). Most Punan groups (including the Aoheng) also chose not to adopt the specific term referring to cooked rice, simply calling it "food," as they do sago and cassava. Rice therefore does not occupy a privileged place in the Punan religious sphere.

It was noted above that the Punan most probably had a core of specific religious beliefs, but that the metaphysical speculations of their farmer neighbors clearly do not interest them. Among the Hovongan, for example, only a few old leaders were able to explain to me their ideas about the world of gods and spirits, or about the origin of the world and human beings, and this proved to be a simplified version of the Kayan cosmogony. Even the Aoheng have only a vague idea of the divinities in their pantheon (possibly of Pin origin), upon which a Kayan deity has been superimposed. Aside from some rare origin myths (one being a tradition of deluge) and a vague idea of a life after death, the Punan have shown no special interest in adopting the farmers' body of beliefs.

It therefore seems reasonable to conclude that the Punan have borrowed rituals in areas where they were forced to do so by their social interactions with the farmers, and not elsewhere. Their evident reluctance to grant a sacred character to a material object like a house or to an economic activity like rice farming (two spheres closely linked and highly ritualized among the settled peoples but secular among the Punan), along with an absence of any inclination toward their neighbors' cosmogonic beliefs and theories, the notable minimalism of the ritual and religious sphere in the Punan traditional culture, and their lack of enthusiasm for borrowed rituals, all lead to the conclusion that Punan societies are fundamentally nonreligious and solidly pragmatic.

Above, I referred to the Punan societies as "secular" and compared them to the Basseri societies studied by Barth (1964). These Basseri are organized in nomadic families, independent from one another and autonomous with regard to their subsistence. Isolated from other nomad families (or bands), they are economically linked to outside markets. Ritual activity is remarkably sparse in their culture.

The Basseri are not the only example of a society poor in religious activity. Fox, studying the Pinatubos of the Philippines, was surprised by the fact that these groups had no religious concepts, no cosmogony, and no interest in what happened to the soul after death (Macdonald, personal communication). The Siriono, nomadic hunter-gatherers of Bolivia (see Holmberg 1969) have a similarly minimal religious life: no marriage ritual (or even marriage payment), highly simplified death rites, no ritual associated with the construction of the hut, no priests, shamans, or healers, no magic, no ancestor cult, no idea of life after death, a virtual absence of folklore and mythology, no spirit cult or propitiation of spirits: their only ritual practices are a few rites of passage for girls and some taboos relating to pregnancy and the couvade. Writing of several groups of nomadic African hunter-gatherers, Woodburn remarks that their beliefs are "rather simple, unstructured and straightforward" (1982:188) and that they "avoid speculating about whether there is a life after death" (1982:198). Similarly, Turnbull says of the BaMbuti pygmies that they are "not a ritualistically minded people" (1961:198). This phrase seems completely adequate as a characterization of the Punan: although it cannot be said that they have no religion, it seems evident that they are not a religiously minded people.

In the context of traditional Punan culture, as it has been outlined, the functioning of the society is based far more upon a system of rules of behavior, of relations between individuals, than upon the experience of a bounded social entity (what Douglas [1982] calls respectively grid and group; Macdonald [1977] seems to have come to a similar conclusion with regard to the Palawan). Indeed, the Punan band is in its essence fluid, the affiliation of families to the band is uncertain and fluctuating, and, in this highly unstable context, interpersonal rela-

tionships play a far more important role than the set of fixed and supposedly transcendent laws, unresponsive to the reality of the individual, that constitutes *adat* in the "closed" society of the stratified farmers. Among the Punan, flexible arrangements are made, taking into
account situations and persons, their choices and respective inclina-
tions, so that society will function smoothly. Because the band is
"open," the opposition between internal and external is not particularly marked, nor is the social concept of an opposition between good
and bad.

I argue, then, that traditional Punan society, with its nomadic way
of life and its flexible social organization, is open, individualistic,
pragmatic, opportunistic, and secular (little inclined to religion and
philosophy). In the course of the conversion of this society to another
way of life, it borrowed from its neighbors sociocultural elements that
were carefully selected and flexibly adapted in order to minimize any
challenge to its intrinsic characteristics and to preserve its type of functioning. The choice of favoring and developing commercial collecting
and, later, mixed systems of subsistence is to be viewed from this perspective of the preservation of a particular type of society. Thus, while
the ideology associated with traditional Punan culture permits the
adaptation of new economic strategies, these in turn act to preserve
the basic values of this ideology in what has been called the new Punan
culture.

Ethnicity

The Punan feeling of ethnic identity remains, as has been said,
fairly vaguely defined, other than by contrast with the farming groups.
The shared memory of an ancient center of dispersal and/or a traditional territory serves to give the Punan group a certain sense of place;
but sometimes this recollection itself is lost.

Writers stress that the Punan attach little importance to time, show
no great interest in their own history (or even in their own genealogies), which they have a hard time remembering, and rarely if ever
speak of heroes or of the exploits of their ancestors (Harrisson 1949:
134; Urquhart 1951:497–498, 500, 530; Urquhart 1959:79; Ellis
1972:237; J. Nicolaisen 1976b:42). In short, they are not interested
in the past. Indeed, the history of the Punan groups is much harder to
reconstruct than that of the farmers, both for reasons pertaining to
their way of life and social organization (the large number of bands
and their impermanence over time) and for this principal reason, their

lack of interest in history. While the farmers often remember their history over ten or even fifteen generations, the Punan sometimes have trouble remembering the names of their own grandparents.

Sometimes a major historic event in the remote past leaves its mark in collective memory. But it proves impossible to link this to a continuous historical tradition; this has its beginning only much later. For example, in the tradition of the Punan Murung, there is a gap of a half-century between the culture hero Lambang and first contacts with the farmers, which have been relegated to a more or less mythical period, and the first band leaders who can be placed genealogically (Sellato 1986b).

In a farmer society, relatively closed and permanent, the sense of identity (if not ethnic, at least cultural) is based on a "charter," which is in part the body of *adat* of the group and in part the body of its historical and mythical traditions. This charter legitimizes current status relationships in the society. In particular, in a stratified society, it legitimizes power (see Sellato 1984a). In traditional Punan society there is nothing to legitimize, neither social status, nor rank, nor territory, nor ancestral house. The open society is as it is, not as it should be. Its present state has no need of legitimization by reference to the past. Interpersonal relations are constantly changing, constantly being redefined; individuals are not part of an all-encompassing scheme within which they exist only by virtue of their social status (the case in stratified societies). For the Punan, history may therefore be irrelevant (see the discussion of this point in Sellato 1986b:54–57).

I suggest that the feeling of "Punan-ness" is based on this set of essential values described above (individualism, pragmatism, and so on). This ideology has no need to be legitimized by tradition or to be upheld by reference to a body of oral texts, because it is rooted in the innermost self of each individual and confirmed by daily life. This feeling being by definition common to all the Punan, it affirms Punan identity in contrast to that of the farmers.

Certainly there does exist a feeling of the family in its widest sense, by which several bands may recognize their kinship, close or distant. The sense of ethnic identity properly speaking is based, then, on nothing more than a concept of a common territory and language. As bands disperse in the course of long-range migrations, and their languages diverge through contact with different farming groups, this feeling of ethnic identity gradually disappears, as it is not supported, as it is among the farmers, by a formalized and socially necessary historical tradition. Thus, for those Bukat who have always remained within their region of origin, it is relatively easy to maintain an awareness of historical roots in the land, a fact that makes it possible to develop ethnohistorical reconstructions covering a period of over a century and a half. Conversely, a group like the present-day Lisum, several times uprooted and having several times changed their ethnonym, no longer feel that they have anything in common with the other nomad groups that once were their kinfolk except for the nomadic way of life, a certain feeling of "Punan-ness."

In the course of Punan sedentarization, the active interface between Punan and farmers seems to act as a catalyzing force. For the groups studied, and for many more, continuous historical tradition begins with the headman of the hamlet where they first trade or settle. Only after a system of values originating in the farmer groups has been extended into Punan society, when there is something to legitimize or transmit (a territorial claim, a status or prestige, a house or goods), does the collective memory take the trouble to retain names and facts. Only after Punan have come to rub shoulders with farmers, and feel the need to affirm their own identity in this relationship, do they begin to take an interest in the exploits of their own heroes. There is indisputably a social-climbing, arriviste mentality (the expression is that of Harrisson, 1967) in this new need to find or invent deep and ancient roots in the ethnic landscape of the region, to elaborate or borrow origin myths, simply in order to justify the group's existence and affirm its cohesion. The plain fact of being, or being there, is no longer enough; it is also necessary to *have been*. Sometimes it is even necessary to have been *there* (see Brosius 1986).

Here I would like to mention the interesting point made by Testart (1981), that enclave hunter-gatherers like the Punan may in reality live a double life: they have an "external" culture more or less modeled on that of their neighbors, but they also preserve an "internal" culture through which they maintain their distinctiveness. In the case of the Punan, this remark seems entirely relevant: the "internal" culture consists of this ideological core of traditional Punan culture, maintained almost unadulterated in the new Punan culture and forming the charter for the "internal" functioning of the society, while the "external" culture consists of fragments of a body of *adat* and mythology borrowed from the farming groups and "activated" particularly in interactions with them.

It seems to me that this "internal culture" may be identified with

Bourdieu's concept of *habitus* (1980), itself drawn from a work by Mauss (1936): a system of lasting and transferable patterns of thought and behavior that regulates social and economic activities and is passed on from generation to generation through all the vicissitudes of history and changes in the "external culture." This is indeed that "core of culture" that Dumont identifies with ideology (1986 and elsewhere).

This internal culture is evident, through one or more external layers of culture, among many other hunter-gatherer groups all over the world. Various expressions have been used to refer to this state of affairs. Zacot speaks of "basic circumstances of the culture" of the Badjo (or Bajau) sea nomads (1986:45); Guillaume, of the "internal dynamics of society" of the Aka pygmies (1986:67); Turnbull similarly mentions this type of dual culture among the BaMbuti pygmies (1961:227); and the same has been said of modern Gypsies (Formoso 1986).

The qualities of the internal culture are expressed, if not by preference then at least most clearly, in the economic sphere. In the literature on hunter-gathers, frequent mention is made of the characteristics noted above: openness, mobility, autonomy, flexibility, opportunism, an inclination to individualism. The Punan, like other groups just referred to, take an immediate and pragmatic view of their economic choices, favoring activities that are temporary and varied (or indeed simultaneous), and that produce as rapid a return as possible for as little investment as possible in time and labor. They maintain the opportunistic attitude of nomadic hunter-gatherers in all their economic activities (see Benjamin 1974), even in those recent activities that no longer have anything to do with their traditional way of life (the case of the Gypsies, studied by Formoso [1986], is particularly striking). Besides this, as stressed above, this duality of culture also extends into the domain of ritual and belief. The Punan, and this is a characteristic of their internal culture, are not given to ritual, and the core of Punan beliefs can be contrasted with the body of borrowed ritual. This opposition between external and internal culture, expressed in the fact that the Punan define themselves by contrast with the farmers, forms the heart of the nomads' feeling of "Punan-ness," a feeling that persists, as does this contrast, in many groups of former nomads.

As stated above, the Punan, in keeping with the ideological characteristics of their traditional society, consistently rejected the social inequality proposed by the model of the society of their stratified farmer neighbors, and in general resisted assimilation to these neighbors. There are few exceptions: one would be the downriver Bukat, who were very early absorbed into the Kayan (though no data exist on the process of assimilation); another, the Bukat (or Ukit) of the Balui, who say they are stratified (though their neighbors find this statement somewhat amusing); a third group were the Lugat of the Mahakam, who joined the Aoheng (though the Aoheng at that time were not yet a truly stratified society). All the other little Punan groups, as they settled, maintained some geographic distance from their stratified neighbors and rejected stratification. In contrast, as has been seen, nomad bands seem to have assimilated much more easily into unstratified farming groups such as the Iban, which offered them the model of a relatively open society, more compatible with their ideological substratum.

What was called the pivotal point at the interface between Punan and farmers may or may not be the site of a shift in ethnicity, according to the type of farmer society involved. When this shift does happen, one consistently finds a flow of population moving downriver from the headwaters, and a flow of culture moving upriver from the farmers' villages, converging on the pivotal point, then diffusing from it again, respectively downward and upward.

The case of the composite ethnic groups, the Aoheng (Sellato 1986b) or the Kajang (I. Nicolaisen 1984), is particularly interesting. In a speculated first stage, the nomads merge with the horticulturalists. These peoples not being stratified, there is no ideological barrier to Punan assimilation. The sharing of geographical space, of ancient ties, and probably of the same lingua franca, and the threat of common enemies contribute to the formation of an ethnic "melting pot" in which nomads and horticulturalists blend. In this process, with the acquisition of food-storage techniques and the subsequent decline in solidarity and collective aspects of production and consumption (discussed above), the Punan move into another socioeconomic system, which incorporates permanent dwellings. There is, no doubt, in the case of these composite ethnic groups a close link between the process of cultural amalgamation and that of the nomads' sedentarization.

At a later stage, the culture of the stratified farmers, imposed by their military power, takes the upper hand. The communities of horticulturalists merged with former nomads take to the cultivation of swidden rice. With rice comes stratification (the historical relationship between rice and stratification calls for investigation), and these communities respond in different ways. The Hovongan introduced rice into their mixed cassava-sago economy but resisted stratification; certain Kajang (the Punan Bah, for example) and some of the Seputan similarly integrated rice into a mixed economy and accepted stratification (the Seputan later evolved an economy centered to a greater extent upon rice, while the Kajang maintained their mixed economy); the Aoheng not only adopted stratification (with, like the Kajang, certain reservations), but they eventually became full-time rice farmers, like their Kayan neighbors.

These composite ethnic groups form village communities, independent from each other, with no common political organization above the level of the village. Nevertheless, they develop a common sense of ethnic identity, which is focused on an ethnonym, such as Kajang or Aoheng, and also on certain specific religious practices. Thus the Aoheng historically rallied around certain religious ideas, such as a prohibition on the use of ironwood *(oheng)* and the *pengosang* festival, preserved and passed down by the Pin elements of the group (Sellato 1986b:385; and 1992b). Despite internal dissention and their inability to establish permanent alliances, these communities affirm their common identity in contrast to the major ethnic groups around them, currently their allies and protectors but historically enemies. Here tradition, whether historical, mythological, or religious, comes to play an important role.

This biphasal assimilation of the Punan—first of the nomads to the horticulturalists and then of the composite ethnic groups thus formed to the rice farmers—may explain the complex ethnic history of certain regions, like the upper basin of the Barito, where ethnic labels are vague and further complicated by the coming of Islam. The nomadic Ot, living on the upper Murung, may first have assimilated into horticulturalists (Ot Danum, equivalent to the Pin of the Mahakam), as the early history of the Punan Murung suggests (Sellato 1986b:225–226). With these Ot Danum, who were in contact with the Hinduized culture-area foyer of the Ngaju farther to the southwest, the nomads then contributed to the constitution of ethnically composite horticultural groups (which later became the present-day Siang and Murung rice farmers). At a later stage, rice was introduced, moving up from the south along the course of the main rivers (independent of the influence of the stratified rice farmers of the Kayan group, which itself no doubt came from the north). Finally, more recently but by the same route,

Islam and the Malay way of life (Bekumpai) penetrated into the interior. The nomad groups of the Murung were therefore subject to three successive waves of cultural influence, which I have elsewhere called "fronts," moving up the Murung: the horticultural front, the rice-farming front, and the Bekumpai front. Cutting across these successive cultural waves proceeding from downriver areas toward the headwaters, a trickle of population flowed downstream (toward the pivotal point and beyond it), eventually to shift into more "downriver" ethnic categories. Thus the nomads, shifting at the pivotal point into the category of horticulturalists, would a little later, as they moved on downstream or came into contact with the cultural front as it moved upward, shifted again first into the category of rice farmers, then into the category of Bekumpai through conversion to Islam and a new, Malay-style way of life (Sellato 1986b:254–257).

The current distribution of ethnic groups gradually became better defined, due to the use of local ethnonyms, tags corresponding to categories based on the criteria of economy, culture, and way of life, leaving the true Ot far upriver, still living as nomads at the beginning of this century. Ethnicity, in this region, is therefore historically determined by cultural factors borne by fronts of diffusion in a mobile, "open," and dynamic social context very different from the "closed" and relatively static stratified societies of the north and east of Borneo.

There exists, as an islandwide autochthonous construction, a sequence of cultural "situations": (1) hunting-gathering, (2) horticulture, (3) swidden rice farming, and (4) irrigated rice farming and/or the Malay way of life. This sequence, oriented overall and in the abstract as Borneo's rivers flow, from the headwaters downward, represents a regional scale of values ranging from the "savage" to the "civilized," from the forest to the town. The savage is always farther upstream.

CHAPTER 6
SUMMARY AND CONCLUSION

OVER THE PAST two centuries, the rainforest nomads of Borneo have been settling, and the nomadic hunting-gathering way of life is now disappearing. In the first part of this work, Chapters 2 and 3 present reconstructions of the history of two nomad groups. These studies, based mainly on data from the traditional oral histories of these groups, demonstrate the usefulness of oral tradition, often denied or at least considerably underestimated, to the historian interested in small acephalous societies. They also show that oral tradition can be the basis for reliable reconstructions, not only of political history, but also of the more subtle fields of economic and social history.

In the second part, Chapter 4 offers an overview of the traditional nomad culture of Borneo in its forest environment, which constitutes a special "economic niche" permitting the nomads who live in it to be totally self-sufficient in food. This "nomad domain" is bounded by its interfaces with the territories of the farming groups.

After examining in detail the subsistence economy of the nomads, including patterns of sago exploitation and specific techniques of hunting and fishing, I suggest that this nomad economy was (and is) capable of existing in complete independence of trade relations with farming populations (and, in consequence, may actually have been independent of all outside contact). In particular, this economy would have been entirely functional before the introduction of metal, basing its technology upon the use of stone tools (for felling sago palms) and plant poisons (used with a hunting weapon). It seems likely that some nomad groups were able to remain outside trade networks until a fairly recent date, perhaps the eighteenth century.

The study of Punan migration patterns and concepts of territory shows that, although the various bands that make up a group may be

215

little concerned with territoriality, the group as a whole often recognizes an ancestral homeland, a center from which it spread. As a matter of principle, the group would not defend this territory or mobilize its constituent bands in a joint action, even against a concrete danger. Commonly, Punan respond to territorial challenge with avoidance and withdrawal, or even long-distance emigration. However, when a direct threat is posed to their food resources, they may take up arms in the defense of their territory, though such reactions are local and restricted to the level of the band.

The nomadic band, a segmentary society in an extreme form, is economically autonomous, and there is no political, economic, or ritual form of organization above band level. The band is generally a composite, with a single core descent group, a number of affines, and a few outsiders. The nuclear family is the residential unit and enjoys a marked autonomy relative to the band, which may undergo fission as the result of family choices. However, band members are bound together by a certain number of collective economic activities, the yield of which is shared equally among them. Leadership is informal, and may at any time be called into question. The leader, who lacks any special status or prerogatives, is chosen among experienced adults according to criteria of competence, and the society is basically egalitarian.

The band is strongly endogamous and incest taboos are fairly vague. Marriage is informally endorsed by the group, without ritual or institutionalized marriage payment. The young couple very soon sets up a neolocal household. Funerary practices are notably minimal, and associated rituals are nearly absent. There is a general tendency to withdraw from a death, both the body and the place of death. Punan groups probably have in common a core of religious beliefs, but these also seem minimal, like all the expressions of their ritual life. Societies such as these, little concerned with the sacred, have been called "secular."

Consideration of these traits of the society, and of characteristic features of the subsistence economy, leads to the conclusion that the "traditional Punan culture" is unique and independent of the farming cultures that surround it.

Subsequently, in Chapter 5, I analyze the mechanisms of the economic transformations that take place in this Punan culture, showing that they originate in the nomads' reorientation from collecting forest products for subsistence to collecting for the market.

In a first stage of the process, the Punan, after the introduction of new elements of technology such as metal, find themselves economically dependent on their farmer neighbors. Thanks to savings in time and energy due to the use of these new tools, they begin the commercial collecting of forest products under the pressure of demand from downriver markets, and are thereby integrated into regional networks of trade.

The farmers, for their part, make attractive profits on trade with the nomads and put into effect a variety of strategies designed to maintain and intensify these trade connections and increase the amount of forest products the nomads supply. These strategies may be purely commercial (the creation of needs among the nomads, competition, credit relationships), political (alliances), or social (the generation of social change among the nomads). Gradually, from their commercial dominance, the farmers gain a political hold over the nomads, establishing an overlord-vassal relationship and making use of them for a variety of services (in particular, for the hunting of heads and slaves).

The better to guarantee continuity in their supply of forest products, the farmers persuade the Punan to settle part-time in a hamlet, where they have their first experience of agriculture. A new type of sexual division of labor emerges, whereby women devote their time to farming, men to commercial collecting. This situation maximizes the yield from collecting. The Punan develop a mixed subsistence economy, based on a combination of cultivated crops and wild sago. Some Punan, however, begin to commit themselves to an ever greater extent to intensive rice cultivation, to the point of becoming heavily dependent upon it. Commercial collecting declines, and the sedentarization of the nomads ultimately produces an effect just opposite to that intended at the start. The farmers' strategy is in reality to settle the nomads, not to convert them to rice farming. This paradoxical response leads to the drying up of the flow of marketable forest products. The Punan themselves, now professional collectors and well aware that it is advantageous to them to remain so, most often refuse to become dependent on rice, developing and refining specific subsistence systems that allow them to continue to practice commercial collecting.

Chapter 5 goes on to examine the process of conversion to agriculture. It appears that in the first stages of sedentarization, the nomads cultivate mainly tubers and fruit trees, their economy being based on a mixed cassava-sago system. At a later stage they begin to cultivate rice, in a threefold system based on rice, cassava, and sago. Reliance on sago may later disappear.

I dismiss the opposition, classic in Borneo ethnography, set up between nomads and rice farmers, showing that there exists instead a continuum of economic situations, based on various combinations of rice farming, horticulture, hunting, and gathering. These economic situations are not to be seen as transitional phases between two polar opposites, nomadism and rice farming, but rather as systems stable and functional in themselves, which have been selected, refined, and maintained over long periods of time because they permit the preservation of profits from commercial collecting. Flexible and secure, these mixed economic systems guarantee permanent supplies of food while permitting the Punan to respond to fluctuations in the market and to take advantage of other opportunities (for example, work for wages). Thus, certain Punan groups have evidently refused to commit themselves fully to rice farming and have maintained over the past century or longer an economic system based in part on combinations of rice, cassava, and sago, and in part on commercial collecting.

To summarize, the following stages of economic transformation have been suggested: the nomadic Punan, in a "traditional" context (hypothetically, before the introduction of metal), collected for subsistence only, lacking time and (perhaps) contacts with farming groups; with iron, these same nomads were able to save time, which they then devoted to commercial collecting; to gain still more time for this activity, they opted for partial sedentarization under the protection of farming groups and developed mixed subsistence economies including some forms of agriculture (horticulture and/or rice farming); finally, often for noneconomic reasons (government pressures), the Punan became heavily dependent upon rice cultivation and were forced to make a sharp reduction in their commercial collecting.

The Punan apparently found it highly advantageous, given the intense demand for forest products, to develop and maintain economic strategies allowing for the highest possible yield. These mixed economic systems seemed to them preferable to a system based principally upon rice farming.

Historical and linguistic evidence suggests the existence in the past of a large culture area of unstratified horticulturalists (called here the Barito Complex), possessors of a sophisticated technology and system of religion. I argue that this culture area covered a large part of Borneo, predating the culture complex of stratified rice farmers (of the Kayan type) of regions in the north and east. It may be that a number of present-day ethnic groups of Sarawak, who have in common mixed subsistence systems and secondary treatment of the dead (the *nulang* arc), as well as a good number of the Barito groups, are the descendants of these horticulturalists.

I then turned to the social transformations experienced in relation to economic changes by the Punan groups in the course of their interactions with the farming peoples. With the development of relatively sedentary residence (at the trading center, later to become a permanent hamlet or village), the following changes must be stressed: the extended family replaces the nuclear family as the residence unit in a more permanent dwelling; the individual's affiliation to a given household and community becomes stronger; the pattern of neolocal postmarital residence shifts toward utrolocal or (locally) uxorilocal patterns; increased population density and an increased mixing of populations lead to a decline in band endogamy, entailing a more precise definition of incest; the concept of territory becomes more clearly defined, on a more legal basis; the concept of private property develops markedly, and at the same time there is a decline in collective activities of food production and the sharing of their yield.

Forms of power and leadership change, exhibiting local tendencies toward the establishment of rank and status and their strictly hereditary transmission, and toward accumulating prestige goods. However, among most groups, this temptation toward social inequality is resisted. Those few groups of composite ethnic origin which adopt a stratified social structure nevertheless maintain a political system in which leaders can be controlled and impeached. It appears that the egalitarian ideology of the Punan groups keeps them from assimilating to any great extent into stratified farmer societies. On the contrary, many are absorbed into more or less egalitarian Iban groups, which offer a social model more acceptable to them.

In the socioreligious sphere, the Punan to a certain extent borrow the farmers' traditions of marriage rituals and marriage gifts, funeral practices and associated rituals, and certain vague concepts of cosmogony. However, they display a distinct reluctance to borrow rituals concerned with the house and rice (two interconnected domains that are highly ritualized among the settled peoples) and a relative lack of interest in their settled neighbors' metaphysical speculations. More than this, they show a certain lack of enthusiasm in the practice of those rituals which they have borrowed. All this, in conjunction with the notable minimalism of the religious and ritual domain in traditional Punan culture, suggests that the Punan are not a religiously minded people.

My argument, based on study of the social, political, economic, and ritual behaviors of the Punan, suggests the following characterization of traditional Punan society. It is individualistic, pragmatic, opportunistic, and secular; its egalitarianism, emphasis on physical mobility, and lack of interest in tradition and the past are manifestations of this ideological system; this underlying ideology is common to nomadic groups of Borneo, and is independent of the ideologies of the farming peoples; and this Punan ideology has been dominant throughout the history of the Punan groups, even through economic change, and has led to innovation in subsistence strategies. What I have called the "new Punan culture," based on a mixed subsistence economy and commercial collecting, plays a role in the maintenance of the essential values of this ideological system by preserving basic principles of Punan life such as family autonomy, mobility, economic versatility, and the "open" nature of the society.

In conclusion, it appears that "Punan" is a relevant sociocultural category in the context of Borneo; that it represents, in its "traditional" form, a specific set of sociocultural features independent of those of the farmers; and that a specifically Punan ideology preserves the contrast, especially in economic choices, between these Punan societies in their modern forms and the societies that surround them. The feeling of "Punan-ness," based upon the ideological premises of the traditional nomad culture, is still alive in today's new Punan culture.

APPENDIX
MAPS AND CHARTS

SETTING

General Key to Maps   222

   1. *Borneo: Political Divisions*   223

   2. *Borneo: Physiography*   224

   3. *Dayak Groups*   225

   4. *Punan Groups*   226

BUKAT

   5. *Present-Day Bukat Villages*   227

   6. *The Upper Kapuas: Physiography and Ethnic Groups*   228

   7. *Bukat Settlements: Relationships of Detail Maps*
      7.1 through 7.8   229

   7.1 *Sibau-Mendalam*   230

   7.2 *Upper Mendalam-Upper Kapuas*   231

   7.3 *Headwaters of the Kapuas*   232

   7.4 *Headwaters of the Mahakam*   233

   7.5 *Upper Mahakam*   234

   7.6 *Bungan*   235

   7.7 *Kapuas-Keriau*   236

   7.8 *Kapuas above Putussibau*   237

   8.1 *Bukat Migrations, 1800–1850*   238

   8.2 *Bukat Migrations, 1850–1900*   239

   8.3 *Bukat Migrations, 1900–1950*   240

   8.4 *Bukat Migrations, 1950–1980*   241

Chronology I: *Bukat of the Kapuas and of Sarawak*   242

Chronology II: *Bukat of the Mahakam*   243

Kinship Chart I: *Bukat Kinship Terminology*   245

221

KEREHO
    9. *Areas Occupied by the Kereho*   246
   10. *Upper Barito: Administrative Divisions*   247
   11. *Kereho in the Upper Busang*   248
   12. *Kereho in the Lower Busang*   249

Chronology III: *Kereho Busang Migrations*   250
Kinship Chart II: *Kereho Kinship Terminology*   251

General Key to Maps

+ – + – + –	state boundary		*Busang* / Metelunai R.	river and rapids
+ + + + + +	provincial boundary		•	present day village or hamlet
– – – – – –	other administrative boundary		•?	same: precise location unknown
	boundary of ethnic group or territory		○	site of abandoned village
MENAKUT △ 1210	watershed, with major peaks (height in meters)		○?	same: precise location unknown
	footpaths		ca 1900	population movement, with date
○ ○ ○ ○ ○ ○	limestone massif; caves		**AOHENG**	name of ethnic group or band
			+	timber company camp

Abbreviations

Lg	Long, river junction (Kayan-Kenyah)		Na	Nanga, river junction (West Kalimantan)
Tb	Tumbang, river junction (Central Kalimantan)		R	Riam, rapids
Ma	Muara, river junction (Indonesian)		P	Pulau, island

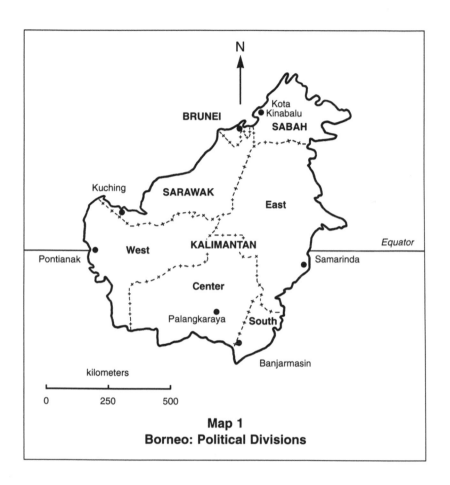

Map 1
Borneo: Political Divisions

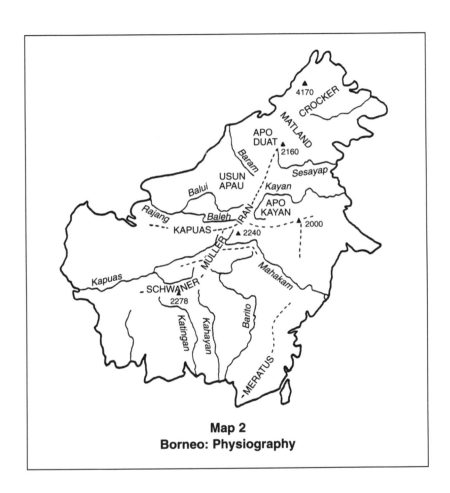

Map 2
Borneo: Physiography

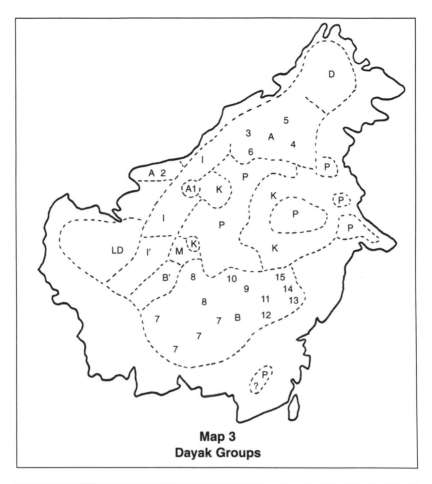

Map 3
Dayak Groups

A	"*Nulang* arc" groups	B	Barito groups		
1	Kajang	7	Ngaju	12	Ma'anyan
2	Melanau	8	Ot Danum	13	Benua'
3	Berawan	9	Siang	14	Bentian
4	Lun Dayeh	10	Murung	15	Tunjung
5	Lun Bawang	11	Luangan		
6	Kelabit				

B'	Melawi groups: Limbai, Melahui, Kebahan, Tebidah
I	Iban groups
I'	Ibanic groups: Kantu', Mualang, Seberuang, Desa
K	Kayan, Kenyah, Modang
D	Dusun (Kedazan)
M	Maloh group: Taman, Kalis, Maloh
LD	Bidayuh (Land-Dayak)
P	Punan groups (nomads and former nomads): Map 4

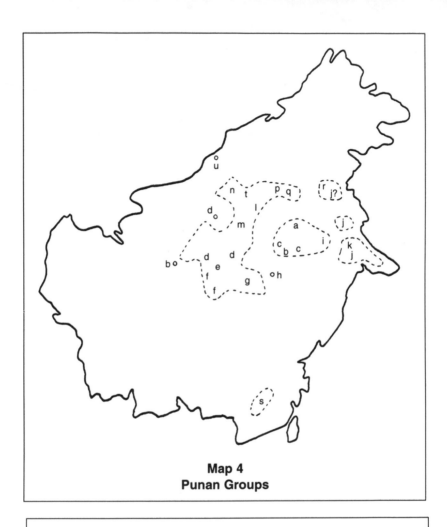

**Map 4
Punan Groups**

a	Aput (Haput)	k	Batu
b	Beketan (Bukitan)	l	Busang (Musang)
c	Lisum	m	Gang and Lusong
d	Bukat	n	Mulu
e	Hovongan (Bungan)	p	Benalui
f	Kereho (Keriau)	q	Tubu and Malinau
g	Murung and Ratah	r	Sesayap
h	Merah (Kohi)	s	Bukit (Meratus)
i	Kelai and Segah	t	Magoh
j	Basap	u	Niah

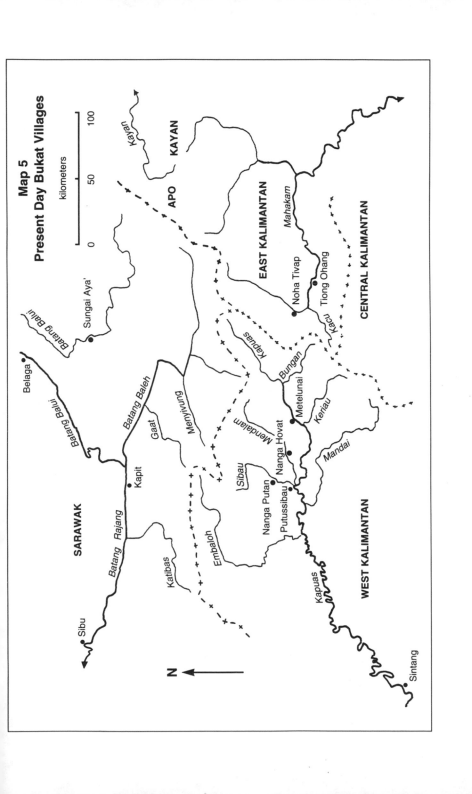

Map 5
Present Day Bukat Villages

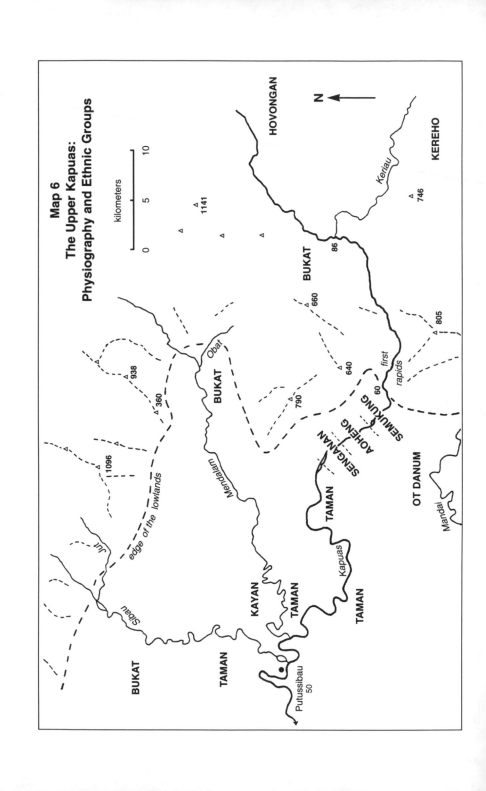

Map 6
The Upper Kapuas:
Physiography and Ethnic Groups

kilometers

0   5   10

HOVONGAN

KEREHO

Keriau

△ 746

△ 1141

△

△

△

BUKAT

86

△ 660

BUKAT

Obat

△ 640

△ 790

first

60

rapids

SEMUKUNG

△ 805

938 △

360 △

△

1096 △

edge of the lowlands

Jui

Mendalam

AOHENG

SENGANAN

OT DANUM

Mandai

TAMAN

Kapuas

TAMAN

Sibau

BUKAT

TAMAN

KAYAN

TAMAN

TAMAN

Putussibau
50

N ←

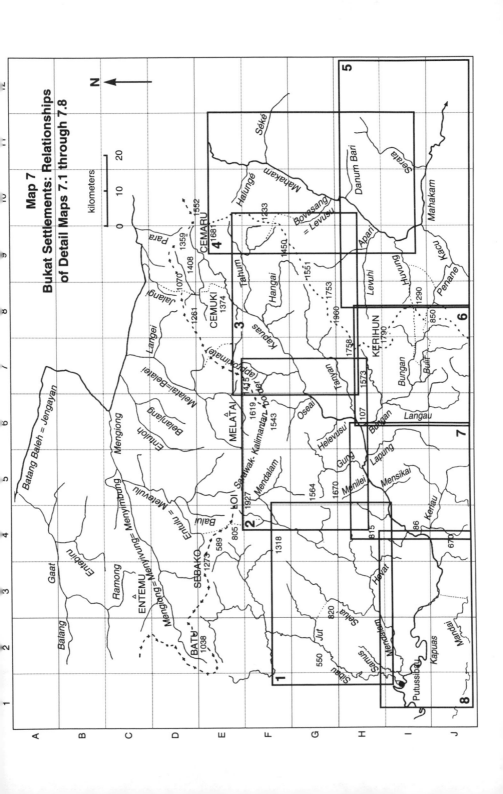

Map 7
Bukat Settlements: Relationships
of Detail Maps 7.1 through 7.8

N

kilometers

0   10   20

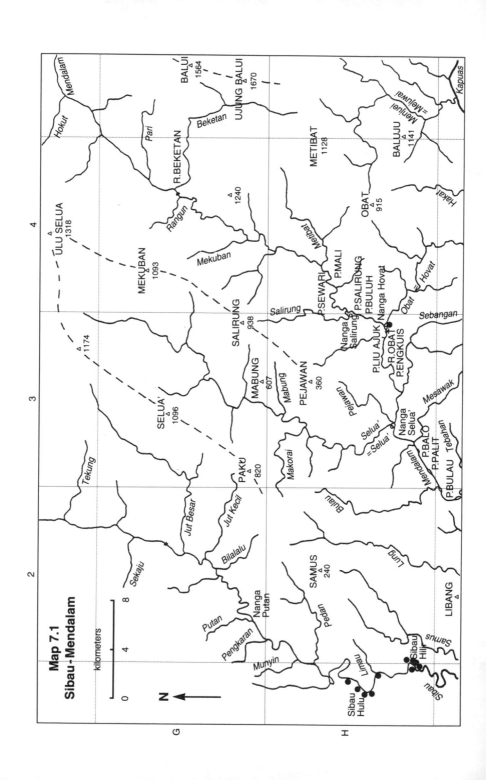

Map 7.1
Sibau-Mendalam

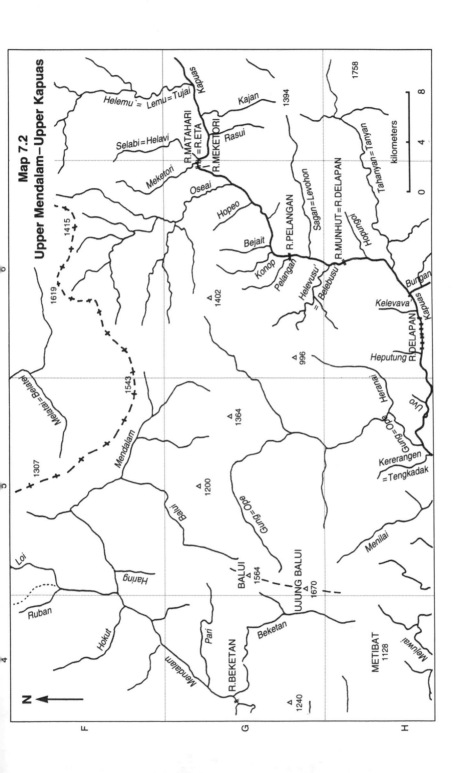

Map 7.2
Upper Mendalam–Upper Kapuas

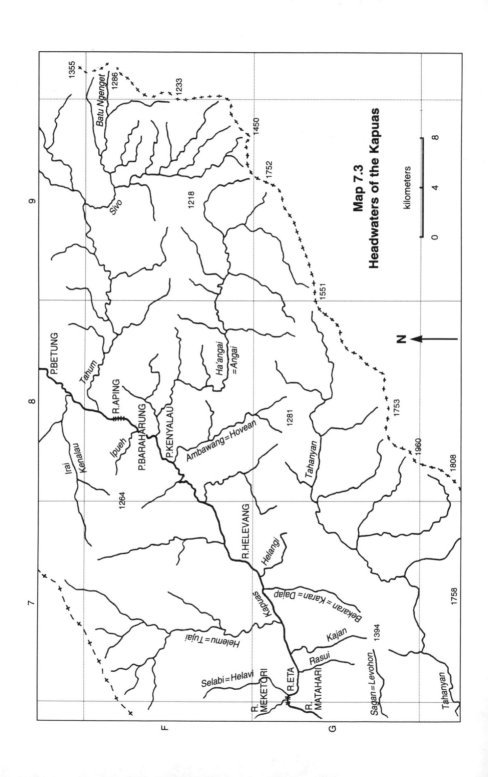

Map 7.3
Headwaters of the Kapuas

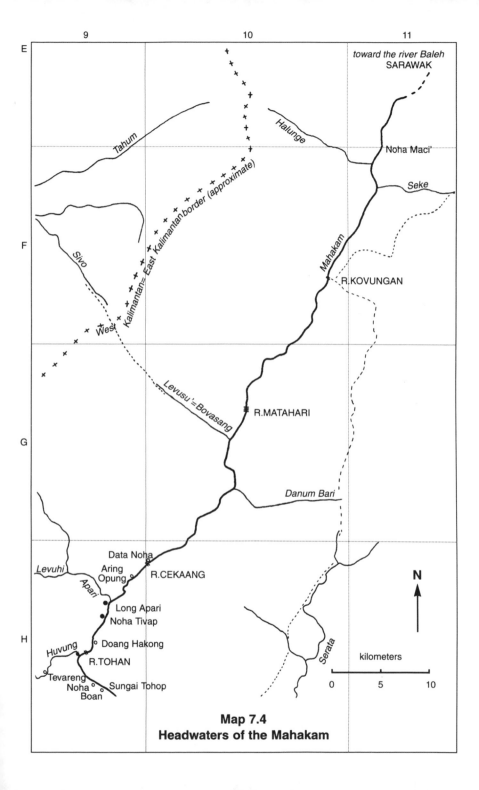

Map 7.4
Headwaters of the Mahakam

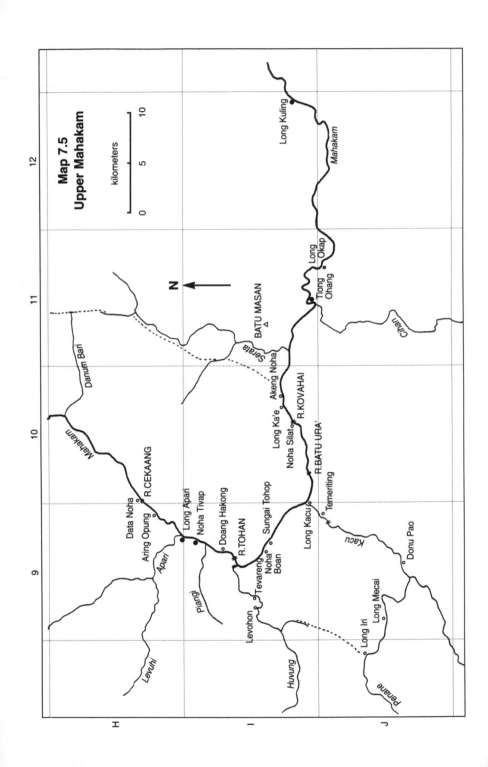

Map 7.5
Upper Mahakam

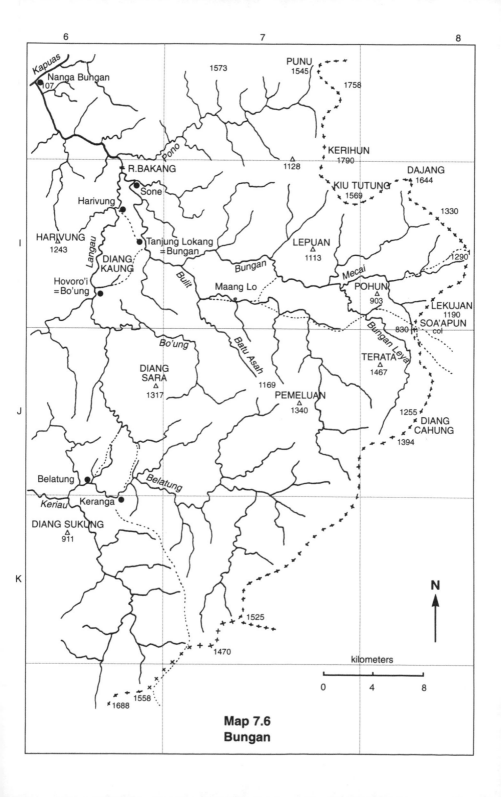

**Map 7.6
Bungan**

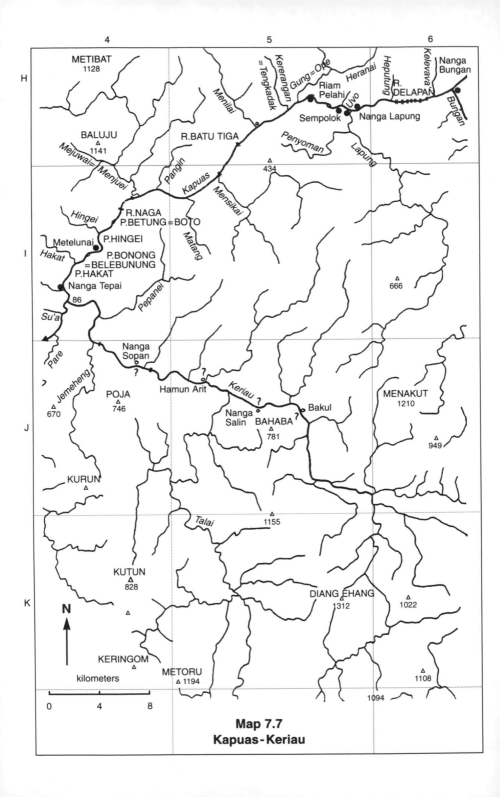

Map 7.7
Kapuas-Keriau

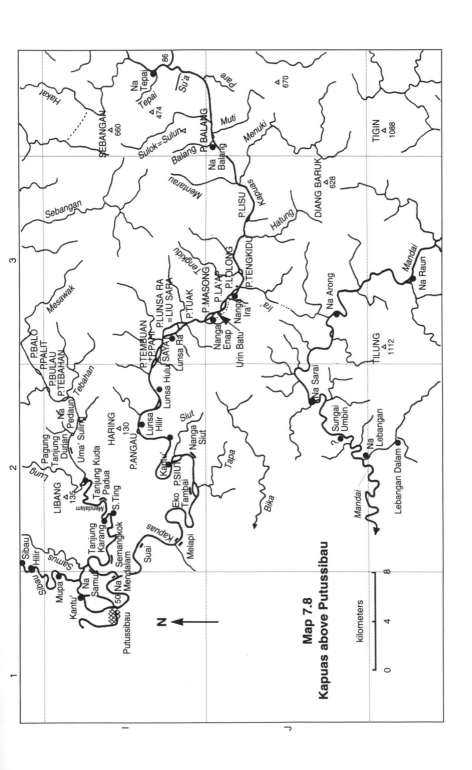

Map 7.8
Kapuas above Putussibau

N

kilometers

0   4   8

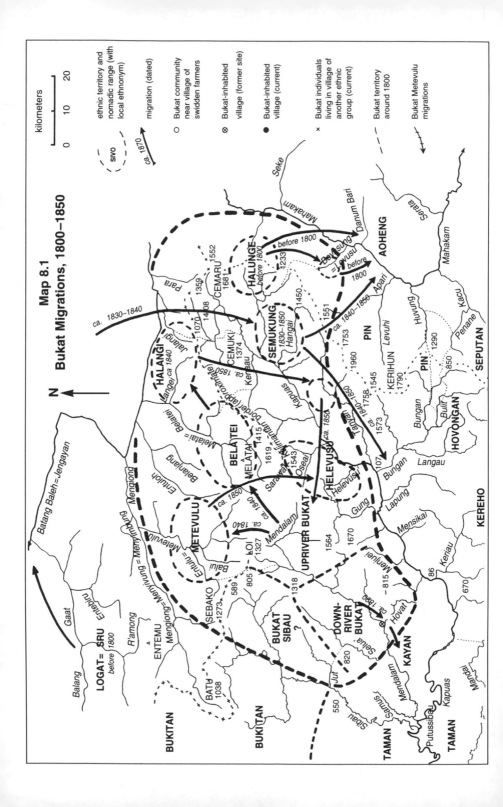

Map 8.1
Bukat Migrations, 1800–1850

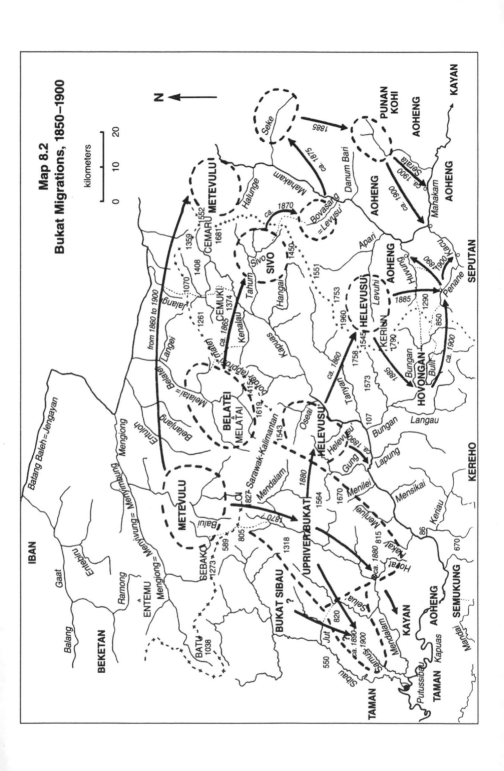

Map 8.2
Bukat Migrations, 1850–1900

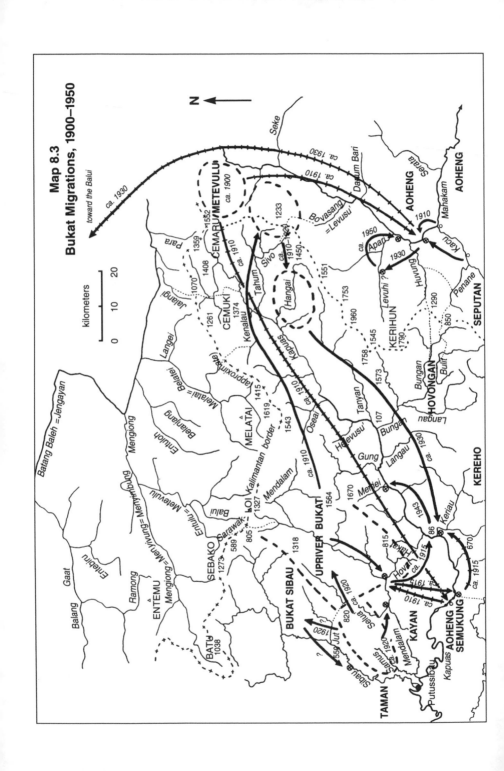

Map 8.3
Bukat Migrations, 1900–1950

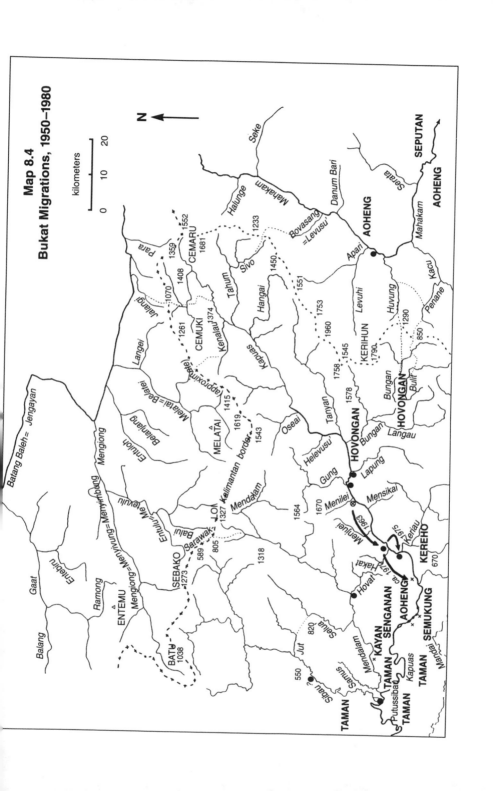

Map 8.4
Bukat Migrations, 1950–1980

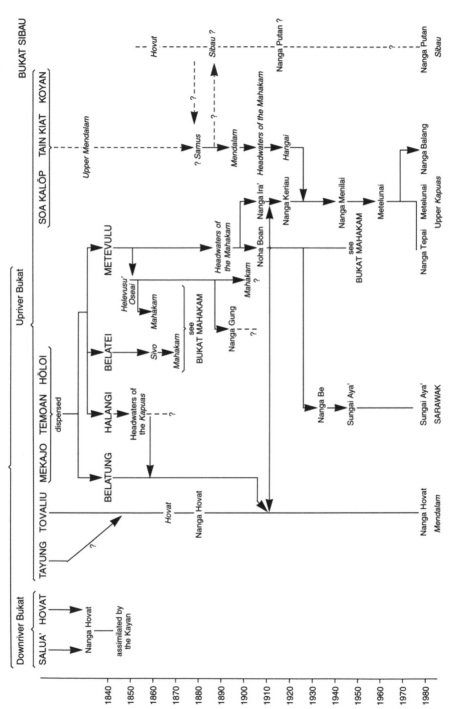

Chronology I
Bukat of the Kapuas and of Sarawak

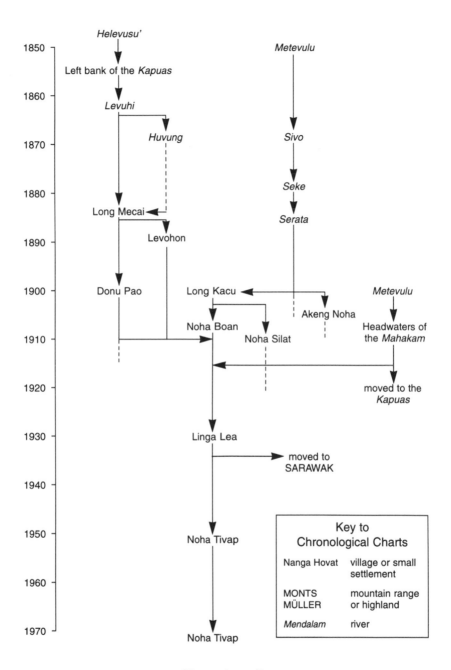

Chronology II
Bukat of the Mahakam

Key to Kinship Charts

F	father		(R: reference
M	mother		(A: address
PB	parent's brother	(uncle)	(B: brother
PZ	parent's sister	(aunt)	(Z: sister
Sb	sibling		(e: elder
Co	cousin		(y: younger
C	child		
PP	parent's parent	(grandparent)	
PPSb	sibling of grandparent		(m: male
PPP	great-grandparent		(f: female
PCo	parent's cousin		
CC	child's child	(grandchild)	
CCC	great-grandchild		
SbC	sibling's child	(nephew, niece)	
CoC	cousin's child		
Sp	spouse		
H	husband		
W	wife		
SpP	spouse's parent	(parent-in-law)	
SpF	father-in-law		
SpM	mother-in-law		
SpPSb	spouse's parent's sibling		
SpPP	spouse's parent's parent		
CSp	child's spouse	(son- or daughter-in-law)	
SbSp	sibling's spouse	(brother- or sister-in-law)	
SpSb	spouse's sibling	(brother- or sister-in-law)	
SpSbSp	spouse's sibling's spouse		
CSpP	child's spouse's parent	(co-parent-in-law)	
location	speaker		
reference	person addressed or referred to		
teknonym	"father/mother of [child's name]"		

Kinship Chart I
Bukat Kinship Terminology

Consanguineal
relationships

F	amön (A: ama')
M	inyön (A: ina')
PP, PPP, PPSb	ake'
PB, PCo (m)	mame'
PZ, PCo(f)	ipui
Sb, Co	'arin
C	kelavi, anak
CC, CCC	usun
SbC, CoC	akön

Affinal relationships

H	lole (A: teknonym)
W	doro (A: teknonym)
SpP, SpPSb	boson
CSp	anak boson, kajan
SbSp, SpSb, CoSp, SpCo:	
loc. m, ref. m	lavet
loc. m, ref. f	langu'
loc. f, ref. m	langu'
loc. f, ref. f	ngaran
CSpP	ave', isan
SpSbSp	duai
all affines	lino ivan

Note: See Key to Kinship Charts on page 244.

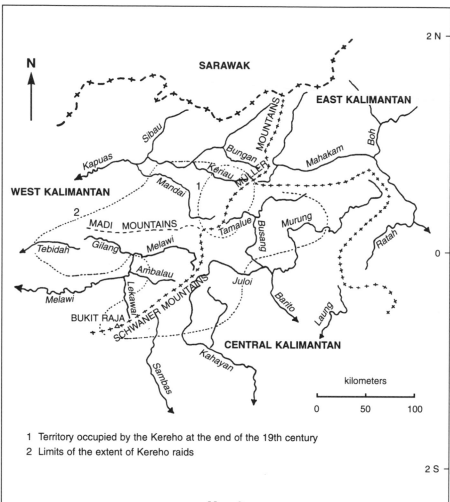

N

SARAWAK

EAST KALIMANTAN

WEST KALIMANTAN

MÜLLER MOUNTAINS

Sibau

Kapuas

Bungan

Keriau

Mandai

1

2

MADI MOUNTAINS

Tamalue

Busang

Murung

Mahakam

Boh

Ratah

0

Tebidah

Gilang

Melawi

Ambalau

Juloi

Barito

Laung

Melawi

Lekawai

SCHWANER MOUNTAINS

BUKIT RAJA

Sambas

Kahayan

CENTRAL KALIMANTAN

kilometers

0   50   100

1 Territory occupied by the Kereho at the end of the 19th century
2 Limits of the extent of Kereho raids

2 N

2 S

Map 9
Areas Occupied by the Kereho

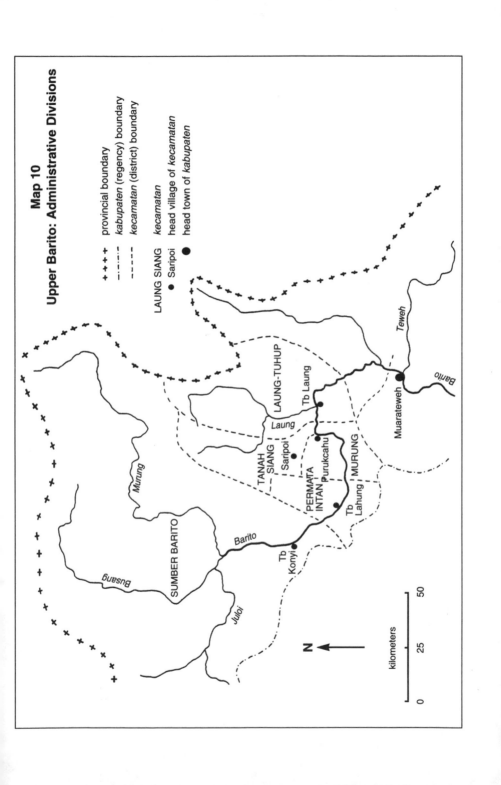

Map 10
Upper Barito: Administrative Divisions

+++	provincial boundary
-··-··-	*kabupaten* (regency) boundary
------	*kecamatan* (district) boundary
LAUNG SIANG	*kecamatan*
Saripoi	head village of *kecamatan*
●	head town of *kabupaten*

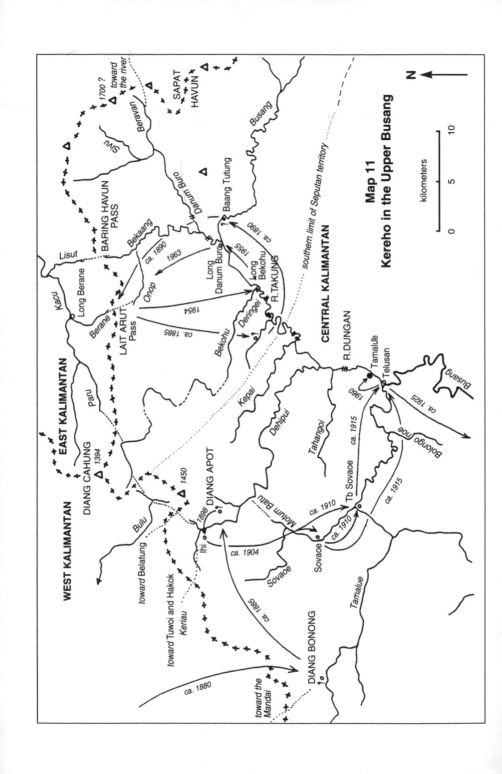

Map 11
Kereho in the Upper Busang

N

kilometers

0   5   10

WEST KALIMANTAN

EAST KALIMANTAN

CENTRAL KALIMANTAN

southern limit of Seputan territory

Paru

Kacu

Lisut

Long Berane

DIANG CAHUNG

Bulu

△ 1394

△ 1450

toward Belatung

toward Tuwoi and Hakok

Keriau

ca. 1885

1898

DIANG APOT

Ihi

ca. 1904

Sovaoe

Sovaoe

Motum Balu

ca. 1910

ca. 1910

ca. 1910

Tb Sovaoe

ca. 1915

ca. 1915

DIANG BONONG

Tamalue

Tamalue

toward the Mandai

ca. 1880

1960

Tamalue

Telusan

R. DUNGAN

Bolongo moe

ca. 1925

Busang

Tahangoi

Dehipui

Kepai

Bekohu

Deringei

R. TAKUNG

ca. 1885

1954

Long Danum Buro

Onop

ca. 1890

1963

Bekaang

Baring Havun Pass

Lait Arut Pass

Berane

Long Berane

Danum Buro

Long Bekohu

1955

ca. 1890

Baang Tutung

△

Busang

Danum Buro

Beravan

Sivu

1700 ?

toward the river

SAPAT HAVUN

△

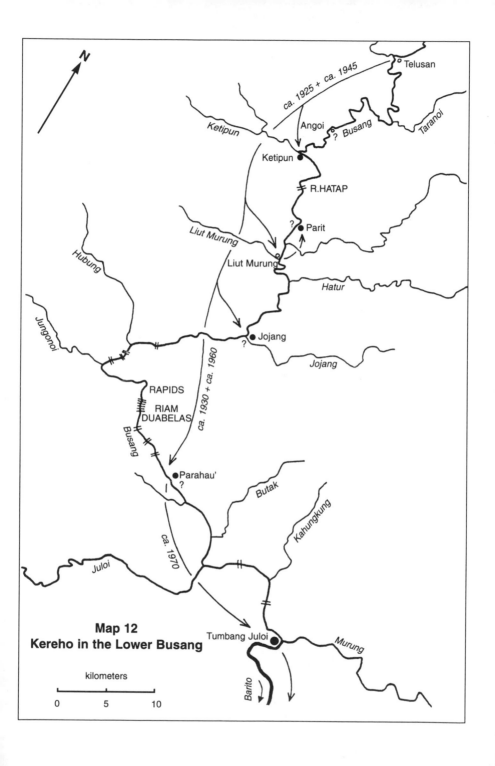

N

ca. 1925 + ca. 1945

Telusan

Ketipun

Angoi

Busang

? Busang

Taranoi

Ketipun

R.HATAP

Liut Murung

? Parit

Hubung

Liut Murung

Hatur

Jungonoi

Jojang

? Jojang

RAPIDS

ca. 1930 + ca. 1960

RIAM
DUABELAS

Busang

Parahau'
?

Butak

Kahungkung

ca. 1970

Juloi

**Map 12
Kereho in the Lower Busang**

Tumbang Juloi

Murung

kilometers

Barito

0   5   10

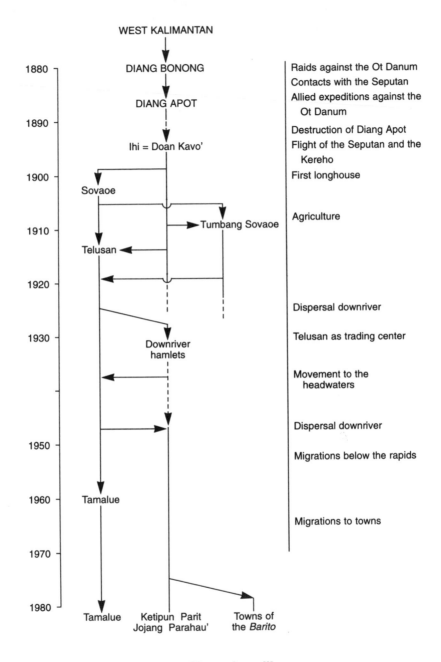

Chronology III
Kereho Busang Migrations

Kinship Chart II
Kereho Kinship Terminology

	KEREHO BUSANG	KEREHO UHENG
Consanguineal relationships		
F	amun (A: ama')	
M	inon (A: ina')	
PP, PPSb	ake'	
PPP	ake'	muyang
PB, PCo(m)	amun okan, aya'	
PZ, PCo(f)	nokan	inon nokan
Sb, Co	doarin	duarin
C	ane'	
CC, CCC	ane' usun	nakon
SbC, CoC	esu	usun
Affinal relationships		
H	saan (A: teknonym)	
W	saan (A: teknonym)	
SpP, SpPSb	dehevan	boson
CSp	ane' evan	boson, ane' evan
SbSp, SpSb, CoSp, SpCo:		
loc. m, ref. m	lango'	lavet
loc. m, ref. f	lavet	lavet
loc. f, ref. m	lavet	lavet
loc. f, ref. f	ngaran	ngaran
CSpP	ave', sange	
SpSbSp	duai	duei

Note: See Key to Kinship Charts on page 244.

Abbreviations

Periodicals

AA	*American Anthropologist,* Washington, D.C.
AE	*American Ethnologist,* Washington, D.C.
Al-Djami'ah	Jakarta
ARB	*Adatrechtbundels,* The Hague
Archipel	Paris
AS	*Anthropologie et Sociétés,* Quebec
ASEMI	*Asie du Sud-Est et Monde Insulindien,* Paris
Ausland (Das)	Munich, Stuttgart
BEFEO	*Bulletin de l'École Française d'Extrême-Orient,* Paris
BIPPA	*Bulletin of the Indo-Pacific Prehistory Association,* Canberra
BKI	*Bijdragen tot de Taal-, Land- en Volkenkunde van Nederlandsch-Indië* (KITLV), Amsterdam, The Hague, Dordrecht, Leiden
BRB	*The Borneo Research Bulletin,* East Lansing, Michigan; Phillips, Maine; Williamsburg, Virginia
BUAE	*Bulletin of the International Committee on Urgent Anthropological and Ethnological Research,* Vienna
CA	*Current Anthropology,* Chicago
CEA	*Cahiers d'Études Africaines,* Paris
EH	*Ethnohistory,* Bloomington, Indiana; Lubbock, Texas; etc.
Folk	Copenhagen
GJ	*Geographical Journal,* London
Homme (L')	Paris

253

IA	*Indisch Archief*, Batavia
Indonesia	Ithaca, New York
Indonesië	The Hague
JIAEA	*Journal of the Indian Archipelago and Eastern Asia*, Singapore
JMBRAS	*Journal of the Royal Asiatic Society, Malaysian Branch*, Singapore
JPS	*Journal of the Polynesian Society*, Wellington
JRAI	*Journal of the Royal Anthropological Institute*, London
JSEAS	*Journal of Southeast Asian Studies*, Singapore
KHG	*Kroniek van het Historisch Genootschap*, Utrecht
KT	*Koloniaal Tijdschrift*, The Hague
Man	London
MNJ	*Malayan Nature Journal*, Kuala Lumpur
NTNI	*Natuurkundig Tijdschrift voor Nederlandsch-Indië*, Weltevreden, Batavia
OA	*Onze Aarde*, Amsterdam
OM	*Objets et Mondes*, Paris
Paideuma	Wiesbaden
PM	*Dr. A. Petermann's Mitteilungen*, Gotha
PQCS	*The Philippine Quarterly of Culture and Society*, Manila
PSR	*The Philippine Sociological Review*, Manila
SA	*Social Analysis*, Adelaide
SG	*The Sarawak Gazette*, Kuching
SMJ	*The Sarawak Museum Journal*, Kuching
SWJA	*Southwestern Journal of Anthropology*, Albuquerque
TBG	*Tijdschrift voor Indische Taal-, Land- en Volkenkunde (Bataviasch Genootschap)*, Batavia
TGLV	*Tijdschrift voor Geschiedenis, Land- en Volkenkunde*, Amsterdam
TN	*Tropisch Nederland*, Amsterdam
TNAG	*Tijdschrift van het Koninklijk Nederlandsch Aardrijkskundig Genootschap*, Amsterdam, Utrecht, Leiden
TNI	*Tijdschrift voor Nederlandsch-Indië*, Batavia
ZAE	*Zeitschrift für Allgemeine Erdkunde*, Berlin

Organizations

AAA	American Anthropological Association
APDN	Akademi Pemerintahan Dalam Negeri, Jakarta and provincial capitals
ASAO	Association for Social Anthropology in Oceania, Ann Arbor, Michigan
CNRS	Centre National de la Recherche Scientifique, Paris
ECASE	Ethnologie Comparative de l'Asie du Sud-Est, CNRS, Paris
EHESS	École des Hautes Études en Sciences Sociales, Paris
HRAF	Human Relations Area Files, New Haven, Connecticut
KITLV	Koninklijk Instituut voor Taal-, Land- en Volkenkunde, Leiden
ORSTOM	Office pour la Recherche Scientifique et Technique Outre-Mer, Paris
P & K	Departemen Pendidikan dan Kebudayaan, Jakarta, and provincial capitals
T.A.D.	Transmigration Area Development Project, Samarinda (Indonesia) and Hamburg

BIBLIOGRAPHY

Anderson, J. A. R., A. C. Jermy, and the Earl of Cranbrook
1982 *Gunung Mulu National Park, Sarawak: A management and development plan.* London: Royal Geographic Society.

Anonymous
1859 "Der Manketta-Häuptling. Ein Sittengemälde aus Borneo." *Das Ausland* 21: 481–485, 516–520, 534–539.
1882 (Note on the nomads). *SG* 12 (no. 185): 10–12 (1 March 1882).
1894 In *Koloniaal Verslag van 1894 (Nederland Oost-Indië),* Bijlage C, 2de Kamer (5–2): 24–26.
1901 In *TNI* 5: 576–578, 847–849.
1907 "The Uma Lisooms." *SG* 37: 135 (5 June 1907).
1920 "A Journey Across Borneo from Banjermasin to Kuching in Sarawak." *GJ* 56:72.
1957 *Daftar kata2 daerah Kalimantan.* Jakarta: Ministry of Education, Instruction and Culture.
1968 "Adat-istiadat dan tata tjara tradisionel suku Punan di ketjamatan Kelay (kab. Berau)." In *Monografi Daerah Propinsi Kalimantan Timur 1968.* Samarinda: P & K, 116–128.
1969 "Adat-istiadat dan tata tjara tradisionel suku Kenyah dan Punan di ketjamatan Tabang kabupaten Kutai." In *Monografi Daerah Propinsi Kalimantan Timur 1969.* Samarinda: P & K, 162–170.

Appell, G. N., ed.
1976a *The Societies of Borneo: Explorations in the Theory of Cognatic Social Structure.* Washington, D.C.: AAA Special Publication no. 6.
1976b *Studies in Borneo Societies: Social Process and Anthropological Explanation.* Northern Illinois University, Center for Southeast Asian Studies, Special Report no. 12.

Arnold, G.
1958 "Nomadic Penan of the Upper Rejang (Plieran), Sarawak." *JMBRAS* 31(1): 40–82.
1967 *Longhouse and Jungle: An Expedition to Sarawak.* Singapore: Donald Moore Press.

257

Asch, M. I.
1979 "The Ecological Evolutionary Model and the Concept of Mode of Production." In *Challenging Anthropology*, ed. D. H. Turner and G. A. Smith. Toronto: McGraw-Hill Ryerson, 81–99.

Avé, J.
1972a "Kalimantan Dayaks." In *Ethnic Groups of Insular Southeast Asia*, ed. F. LeBar. New Haven, Conn.: HRAF Press, 185–187.
1972b "Ot Danum Dayaks." In *Ethnic Groups of Insular Southeast Asia*, ed. F. LeBar. New Haven, Conn.: HRAF Press, 192–194.
1977 "Sago in Insular Southeast Asia: Historical Aspects and Contemporary Use." In *Papers of the First International Sago Symposium 1976*, ed. Koonlin Tan. Kuala Lumpur, 21–30.

Avé, J., and V. T. King
1986 *Borneo: The People of the Weeping Forest, Tradition and Change in Borneo.* Leiden: National Museum of Ethnology.

A.Y.H.
1980 *Kabupaten Daerah Tingkat II Kapuas Hulu.* Putussibau.

Bailey, D. J. S.
1963 "The Sru Dyaks (2nd Division)." In *The Sea-Dyaks and Other Races of Sarawak*, ed. A. Richards. Kuching: Borneo Literature Bureau, 331–340. Reprinted from *SG* 31 (1901): 48–50, 179.

Baling Avun
1961 MS map of villages of the Upper Kapuas. Archives of Tom Harrisson. (Courtesy of Jérôme Rousseau.)

Barclay, J.
1980 *A Stroll Through Borneo.* London: Hodder and Stoughton.

Barth, F.
1964 *Nomads of South Persia: The Basseri Tribe of the Khamseh Confederacy.* London: Allen & Unwin.

Barth, F. (ed.)
1969 *Ethnic Groups and Boundaries.* Boston: Little, Brown & Co.

Barth, J. P. J.
1904 "Report Boven-Mahakam." Archives of the Colonial Ministry, April 1904.
1910 *Boesangsch-Nederlandsch Woordenboek.* Batavia: Landsdrukkerij.

Battan, H. M.
1976 "Masalah kehidupan sosial ekonomi masyarakat kecamatan Long Apari kabupaten Kutai." Samarinda: APDN.

Becker, J. F.
1849a "Het District Poelopetak, Zuid- en Oost-Kust van Borneo." *IA* 1(1): 421–473.
1849b "Reis van Poelopetak naar de Binnenlanden van Borneo langs de Kapoeas Rivier." *IA* 1(1): 318–330.

Bellwood, P.
1983 "New Perspectives on Indo-Malaysian Prehistory." *BIPPA* 4: 17–83.

Benjamin, G.
1974 *Indigenous Religious Systems of the Malay Peninsula*. Singapore: National University, Department of Sociology, Working Papers no. 28. Published in *The Imagination of Reality: Essays in Southeast Asian Coherence Systems*, ed. A. L. Becker and A. A. Yengoyan. Norwood, N.J.: Ablex, 1979, 9–27.
1985 "Between Isthmus and Islands: Notes on Malayan Palaeo-Sociology." Communication, 12th Congress of the Indo-Pacific Prehistory Association, Peñablanca (Philippines), Jan.–Feb. 1985. Published as *Between Isthmus and Islands: Reflections on Malayan Palaeo-Sociology*. Singapore: National University, Department of Sociology, Working Papers no. 71, 1986.

Black, I.
1984 "The 'lastposten': Dutch Penetration of Eastern Kalimantan and the Local Responses." Communication, 5th National Conference of the Asian Studies Association of Australia, Adelaide, May 1984.

Blust, R. A.
1976 "Austronesian Culture History: Some Linguistic Inferences and the Relations to the Archaeological Record." *World Archaeology* 8 (1):19–43.

Bock, C.
1887 *Chez les cannibales de Bornéo*. Tours: Alfred Mame.
1985 (1881) *The Head-Hunters of Borneo: A Narrative of Travel up the Mahakam and down the Barito*. Singapore: Oxford University Press.

Bouman, M. A.
1924 "Ethnografische aanteekeningen omtrent de Gouvernementslanden in de boven-Kapoeas, Westerafdeeling van Borneo." *TBG* 64:173–195.
1952 "Gegevens uit Smitau en Boven-Kapoeas." *ARB* 44:47–86.

Bourdieu, P.
1980 *Le Sens pratique*. Paris: Éditions de Minuit.

Brooke, C.
1866 *Ten Years in Sarawak*. London: Tinsley.

Brosius, J. P.
1986 "River, Forest and Mountain: The Penan Gang Landscape." *SMJ* 36 (57): 173–184.
1992 "The Axiological Presence of Death: Penan G@ng Death Names." Ph.D. diss., University of Michigan, Ann Arbor.

Bücher, A.
1970 (June) Series of fourteen articles in *The Djakarta Times*.

Budowski, G.
1978 "Food from the Forest." Communication, 8th World Forestry Congress, Jakarta, 1978.

Bulbeck, D.
1976 Personal communication.

Burkill, I. H.
1924 "A List of Oriental Vernacular Names of the Genus *Dioscorea*." *The Gardens' Bulletin, Straits Settlements* 3 (4–6): 121–244.
1951 "*Dioscoreaceae*." *Flora Malesiana* 4/3 (1):293–335.

Burns, R.
1849 "The Kayans of Northwest Borneo." *JIAEA* 3:138–152.

Büttikofer, J.
1894–1895 "Toch naar de Boven Kapoeas op het eiland Borneo." *TNAG* 11:289–292, 432–438, 642–643, 749–751, 858–859, 965–972, 1008–1012; 12: 113–133.

Cashdan, E.
1983 "Territoriality among Human Foragers: Ecological Models and an Application to Four Bushman Groups." *CA* 24 (1): 47–66.

Cense, A. A., and E. M. Ühlenbeck
1958 *Critical Survey on the Languages of Borneo*. The Hague: Nijhoff, KITLV Bibliographical Series no. 2.

Chai, P. P. K.
1975 "Ethnobotany (Part I)." *SMJ* 23 (44): 37–51.
1978 "Ethnobotany (Part II)." *SMJ* 26 (47): 243–270.

Chin, L., and R. Nyandoh
1975 "Archaeological Work in Sarawak." *SMJ* 23 (44): 1–7.

Combanaire, A.
Undated: ca. 1910 *Au pays des coupeurs de têtes: À travers Bornéo*. Paris: Plon-Nourrit.

Condominas, G.
1977 *We Have Eaten the Forest: The Story of a Montagnard Village in the Central Highlands of Vietnam*. Translated from the French by Adrienne Foulke. Photographs, maps, and diagrams by the author. New York: Hill & Wang; Harmondsworth, U.K.: Penguin Books.
1980 *L'Espace social: À propos de l'Asie du Sud-Est*. Paris: Flammarion.

Coomans, M. C. C.
1980 *Evangelisatie en Kultuurverandering*. St. Augustin: Steyler Verlag.

Daftar Kata-2 (List of Words) Daerah Kalimantan
1957 Jakarta: Ministry of Education, Instruction and Culture.

Dahlberg, F. (ed.)
1981 *Woman the Gatherer*. New Haven and London: Yale University Press.

Deshon, H. F.
1901a "The Attack on Some Lisums." *SG* 31: 8.
1901b "The Lisums." *SG* 31: 117 (1 June 1901).

Dewall, H. von
1849 "Extract uit de dagelijksche aanteekeningen van den civielen gezaghebber voor Koetei en de oostkust van Borneo, H. von Dewall, op eene reis van Bandjarmassin naar Koetei, Passier, en van daar terug naar Bandjarmassin; van 1 Nov. 1846 tot 2 Sept. 1847." *IA* 1 (1): 85–105, 123–160.
1855 "Aanteekeningen omtrent de Noordoostkust van Borneo." *TBG* 4: 423–464.

Ding Ngo, A. J.
1977 "Mengunjungi Mahakam." Unpublished MS.

Dormeier, J. J.
1952 "Gebruiken bij huwelijk en sterfgeval: Adatdelicten der Ponjawung, Heban en Mantuwah-Dajaks (Kuala Kapuas)." *ARB* 44: 230–238.

Douglas, M.
1982 *Natural Symbols: Explorations in Cosmology.* New York: Pantheon.

Dumont, L.
1986 "Are Cultures Living Beings? German Identity in Interaction." *Man* 21 (4): 587–604.

Dyson-Hudson, R., and E. A. Smith
1978 "Human Territoriality: An Ecological Reassessment." *AA* 80: 21–41.

Eder, J. F.
1977 "Portrait of a Dying Society: Contemporary Demographic Conditions among the Batak of Palawan." *PQCS* 5: 12–20.

Eisenberger, J.
1936 *Kroniek de Zuider- en Oosterafdeeling van Borneo.* Bandjermasin: Liem Hwat Sing.

Ellis, D. B. (ed.)
1972 "A Study of the Punan Busang." *SMJ* 20 (40–41): 235–299.

Elshout, J. M.
1926 *De Kenja-Dajaks uit het Apokajan gebied.* The Hague: Nijhoff.

Engelhard, H. E. D.
1897 "Aanteekeningen betreffende de Kindjin Dajaks in het landschap Baloengan." *TBG* 39: 458–495.

Enthoven, J. J. K.
1903 *Bijdragen tot de Geographie van Borneo's Westerafdeeling.* 2 vols. Leiden: Brill.

Estioko, A. A., and P. B. Griffin
1975 "The Ebuked Agta of Northern Luzon." *PQCS* 3:237–244.

Evans, I. H. N.
1970 (1923) *Studies in Religion, Folk-Lore and Custom in British North Borneo and the Malay Peninsula.* London: Frank Cass.

Formoso, B.
1986 *Tsiganes et sédentaires: La reproduction culturelle d'une société.* Paris: L'Harmattan.

Fox, R. B.
1957 "A Consideration of Theories Concerning Possible Affiliations of Mindanao Cultures with Borneo, the Celebes, and Other Regions of the Philippines." *PSR* 5 (1):2–12.

Freeman, J. D.
1970 *Report on the Iban.* London School of Economics, Monographs on Social Anthropology no. 41. New York: Athlone Press.

Friedman, J.
1975 "Dynamique et transformations du système tribal: L'exemple des Katchin." *L'Homme* 15 (1): 63–92.

Gennep, A. van
1960 *The Rites of Passage.* Chicago: University of Chicago Press.

Gerlach, L. W. C.
1881 "Reis naar het meergebied van den Kapoeas in Borneo's Westerafdeeling." *BKI* 29: 285–322.

Guerreiro, A.
1984 "Min, 'maisons' et organisation sociale: Contribution à l'ethnographie des sociétés Modang de Kalimantan-Est, Indonésie." Ph.D. diss., Paris: EHESS.
1987 "The Lahanan: Some Notes on the History of a Kajang Group." Unpublished MS.

Guillaume, H.
1986 "Mobilité et flexibilité chez les chasseurs-collecteurs pygmées Aka." In *Nomadisme: Mobilité et flexibilité?* Paris: ORSTOM, Départment H, Bulletin de Liaison no. 8, 59–85.

Haddon, E. B.
1905 "The Dog-motif in Bornean Art." *JRAI* 35:113–125.

Hang Nyipa
1956 "Migrations of the Kayan People." *SMJ* 7 (7):82–88.

Harrisson, T.
1949 "Notes on Some Nomadic Punans." *SMJ* 5 (1):130–146.
1965 "The Maloh of Kalimantan: Ethnological Notes." *SMJ* 12 (25–26): 236–350.
1967 "Ethnological Notes on the Muruts of the Sapulut River, Sabah." *JMBRAS* 40:111–129.
1984 (1970) "The Prehistory of Borneo." In *Prehistoric Indonesia,* ed. P. van de Velde. Dordrecht: Foris, 297–326.
Undated "The last of the Serus: A Study in Dynamic Decay." Unpublished MS. (Courtesy of Jérôme Rousseau.)

Harrisson, T. (ed.)
1959 *The Peoples of Sarawak.* Kuching: Sarawak Museum.

Hartman, J. F.
1864 "Beschrijving van eenen togt naar de bovenlanden van Bandjermassin enz. in het jaar 1790." *KHG* 20: 331–404.

Haudricourt, A. G., and L. Hédin
1987 (1943) *L'Homme et les plantes cultivées*. Paris: Métailié.

Headland, T. N.
1975 "The Casiguran Dumagats Today and in 1936." *PQCS* 3: 245–257.

Heine-Geldern, R.
1946 "Research on Southeast Asia: Problems and Suggestions." *AA* 48: 149–175.

Heppell, M.
Undated "Report on the Bukat (Ukit) of Long Ayak." Unpublished MS.

Hildebrand, H. K.
1982 *Die Wildbeutergruppen Borneos*. Munich: Minerva Publikation, Münchner Ethnologische Abhandlungen no. 2.

Hoffman, C. L.
1983 "Punan." Ph.D. diss., University of Pennsylvania. Published as *The Punan: Hunters and Gatherers of Borneo*. Ann Arbor: UMI Research Press, Studies in Cultural Anthropology no. 12, 1986.
1984 "Punan Foragers in the Trading Networks of Southeast Asia." In *Past and Present in Hunter-Gatherer Studies*, ed. C. Schrire. London: Academic Press, 123–149.

Holle
1916 "Woordenlijst 145 (Penyabong)." Unpublished MS.

Holmberg, A. R.
1969 *Nomads of the Long Bow: The Siriono of Eastern Bolivia*. New York: Natural History Press.

Hose, C.
1894–1895 "The Natives of Borneo." *SG* 24:172–173, 192–193, 214–215; 25: 18–19, 39–40.

Hose, C., and W. McDougall
1912 *The Pagan Tribes of Borneo*. 2 vols. London: Macmillan.

Hudson, A. B.
1967 *The Barito Isolects of Borneo*. Ithaca, N.Y.: Cornell University Press.
1978 "Linguistic Relations among Bornean Peoples with Special Reference to Sarawak: An Interim Report." In *Sarawak: Linguistics and Development Problems*. Studies in Third World Societies 3:1–44.

Huehne, W. H.
1959–1960 "A Doctor among 'Nomadic' Punans." *SMJ* 9 (13–14):195–202.

Israel, M. E. L.
1938 "Vervolgmemorie van overgave van de afdeeling Samarinda, 1938." Archives Koningklijk Instituut voor de Tropen.

Ivanoff, J.
1985 "L'Épopée de Gaman: Histoire et conséquences des relations Moken/Malais et Moken/Birmans." *ASEMI* 16 (1–4):173–194.

Jackson, J. C.
1968 *Sarawak: A Geographical Survey of a Developing State*. London: University of London Press.

Jayl Langub
1972 "Structure and Progress of the Punan Community of Belaga Subdistrict." *SG* 97 (1378): 219–221.
1974 "Adaptation to a Settled Life by the Punan of the Belaga Sub-District." In *The Peoples of Central Borneo,* ed. J. Rousseau. Special Issue of the *SMJ* 22 (43): 295–301.

Johnson, D.
1977 "Distribution of Sago Making in the Old World." In *Papers of the First International Sago Symposium 1976,* ed. Koonlin Tan. Kuala Lumpur.

Jongejans, J.
1922 *Uit Dajakland.* Amsterdam: Meulenhoff.

Kater, C.
1867 "Rapport aangaande eene op de Boven-Kapoeas plaats gehad hebbende sneltogt." *TNI* 16: 252–258.

Kay, J.
1984 "The Fur Trade and Native American Population Growth." *EH* 31 (4): 265–287.

Kedit, P. M.
1982 "An Ecological Survey of the Penan." *SMJ* 30 (51): 225–279.

Kennedy, R.
1974 (1935) *A Bibliography of Indonesian Peoples and Cultures.* Rev. ed. New Haven, Conn.: Yale University (HRAF).

Kessel, O. von
1849–1850 "Statistieke aanteekeningen omtrent het stroomgebied der rivier Kapoeas (Westerafdeeling van Borneo)." *IA* 1 (2): 165–204.
1857 "Über die Volkstämme Borneos." *ZAE* n.s. 3: 377–410.

King, V. T.
1974a "Some Suggestions for Future Research in West Kalimantan." *BRB* 6 (2): 31–38.
1974b "Notes on Punan and Bukat in West Kalimantan." *BRB* 6 (2):39–42.
1975a "A Note on Bukitan in West Kalimantan." *SG* 101 (1403), 2–3.
1975b "Bukitan in Enthoven: A Further Note." *SG* 101 (1407), 94–95.
1976 "Some Aspects of Iban-Maloh Contact in West Kalimantan." *Indonesia* 21: 85–114.
1979a *Ethnic Classification and Ethnic Relations: A Borneo Case Study.* University of Hull, Centre for South-East Asian Studies, Occasional Paper no. 2.
1979b "Research on Former Nomads in West Kalimantan (Western Indonesian Borneo)." *BUAE* 21:89–98.
1985 *The Maloh of West Kalimantan.* Dordrecht: Foris (Verhand. KITLV no. 108).

King, V. T. (ed.)
1978 *Essays on Borneo Societies.* Hull Monographs on South-East Asia no. 7. Oxford: Oxford University Press.

Klausen, A. M.
1957 *Basket-work Ornamentation among the Dayak*. Oslo: Forenede Trykkerier.

Knappert, S. C.
1905 "Beschrijving van de onderafdeeling Koetei." *BKI* 58: 575–654.

Kuehlewein, M. von
1930 *Rapport over een reis naar de onderafdeeling Boven-Mahakam (Borneo) Februari–Mei 1929*. Weltevreden: G. Kolff & Co. Also published in *Mededeelingen van den Dienst der Volksgezondheid in Ned.-Indië* 19: 65–155, 1930.

Leach, E. R.
1948 *Report on the Possibilities of a Social Economic Survey of Sarawak*. London. Mimeograph.
1965 (1954) *Political Systems of Highland Burma*. Boston: Beacon Press.

LeBar, F. M. (ed.)
1972 *Ethnic Groups of Insular Southeast Asia, vol. 1: Indonesia*. New Haven, Conn.: HRAF Press.

Lee, R. B., and I. DeVore (eds.)
1982 (1968) *Man the Hunter*. New York: Aldine.

Lijnden, D. W. C. van, and J. Groll
1851 "Aanteekening over de landen van het stroomgebied der Kapoeas." *NTNI* 2: 537–636.

Low, H. B.
1882 "Journal of a Trip up the Rejang." *SG* 12:52–54, 62–65, 72–73, 81–83, 93–96.

Lowie, R. H.
1915 "Oral Tradition and History." *AA* 17: 597–599. Cited in Willis 1980:28.

Lumholtz, C.
1920 *Through Central Borneo*. 2 vols. London: T. F. Unwin.
Undated Word list: English, Aoheng, Saputan, Penyabong Punan, Omasuling, Busang, Longglat, Duhoi, Katingan, Tamoan. Unpublished MS. (Courtesy Steinar Sörensen).

MacCarthy, F. D.
1953 "The Oceanic and Indonesian Affiliations of Australian Aboriginal Culture." *JPS* 62: 243–261.

Macdonald, C.
1977 *Une Société simple: Parenté et résidence chez les Palawan (Philippines)*. Paris: Musée de l'Homme, Institut d'Ethnologie.
1986 Personal communication.

Maceda, M. N.
1975 "Culture Change among a Mamanua Group of Northeastern Mindanao." *PQCS* 3: 258–276.

McKinley, R.
1978 "Pioneer Expansion, Assimilation and the Founding of Ethnic Unity among the Iban." *SMJ* 26 (47): 15–27.

Mallinckrodt, J.
1927 "De stamindeeling van de Maanjan-Sioeng-Dajaks der Zuider- en Ooster-Afdeeling van Borneo." *BKI* 83: 552–592.

Marcus Sinau
1970 "Usaha meningkatkan taraf kehidupan dan penghidupan suku Dajak Punan Ketjamatan Malinau Kabupaten Bulungan." Samarinda: APDN.

Martinoir, B. de
1974 "Notes on the Kajang." In *The Peoples of Central Borneo*, ed. J. Rousseau. Special Issue of the *SMJ* 22 (43): 267–273.

Massey, B. W. E.
1919 "Bandjermasin-Kuching, via central Borneo." *SG* 49: 18–19, 31–33.
1920 *See* Anonymous, 1920.

Mauss, M.
1983 (1950) "Les Techniques du corps" (1936). In *Sociologie et Anthropologie*. Paris: Quadrige-PUF.

Metcalf, P.
1975 "The Distribution of Secondary Treatment of the Dead in Central North Borneo." *BRB* 7 (2): 54–59.
1982 *A Borneo Journey into Death: Berawan Eschatology from Its Rituals*. Philadelphia: University of Pennsylvania Press.

Meyners d'Estrey, Comte
1891 *A travers Bornéo*. Paris: Hachette.

Miller, C. C.
1946 *Black Borneo*. London: Museum Press.

Mjöberg, E.
1934 *Bornéo: L'Île des chasseurs de têtes*. Paris: Plon.

Molengraaff, G. A. F.
1895a "De Nederlandsche expeditie naar Centraal-Borneo in 1894." In *Handelingen van het 5de Nederlandsche Natuur- en Geneeskundig Congres, Amsterdam, April 1895*. Haarlem: Kleynenberg, 498–506.
1895b "Die niederländische Expedition nach Zentral Borneo in den Jahren 1893 und 1894." *PM* 41: 201–208.
1900 *Borneo Expeditie: Geologische Verkenningstochten in Centraal Borneo (1893–1894)*. Leiden: Brill; Amsterdam: Gerlings.
1902 *Borneo Expedition: Geological Explorations in Central Borneo (1893–1894)*. Leiden: Brill; London: Kegan Paul, Trench, Trubner & Co.

Monografi Daerah Kalimantan Tengah, 1979. Jakarta: Proyek Media Kebudayaan, P & K.

Monografi Daerah Propinsi Kalimantan Timur, 1968. See Anonymous 1968.

Morgan, S.
1968 "Iban Aggressive Expansion: Some Background Factors." *SMJ* 16 (32–33): 141–185.

Morris, H. S.
1978 "The Coastal Melanau." In *Essays on Borneo Societies,* ed. V. T. King. Hull Monographs on South-East Asia no. 7. Oxford: Oxford University Press, 37–58.
1983 "Kinship and Rank among the Coastal Melanau of Sarawak." In *Cognatic Forms of Social Organization in Southeast Asia.* Proceedings of the Symposium on Cognatic Forms of Social Organization in Southeast Asia, January 1983. 2 vols. Amsterdam: University of Amsterdam.

Naerssen, F. H. van
1951–1952 "Een streekonderzoek in West-Borneo." *Indonesië* 5:133–166.

Needham, R.
1954a "A Note on Some Nomadic Punan." *Indonesië* 7: 520–523.
1954b "Siriono and Penan: A Test of Some Hypotheses." *SWJA* 10: 228–232.
1954c "The System of Teknonyms and Death-names of the Penan." *SWJA* 10: 416–431.
1966 "Age, Category and Descent." *BKI* 122:1–35.
1971 "Penan Friendship-names." In *The Translation of Culture,* ed. T. O. Beidelman. London: Tavistock, 203–230.
1972 "Punan-Penan." In *Ethnic Groups of Insular Southeast Asia, vol. 1: Indonesia,* ed. F. M. LeBar. New Haven, Conn.: HRAF Press, 176–180.

Nicolaisen, I.
1976 "Form and Function of Punan Bah Ethno-historical Tradition." *SMJ* 24 (45): 63–95.
1986 "Pride and Progress: Kajang Response to Economic Change." *SMJ* 36 (57): 75–116. MS 1984.

Nicolaisen, J.
1976a "The Penan of Sarawak: Further Notes on the Neo-evolutionary Concept of Hunters." *Folk* 18: 205–236.
1976b "The Penan of the Seventh Division of Sarawak: Past, Present and Future." *SMJ* 24 (45): 35–62.
1978 "Penan Death-names." *SMJ* 26 (47): 29–41.

Nieuwenhuis, A. W.
1900a *In Centraal Borneo.* 2 vols. Leiden: Brill.
1900b "Tweede reis van Pontianak naar Samarinda in 1898 en 1899." *TNAG* 2d ser., 17: 177–204, 411–435.
1902 "Een schets van de bevolking in Centraal Borneo." *TGLV* 17: 178–208.
1904–1907 *Quer durch Borneo.* 2 vols. Leiden: Brill.
1928 *Ten Years of Hygiene and Ethnology in Primitive Borneo (1891–1901).* Weltevreden.

O'Hanlon, R.
1985 *Into the Heart of Borneo.* Harmondsworth, U.K.: Penguin Books.

Padoch, C.
1982 *Migration and Its Alternatives among the Iban of Sarawak.* The Hague: Nijhoff (Verhand. KITLV no. 98).
1983 "Agricultural Practices of the Kerayan Lun Dayeh." *BRB* 15 (1): 33–38.

Pauwels, P. C.
1935 "Poenan's in de onderafdeeling Boeloengan." *KT* 24: 342–353.

Perelaer, M. T. H.
1870 *Ethnographische beschrijving der Dajaks.* Zalt-Bommel: J. Norman.
1881 *Borneo van Zuid naar Noord.* 2 vols. Rotterdam: Elsevier.

Peterson, N.
1975 "Hunter-Gatherer Territoriality: The Perspective from Australia." *AA* 77: 53–68.

Pfeffer, P.
1963 *Bivouacs à Bornéo.* Paris: Flammarion.

Pfeffer, P., and J. Caldecott
1986 "The Bearded Pig *(Sus barbatus)* in East Kalimantan and Sarawak." *JMBRAS* 59 (2): 81–100.

Pringle, R.
1970 *Rajahs and Rebels: The Ibans of Sarawak under Brooke Rule (1841–1941).* London: Macmillan.

Puri, R. K.
1992 "Mammals and Hunting on the Lurah River." Paper presented at the Borneo Research Council's Second Biennial International Meeting, Kota Kinabalu, Sabah, Malaysia, 13–17 July 1992.

Ray, S. H.
1913 "The Languages of Borneo." *SMJ* 1 (4):1–196.

Revel-Macdonald, N.
1978 "La danse des *hudoq.*" *OM* 18: 31–44.

Rosaldo, R.
1980 *Ilongot Headhunting 1883–1974: A Study in Society and History.* Stanford, Calif.: Stanford University Press.

Roth, H. L.
1968 (1896) *The Natives of Sarawak and British North Borneo.* 2 vols. Singapore: University of Malaya Press.

Rousseau, J.
1971 Word list from the Bukat of the Balui. Unpublished MS.
1974 "The Baluy Area." In *The Peoples of Central Borneo,* ed. J. Rousseau. Special Issue of the *SMJ* 22 (43):17–27.
1975 "Ethnic Identity and Social Relations in Central Borneo." In *Pluralism in Malaysia: Myth and Reality,* ed. J. A. Nagata. Leiden: Brill, 32–49.
1977 "Kayan Agriculture." *SMJ* 25 (46):129–156.
1984 "Review Article: Four Theses on the Nomads of Central Borneo." *BRB* 16 (2):85–95.
1985 "The Ideological Prerequisites of Inequality." In *Development and Decline: The Evolution of Socio-political Organization,* ed. H. M. J. Claessen, P. van de Velde, and E. Smith. South Hadley, Mass.: Bergin & Garvey, 36–46.

1990 *Central Borneo: Ethnic Identity and Social Life in a Stratified Society.* Oxford: Clarendon Press.
Undated "Central Borneo and Its Relations with Coastal Malay Sultanates." Unpublished MS.

R[ozario], F. de
1963 "The Sru Dyaks." In *The Sea-Dyaks and Other Races of Sarawak,* ed. A. Richards. Kuching: Borneo Literature Bureau, 341–343. Reprinted from *SG* 31 (1901):175.

Rutten, M. L. R.
1916 "Reisherinneringen uit Zuid-Oost Boelongan (Oost-Borneo)." *TNAG* 33: 236–253.

Salzner, R.
1960 *Sprachenatlas des Indopazifischen Räumes.* Wiesbaden: Harrassowitz.

Sandin, B.
1956 "The Westward Migration of the Sea Dayaks." *SMJ* 7 (7):54–81.
1957 "The Sea Dayak Migration to Niah River." *SMJ* 8 (10): 133–135.
1965 "Punan La'ong (Two Notes)." *SMJ* 12 (25–26): 185–187.
1967–1968 "The Baketans." *SMJ* 15 (30–31):228–242; 16 (32–33):111–121.

Sarwoto Kertodipoero
1963 *Kaharingan, Religi dan Penghidupan.* Bandung: Sumur Bandung.

Schärer, H.
1963 *Ngaju Religion: The Conception of God among a South Borneo People.* The Hague: Nijhoff (KITLV Translation Series 6).

Schebesta, P.
1973 (1928) *Among the Forest Dwarfs of Malaya.* Kuala Lumpur, Singapore: Oxford University Press.

Schneeberger, W. F.
1933 "Globaal Geologisch Onderzoek, Boven-Mahakam-Belajan." MS: Geolog. Rapport no. 14115, Archief GA Batavia no. 10318, Balikpapan.

Schrire, C. (ed.)
1984 *Past and Present in Hunter Gatherer Studies.* London, Orlando: Academic Press.

Schwaner, C. A. L. M.
1853–1854 *Borneo: Beschrijving van het stroomgebied van den Barito.* 2 vols. Amsterdam: P. N. van Kampen.
1968 (1896) "Ethnographical Notes by Dr. Schwaner." In *The Natives of Sarawak and British North Borneo,* by H. L. Roth. Singapore: University of Malaya Press, 2:CLXI–CCVII.

Seitz, S.
1981 "Die Penan in Sarawak und Brunei: Ihre Kultur-historische Einordnung und Gegenwärtige Situation." *Paideuma* 27: 275–311.

Sellato, B. J. L.
1980 "The Upper Mahakam Area." *BRB* 12 (2): 40–46.
1981a "La Région de la haute Mahakam, Est-Kalimantan." *Archipel* 22: 21–42.

1981b "Three-gender Personal Pronouns in Some Languages of Central Borneo."
     BRB 13 (1): 48–49.
1983a "Le Mythe du Tigre au centre de Bornéo." *ASEMI* 14 (1–2): 25–49.
1983b "Nomadism, Utrolocal Residence and Affinal Terminology in Borneo." In
     Cognatic Forms of Social Organization in Southeast Asia. Proceedings of the
     Symposium on Cognative Forms of Social Organization in Southeast Asia, Janu-
     ary 1983. Amsterdam: University of Amsterdam, 1: 82–91.
1984 "Mémoire collective et nomadisme." *Archipel* 27: 85–108.
1986a "An Ethnic Sketch of the Melawi Area, West Kalimantan." *BRB* 18 (1):
     46–58.
1986b "Les Nomades forestiers de Bornéo et la sédentarisation: Essai d'histoire
     économique et sociale." Ph.D. diss., Paris: EHESS.
1987 "Note préliminaire sur les sociétés 'à maison' de Bornéo" and "Maisons et
     organisation sociale en Asie du Sud-Est." In *De la hutte au palais: Sociétés "à
     maison" en Asie du Sud-Est insulaire,* ed. C. Macdonald. Paris: CNRS-ECASE,
     14–44, 195–207.
1988 "The Nomads of Borneo: Hoffman and 'Devolution.' " *BRB* 20 (2):106–120.
     Review of Carl L. Hoffman's "Punan," 1983.
1989 *Hornbill and Dragon (Naga dan Burung Enggang): Kalimantan, Sarawak,
     Sabah, Brunei.* Bilingual text (English and Indonesian/Malay), 176 color photo
     plates (550 photographs), 100 ink drawings. Jakarta: Elf Aquitaine. 2d ed. in
     English: *Hornbill and Dragon: Arts and Culture of Borneo.* Singapore: Sun Tree
     Publishing, 1992.
1990 "A Note on the Penan of Brunei." *BRB* 22 (1): 37–42.
1992a "The Punan Question and the Reconstruction of Borneo's Culture History."
     In *Change and Development in Borneo: Selected Papers from the First Extraor-
     dinary Conference of the Borneo Research Council, Kuching, Sarawak,* ed.
     V. H. Sutlive, Jr. Williamsburg, Va.: The Borneo Research Council, 47–81.
1992b "Rituel, politique, organisation sociale et ethnogenèse: Les Aoheng de
     Bornéo." *BEFEO* 79 (2):45–66.
1993 "Myth, History, and Modern Cultural Identity among Hunter-Gatherers: A
     Borneo Case." *JSEAS* 24 (1): 18–43.
In press (a) "Salt in Borneo." In *Le Sel de la vie en Asie du Sud-Est,* ed. P. Le Roux
     and J. Ivanoff. Patani: Prince of Songkla University Press, "Grand Sud" no. 4.
In press (b) "Spatial Organization and Provincial Cultural Identity: Historical Fac-
     tors and Current Trends in Kalimantan." In *Centres and Peripheries in Insular
     Southeast Asia,* ed. M. Charras. Paris: CNRS.

Service, E. R.
1966 *The Hunters.* Englewood Cliffs, N.J.: Prentice-Hall (Foundations of Modern
     Anthropology Series).

SG 1885, 1886, 1887, 1890, 1891 Selections from the *Sarawak Gazette.*

Simandjuntak, M.
1967 "Masjarakat Punan Ketjamatan Kelaij Kabupaten Berau Propinsi Kaliman-
     tan Timur." Samarinda: APDN.

Sloan, C.
1975 "A Study of the Punan Busang, III: Punan Hunting Methods." *MNJ* 28 (3–4): 146–151.

Smith, J. G. E.
1974 "Proscription of Cross-Cousin Marriage among the Southwestern Ojibwa." In *Uses of Ethnohistory in Ethnographic Analysis*. Special Issue of *AE* 1 (4): 751–762.

Stöhr, W.
1959 *Das Totenritual der Dajak*. Cologne: Brill (Ethnologica, n.s., vol. 1).

Stolk, J. J.
1907 "Opsporing van de zwervende stam der Penjabong-Poenan's, op de waterscheiding der Barito met de Mahakam en Kapoeas (Midden-Borneo) in Oct. 1905." *TNAG* 24: 1–27.

Strickland, S. S.
1986 "Long-term Development of Kejaman Subsistence: An Ecological Study." *SMJ* 36 (57):117–171.

Sulaiman Ring
1968 "Hasil Survey Terhadap Suku Punan." *Al-Djami'ah* 8 (1):3–53.

T.A.D.
Undated (ca. 1981) *Forest for Food, Phase 1*. T.A.D.-Materielen 11, East Kalimantan.

Testart, A.
1981 "Pour une typologie des chasseurs-cueilleurs." *AS* 5 (2):177–221.

Tillema, H. F.
1934–1935 "Naar Apo-Kajan." *TN* 7:184–188, 194–201, 210–216.
1939 "Jagerstammen op Borneo." *OA* 12:76–83, 135–142, 203–212, 228–232, 262–269.

Tjilik Riwut
1979 *Kalimantan membangun*. Jakarta.

Tromp, S. W.
1889 "Een reis naar de bovenlanden van Koetei." *TBG* 32: 273–304.

Turnbull, C. M.
1961 *The Forest People: A Study of the Pygmies of the Congo*. New York: Simon & Schuster.

Tuton Kaboy
1974 "The Penan Aput." In *The Peoples of Central Borneo*, ed. J. Rousseau. Special Issue of the *SMJ* 22 (43): 287–293.

Urquhart, I. A. N.
1951 "Some Notes on Jungle Punans in Kapit District." *SMJ* 5 (3): 495–533.
1955 "Some Interior Dialects." *SMJ* 6 (5):193–204.
1957 "Some Kenyah-Pennan Relationships." *SMJ* 8 (10):113–116.

1958 "The Peoples of Sarawak: Nomadic Punans and Pennans." *SG* 84 (1209): 205–207.
1959 "Nomadic Punans and Pennans." In *The Peoples of Sarawak*, ed. T. Harrisson. Kuching: Sarawak Museum, 73–83.

Valentinus T.
1977 "Beberapa masalah penduduk yang mempengaruhi perkembangan masyarakat kecamatan Long Apari Kabupaten Kutai." Samarinda: APDN.

Vansina, J.
1961 *De la tradition orale: Essai de méthode historique.* Tervuren: Musée Royal de l'Afrique Centrale, Annales, Sciences Humaines no. 36. English translation: *Oral Tradition: A Study in Historical Methodology,* trans. H. M. Wright. London: Routledge & Kegan Paul, 1965.

Vayda, A. P.
1961 "Expansion and Warfare among Swidden Agriculturalists." *AA* 63:346–358.

Velde, P. van de (ed.)
1984 *Prehistoric Indonesia.* Dordrecht: Foris.

Veth, P. J.
1854–1856 *Borneo's Wester-Afdeeling: Geographisch, Statistisch, Historisch, voorafgegaan door eene algemeene schets des ganschen eilands.* 2 vols. Zaltbommel: Joh. Noman en Zoon.

Vorstman, J. A.
1927 "Memorie van overgave der onderafdeeling Boven–Mahakam, 1927." KITLV Archives (Korn Collection).
1952 "Adatrechtelijke en andere gegevens uit de onderafdeeling Boven-Mahakam der Zuider- en Ooster-afdeeling van Borneo (1927)." *ARB* 44: 202–220 (The Hague: Nijhoff).

Vrocklage, B. A. G.
1936 *Die sozialen Verhältnisse Indonesiens.* Münster.

Walchren, E. W. F. van
1907 "Een reis naar de bovenstreken van Boeloengan, Midden-Borneo." *TNAG* 24: 755–844.

Wariso, R. A. M.
1971 "Suku Daya Punan." Pontianak: Universitas Tanjungpura (Fakultas Sosial dan Politik).

Weddik, A. L.
1849–1850 "Beknopt overzigt van het Rijk van Koetai op Borneo." *IA* 1 (1):78–105; *IA* 1 (2):123–160.

Whittier, H. L.
1974 "The Distribution of Punan in East Kalimantan." *BRB* 6 (2):42–48.

Willis, R.
1980 "The Literalist Fallacy and the Problem of Oral Tradition." *Social Analysis* 4: 28–37.

Woodburn, J.
1982 "Social Dimensions of Death in Four African Hunting and Gathering Societies." In *Death and the Regeneration of Life,* ed. M. Bloch and J. Parry. Cambridge: Cambridge University Press, 187–210.

Wurm, S. A., and S. Hattori (eds.)
1983 *Language Atlas of the Pacific Area, Part II: Japan Area, Philippines and Taiwan, Mainland and Insular Southeast Asia.* Canberra: The Australian Academy of the Humanities; Tokyo: The Japan Academy (Stuttgart: Internationales Landkartenhaus, GeoCenter).

Zacot, F.
1986 "Mobilité et flexibilité: Le cas des Badjos, nomades de la mer." In *Nomadisme: mobilité et flexibilité?* Paris: ORSTOM, Départment H, Bulletin de Liaison no. 8:41–57.

INDEX

(A) indicates an Aoheng subgroup
(B) indicates a Bukat subgroup
(P) indicates a Punan group

Names of individuals are followed by
the name of their ethnic group
within parentheses.

abandonment (of dead, of camp), 74,
  158–161, 216
Acue (A), 23, 30, 55, 136, 137, 171,
  190
Acue, Long, 229 (Map 7 H–10)
adat, 43, 72, 118, 154, 193, 204, 208,
  209; *adat torai,* 98; *kepala adat,* 43,
  47
affine, affinal (kinship), 71, 95, 154,
  195
aggression, 78, 132, 138, 141–142
alliance, 51–52, 139, 166, 170, 201;
  by blood pact, 36, 51, 166; by
  marriage, 33, 36, 51, 166, 201
Alung (B), 24, 48, 53, 60
Amue (A), 30, 55
Angoi, Tumbang, 249 (Map 12)
animal (domestic), 13, 67, 184; as
  sacrifice, 98, 159
Aoheng, 6, 16, 20, 23, 25, 27, 30–35,
  37, 43–51, 53, 54, 58, 62, 63, 65–
  68, 72, 73, 74, 78–81, 89, 90, 95,
  96, 117, 125, 126, 128, 139, 140,
  141, 145, 150, 152, 153, 159, 160,
  161, 171, 174, 183, 189, 190, 193,
  196–199, 201, 202, 206, 212, 213.
  See also individual entries marked
  (A)

Apari, Long, 229 (Map 7 H–9)
Aput (P), 16, 135, 138, 146, 150, 156,
  161
Aring Opung, 229 (Map 7 H–9/10)
aristocrat, aristocratic, 69, 188, 189,
  194, 197, 200, 201
attack, 35, 37, 78, 141
autonym. *See* name
Auva (A), 30
Aya', Long, 227 (Map 5)

Baang Tutung, 248 (Map 11)
Bahau (P), 139, 140, 204
Balang, Nanga, 229 (Map 7 J–3/4)
banana (tree), 60, 171, 178, 179, 185
Bang Juk (Long Gelat), 142
Barito Complex, 187, 188, 189, 218
Basap, 16, 135
Batang Lupar. *See* Iban
Batu (P), 156, 184
Batu Ura, 229 (Map 7 I/J–10)
Bekaang river, 248 (Map 11)
Beketan, 16, 19–23, 26, 28–31, 36–
  39, 49, 50, 52, 53, 54, 56, 57, 58,
  60, 64, 86, 121, 134, 135, 136,
  138, 140, 141, 151, 155, 159, 161,
  174, 175, 179, 181, 183, 184, 190,
  198, 199, 203
Bekohu river, 248 (Map 11)
Belatei river, 229 (Map 7 D–7)
Belatung (B), 28, 29, 37, 40, 41, 48,
  55, 70
Belatung river, 235 (Map 7.6)
Benalui (P), 155, 159, 190
Benyawung (P), 156

Berane, Long, 248 (Map 11)
Berawan, 12, 177, 188, 189, 190
Berun (P), 156
bezoar stone, 56, 167
bilateral. *See* kinship
Binai (P), 156
bird nests, 47, 56, 87
blowpipe, 65, 123–124, 126, 127, 147, 165; as marriage gift or payment, 73, 94, 157
Boan, Noha, 229 (Map 7 I–9)
Boh river, 246 (Map 9)
Bovasang river, 229 (Map 7 G–10)
bridewealth, 73, 94
Brunei (P), 171
Bukit, 17, 183
Bukitan. *See* Beketan
Bulan Jihat (Punan Ratah), 198
Bungan, Nanga, 229 (Map 7 H–6)
Bungan (P). *See* Hovongan
Bungan river, 229 (Map 7 H/I–6)
Busang (P), 16, 65, 68, 127, 136, 146, 161, 168
Busang river, 246–249 (Maps 9–12)
bush knife, 67, 92, 94, 124, 127, 156

camp, 66, 132–133, 149, 192. *See also* abandonment
canoe, 53, 67, 92, 129
cash crop, 13, 63
cassava, 171, 172, 178–179, 180, 181, 185, 217–218
categories: ethnic, 15–17, 152, 183, 214; social, 71, 92–93, 150, 152, 153, 184, 201, 220
caves, 9, 55, 66, 87, 149–150
chicken, 13, 67, 89, 92, 184
Cihan (A), 33
classification (ethnic). *See* categories
cognatic. *See* kinship
colonial (administration, government), 10, 37, 40, 45, 59, 170, 174
commoner, 93, 189, 197, 201-202
composite (ethnic group), 153, 185, 190, 202, 212–213, 216, 219
consanguine, consanguineal. *See* kinship
credit (system of), 86, 88, 89, 166, 169, 217

Danum Buro river, 248 (Map 11)
Data Noha, 229 (Map 7 H–10)
death, 74, 95, 97–98, 158–161, 204–205, 207, 216. *See also* funerals; soul
debt. *See* credit
defense, 95, 118, 136–139, 142, 194, 216
Dehipui river, 248 (Map 11)
deity. *See* god
demography. *See* population
Deringei river, 248 (Map 11)
desa, 40, 42, 43, 70, 76, 87, 88, 93
devolution, 116, 128, 180
dialect. *See* language
Diang Apot, 248 (Map 11)
Diang Bonong, 248 (Map 11)
Dioscorea, 122, 178, 179
divinity. *See* god
Doan Kavo'. *See* Ihi
Doang Hakong, 229 (Map 7 I–9)
dog, 65, 92, 126–127, 131, 147, 164–165
Donu Pao, 229 (Map 7 J–9)

egalitarian, egalitarianism, 93, 150, 153, 197, 216, 220
Enap, Nanga, 229 (Map 7 J–3)
enclave, 119, 137, 195, 210
endogamy, 72, 155; of band, 72, 145, 153, 154–156, 219; of hamlet, 194; of rank, 200
environment (natural), 119–121, 132, 144, 215
equality. *See* egalitarian
ethnicity, 49–56, 135–136, 189, 208–214
ethnonym. *See* name
exonym. *See* name

family: extended, 68–69, 93, 143, 145, 219; nuclear, 68, 93, 145–146, 152, 216, 219; stem, 143
fishing, 65-66, 128–130
fission (of band), 146, 152, 216
footpath. *See* path
forest: primary, 118–120; secondary, 13
fruit, 122, 179; fruit tree, 13, 176, 179, 217

funerals, funerary: festivals, 187, 188,
205; funeral post, 84, 97; grave hut,
188; rituals, 11, 12, 57, 97–99,
187, 188, 205; two-stage ceremony,
11, 12, 97, 187–188

Gaat (= Lugat) river, 229 (Map 7 A–4)
Gang (P), 125, 131, 157, 160, 172,
178, 181
Gasai Butek (B), 46
Gemala (B), 36, 39, 42, 43, 46, 48, 55,
60, 63, 65, 69, 70
god, 73, 96, 161, 162, 206
gold, 44, 47, 56, 59, 85, 87, 88
guerrilla. See war
Gung river, 229 (Map 7 H–5)

Hakat, Nanga, 229 (Map 7 I–4)
Halangi (B), 29
Halunge (B), 23, 30, 31, 55, 136, 151
Halunge river, 229 (Map 7 F–10)
Hangai (B), 41
Hangai river, 229 (Map 7 F–8)
head (human), 54, 57, 59, 140, 141,
169
head house, 12
headhunting, 54, 136, 137, 141
headman. See leadership
healing, 74, 96, 161, 205, 207
Helangi river, 229 (Map 7 G–7)
Helevusu' (B), 29, 31, 32, 35, 36, 41
Helevusu' river, 229 (Map 7 G–6)
hero (culture), 6, 199, 208, 209, 210
hierarchy, hierarchized, 43, 55, 150,
188, 205
Hindu, Hinduized, 9, 11, 213
Höloi (B), 24, 27, 28, 48
horticulture, 177–180, 187–191, 202,
212, 214, 218–219
house, 60, 66, 69, 82, 89, 145, 149,
192, 204, 209; "house" as descendant line of leaders, 200; rituals,
204, 206, 219. See also head house;
longhouse
household, 89, 145, 192, 196, 219;
spirits and rituals, 206
Hovat (B), 24, 26, 27, 38
Hovat, Nanga, 229 (Map 7 H–3)
Hovongan, 16, 18, 22, 25, 27, 35, 36,
44, 45, 53, 54, 55, 61–65, 67, 68,

71, 73, 74, 76, 78–81, 90, 92, 96,
127, 128, 129, 135, 136, 142, 145,
155, 156, 172, 175, 181, 182, 185,
186, 190, 199, 202, 206, 213
Hovorit, 35
Hovut (B), 24, 29, 30, 38, 39, 40, 48,
59
hunting, 65, 92, 122–128, 131, 147
hut. See house
Huvung (A), 23, 31, 33, 34, 35, 44,
45, 51, 52, 139
Huvung river, 229 (Map 7 I–9)

Iban, 11, 19, 20, 23, 24, 26, 28–33,
35, 37–39, 44, 45, 50, 52, 54, 60,
62, 64, 68, 86, 90, 119, 134, 138–
140, 142, 150, 174, 183, 190, 198,
203, 212, 219
identity. See ethnicity
ideology, 204, 207–208, 209, 220
Ihi, 248 (Map 11)
incest, 155, 156, 195, 216, 219
individualism, 203, 208, 209, 211, 220
inequality, 199–202
interface: active, 132, 139–140, 168,
176; static, 138
intermarriage, 72–73, 191, 194–195.
See also alliance; marriage
Ira', Nanga, 229 (Map 7 J–3)
Irang Ubung (A), 33
iron. See metal
irrigated agriculture, 12, 176, 214
Islam, Islamized, 9, 10

Jalangi river, 229 (Map 7 D–8)
jar (ceramic), 58, 130, 188
Jojang, 249 (Map 12)
Juba' (Hovongan), 78

Kacu, Long, 229 (Map 7 I–10)
Kacu river, 229 (Map 7 J–9)
Kajang, 12, 50, 173, 177, 185, 186,
188–189, 190, 196, 201, 202, 212,
213
Kaki Merah (P), 80
Kanowit, 23
Kaya (A), 34, 44
Kayan, 9, 12, 18, 20, 21, 23–30, 32,
35–38, 40, 41, 44, 45, 48–62, 65–
73, 81, 84, 90, 91, 92, 94, 95–98,

127, 130, 137, 139, 140, 141, 150,
164, 165, 169, 170, 173, 174, 184,
187–190, 201, 202, 205, 206, 212,
213, 219
Kebahan, 12
Kelabit, 12, 125, 127, 189
Kelai (P), 16, 136, 155, 156, 160, 177
Kenyah, 12, 20, 70, 139, 140, 161,
175, 177, 184, 185, 201
Kerasut (Kereho), 82, 83, 91, 93
Keriau, Nanga, 229 (Map 7 I–4)
Keriau river, 229 (Map 7 J–4)
Ketipun, 249 (Map 12)
kidnapping, 35, 57
killing, 54
kinship, 71, 95, 153–154, 195
Kohi (P), 16, 32, 170
Koyan (B), 24, 27, 37, 41, 48
Kuhi. See Kohi
Kwing Irang (Mahakam Kayan), 165

La'ong (P), 159
labor: corvée, 170, 200, 201; sexual
division of, 61, 70–71, 95–96, 122,
147–148, 173, 196, 217; wage,
186, 218
Lambang (Punan Murung), 209
Langasa (P), 16, 170
Langei river, 229 (Map 7 D–7)
language, 17, 21, 77, 209
leadership, 43–44, 55, 69–70, 93,
150–153, 189, 191, 196–202, 216,
219
Lekawai river, 246 (Map 9)
Lepo' Tau, 20, 139
Levuhi river, 229 (Map 7 H–8)
Levusu'. See Helevusu'
Liju Li' (Long Gelat), 24, 25, 26, 27,
51, 52, 60, 199
Lisum (P), 16, 20, 21, 49, 135, 136,
138, 139, 140, 151, 153, 155, 161,
190, 199, 210
Liut Murung, 249 (Map 12)
Logat. See Lugat
Long Apari (A), 31–35, 44, 45, 47, 53,
62
Long Gelat, 21, 24, 25, 68, 90, 91, 96,
97, 124, 140–142, 150, 156, 157,
171, 199, 201, 204–206
longhouse, 13, 66, 82, 83, 172, 192,
206

Lugat, 16, 20, 49, 161, 183, 203, 212.
See also Gaat
Lun Dayeh, 12, 189, 190
Lusong (P), 131, 151, 157, 174

Maci', Noha, 229 (Map 7 F–11)
Magoh (P), 131
Malay, 10, 40, 78, 214; language / dia-
lect, 10, 40
Malinau (P), 177
Maloh, 12, 19, 20, 22, 24–25, 26, 37,
38, 53, 57, 68, 184
Mandai river, 229 (Map 7 J–2), 246
(Map 9)
manioc. See cassava
Mankettan. See Beketan
marriage, 71, 72, 95, 154–156, 192,
194, 195, 200, 216; rituals, 73, 93,
94, 95, 156–157, 196–197, 199,
204–205, 207, 216, 219. See also
alliance; intermarriage; residence
Mbau, 78
Mecai, Long, 229 (Map 7 J–9)
Mekajo (B), 24, 27, 28, 48
Menawan (P), 151
Mendalam river, 229 (Map 7 I–2)
Menilei, Nanga, 229 (Map 7 H–5)
Menjuei, Nanga, 229 (Map 7 I–4)
Mensikei, Nanga, 229 (Map 7 I–5)
Menyivung river, 229 (Map 7 C–4)
Merah (P), 16, 136, 140, 161, 181
Mesio. See Sio
metal, 9, 57, 65, 120, 123–126, 131,
164–165, 217
Metelunai, 229 (Map 7 I–4)
Metevulu river, 229 (Map 7 C–5)
migration, 120, 133, 141, 143, 146,
209, 215–216. See also mobility
mobility, 132–134, 168, 176, 212,
214, 220. See also migration
Modang, 12, 140, 177, 184
movement (of band). See mobility
Mulu (P), 135, 145, 150, 182
Murung (P), 11, 17, 79, 80, 117, 124,
129, 134–143, 145, 146, 149, 150,
151, 155–157, 174, 175, 178, 179,
182, 183, 190, 197, 198, 201, 202,
204, 205, 209, 213
Musang (P). See Busang
Muti river, 229 (Map 7 J–4)
myth, mythology, 207, 209, 210, 212

name (ethnic), 14, 16, 18–21, 135–136, 213
necronym, 95, 154
Neolithic. *See* prehistory
net. *See* fishing
Niah (P), 159, 175, 180, 182
noble. *See* aristocrat
nulang arc, 12, 189, 219
Nya'an (P), 16
Nyagang (A), 27, 37
Nyawong, 16, 76, 77, 79, 98

Obat. *See* Hovat
Okap, Long, 229 (Map 7 J–11)
Olo Ot(t), 16, 75, 76, 77, 79
opportunism, 208, 211, 220
orchard. *See* fruit
Oseai river, 229 (Map 7 G–6)
Ot Danum, 11, 21, 22, 23, 25, 78, 79–86, 90–92, 95, 97–99, 129, 137, 139, 187, 190, 204, 205, 206, 213
Ot Punan, 78
Ot, 59, 94, 135, 140, 157, 159, 174, 203, 213, 214
overlord, overlordship, 53, 140, 169, 217

palm, coconut and oil, 13. *See also* sago
Parahau', 249 (Map 12)
Pari, 26, 57
Parit, 249 (Map 12)
path, 120, 133
peace (treaty), 31, 32, 36, 37, 39, 41, 46, 52
Penane river, 229 (Map 7 J–8)
Penganun (B), 30, 151
Penihing. *See* Aoheng
pig: domestic, 13, 67, 89, 92; as sacrifice, 95, 97; wild, 122, 123, 125, 127, 147, 151
Pin, 23, 27, 96, 98, 141, 187, 189, 190, 206, 213
Pinang (Kereho), 77, 83
pioneer (farmer), 11, 81, 138
Pisa (Kereho), 82, 84, 92, 98
poison, 56, 57, 66, 124, 126–127, 128–129, 215
polygamy, 71
population (figures), 8, 42, 43, 46–49, 75, 84, 87, 143–144

prehistory, 9
prestige. *See* status
prohibition, 65, 74, 82, 96, 97, 155
property, 192; collective, 193, 194; private, 192, 193, 195, 219
protection, 51, 139, 169, 174, 218
Punan Bah, 129, 180, 189, 201, 202, 213
Purukcahu, 247 (Map 10)
Putan, Nanga, 229 (Map 7 G–2)
Putussibau, 229 (Map 7 I–1)

raid. *See* attack
Rajang (B), 46
Ratah (P), 139, 204
religion, 73, 96–99, 160–162, 206–208, 219, 220
residence: ambilocal, 157, 158; neolocal, 72, 157, 158, 195, 216, 219; patterns, 99, 149–150, 192–193, 194–196; postmarital, 49, 72–73, 94, 157–158, 195, 197, 219; unit, 132, 143, 145, 149, 194, 219; utrolocal, 72, 158, 195, 197, 219; uxorilocal, 49, 72–73, 94, 100, 157, 158, 195, 197, 219. *See also* house; household
Riam Pelahi, 229 (Map 7 H–5)
rice (cultivation), 9, 10, 13, 60–64, 179–187, 214
ritual, 51, 57, 74, 96–99, 154–162, 204–207, 220. *See also* funerals; marriage: rituals
rotan (rattan), 56, 59, 88

sacrifice, 57, 63, 95, 97, 98
sago, sago flour, 13, 60–61, 119, 121–122, 177; extraction and processing, 70, 121–122, 125, 131, 147; storage, 61, 130
Sahidal, Raden (Barito), 34, 51
salt, 57, 131
Salua' (B), 24, 26
Samus river, 229 (Map 7 H–2)
Savaoe, 248 (Map 11)
schooling, 42, 47, 62, 88, 170
Segah (P), 17
Segai, 174
Sekudan (Bukat), 31, 40–42, 44, 45, 48, 54, 55, 70, 146, 198
Selimbau. *See* Mbau

Selirung, Nanga, 229 (Map 7 H–3)
Selua', Nanga, 229 (Map 7 H–3)
Selua' (Ulu) mountains, 229 (Map 7
    F–4)
Selua' river, 229 (Map 7 H–3)
Sempolok, 229 (Map 7 H–5)
Semukung, 25, 27, 31, 35, 41, 43, 53,
    90, 139
Senganan, 40, 43
Seputan, 16, 23, 34, 54, 67, 68, 77–
    84, 86–100, 139, 145, 149–150,
    155, 156, 157, 175, 182, 190, 197,
    199–206, 213
Serata (P), 16
Serata river, 229 (Map 7 I–11)
shamanism, 96, 161, 205, 207
sharing, 122, 128, 145, 148, 193, 216,
    219
Si Hebar. See Sahidal
Siau. See Sio
Sibau river, 229 (Map 7 H–1)
Silam, Temanggung (Siang), 82, 84, 98
Silat, Noha, 229 (Map 7 I/J–10)
Sio, 80, 81
Sivo (B), 31, 35, 46
Sivo river, 229 (Map 7 F–9)
slave, slavery, 12, 51, 54, 141, 169,
    217
Soa Kalöp (B), 24, 27, 37, 41, 48
soul, 73, 74, 97, 160–161, 205, 207
Sovaoe, Tumbang, 248 (Map 11)
spirit, 73, 74, 96, 97, 160–161, 205,
    207
Sru, 16, 20–21, 49, 50, 183, 203
status, 151–152, 191, 193, 197, 199–
    201, 209, 219
stone: sculpture, 187; tool, 9, 125,
    131, 164, 166, 215
storage, 61, 130, 180, 212
stratification (social), 12, 69, 192, 193,
    200–204, 205, 212–213
sultanate, 8–10, 22, 184
Sung (A), 33, 34, 35
swidden agriculture, 10, 12, 13, 214

taboo. See prohibition
Tain Kiat (B), 24, 27, 37, 41, 48
Talai, Nanga, 229 (Map 7 J–5)

Tamalue, 248 (Map 11)
Taman, 12, 21, 22, 24–25, 26, 29, 30,
    36–40, 50–56, 58–60, 68, 90
Tayung (B), 24, 27, 48
Telusan, 248–249 (Maps 11–12)
Temoan (B), 24, 27, 28, 48
Tepai, Nanga, 229 (Map 7 I–4)
territoriality, 53, 132–140, 142, 192–
    194, 215–216
timber, 44, 48, 88, 89
Tingang Kuhi (A), 44, 45
Tingang Senean (A), 30, 198
Tiong Bu'u (A), 32, 35, 44, 46
Tiong Ohang, 229 (Map 7 J–11)
title, 42, 43, 69, 84, 86, 150, 199
Tivap, Noha, 229 (Map 7 H/I–9)
tobacco, 57, 68, 100, 132, 165, 166
Tomong Mo'ong, 229 (Map 7 H–10)
Tovaliu, 24, 27, 28, 48, 60
trade, 47–48, 56–59, 88–89, 130–
    132, 164–168, 169–170, 173–174,
    217; silent, 52, 59, 167
tradition, 5–6, 209–210, 215
tubers, 122, 176, 178–179, 187
Tubu (P), 178
Tukung, Nanga, 229 (Map 7 J–3)

Uheng. See Semukung
Ukit, 16, 19, 21, 29, 31, 39, 46, 57,
    59, 64, 135, 138, 179, 212
Ulu Air, 22
Uma' Aging, 23, 24, 25
Uma' Laran, 140
Uma' Long, 129
Uma' Pagung, 37
Uma' Suling, 25, 170
Uma' Wak, 25
Ut (B), 23
Utot (B), 30
Uut (P), 80

vassal, 217. See also overlord

war, 54, 81, 176
warrior, 54, 79, 137, 141
withdrawal, 137–138, 160, 216. See
    also abandonment